MY HEART

WILL CROSS

THIS OCEAN

MY HEART
WILL CROSS
THIS OCEAN

My Story,
My Son,
Amadou

KADIATOU DIALLO
and
Craig Wolff

ONE WORLD
BALLANTINE BOOKS · NEW YORK

A One World Book
Published by The Random House Ballantine Publishing Group
Copyright © 2003 by Kadiatou Diallo and Craig Wolff

All rights reserved under International and Pan-American Copyright Conventions.
Published in the United States by The Random House Ballantine Publishing Group,
a division of Random House, Inc., New York, and simultaneously in
Canada by Random House of Canada Limited, Toronto.

One World and Ballantine are registered trademarks
and the One World colophon is a trademark of Random House, Inc.

www.ballantinebooks.com/one/

Library of Congress Cataloging-in-Publication Data
is available from the publisher upon request.

ISBN 0-345-45600-9

Manufactured in the United States of America

Text design by Julie Schroeder

First Edition: May 2003

10   9   8   7   6   5   4   3   2   1

To Amadou and Fifi, my two beautiful angels who are now together. When tomorrow comes, we will find you waiting at the gate of Al-Jannah. To humanity: love and wisdom.

CONTENTS

MY HEART
WILL CROSS
THIS OCEAN

$\mathcal{T}$he first thing you should know about me is that I have been given away many times. I have been borne on the shoulders of men who were willing to see me left and forsaken. I have been sacrificed, transferred, and conveyed so often, I know the feeling of being lifted and carried away. I know how the broken river branch feels.

I have the knowledge, too, that I can stand erect and change the order of things, but that came much later. For a long time, I knew myself merely as an offering, to be handed over like a parcel.

My father gave me away when I was three days old. That was the first time. He wrapped me in a blanket and swung me over the lip of a balcony on the fourth floor of the main hospital in Conakry, Guinea. The blanket fell away and floated to the street. I dangled in the sky. A French woman, a doctor, came from behind and convinced him not to throw me to the street. He was not in his right mind.

"Take my child," he told her. "Please take her and raise her. I cannot give her what she needs." The woman accepted the gift and was willing to keep me for her own, until my mother found her.

"My husband doesn't know what he is doing," my mother cried. "Please give me back my baby. Please. She is my daughter, and I need her."

When I was thirteen, my father gave me away again, to be married. My husband appeared in a doorway, more serious, I thought, than he showed in the photograph he had sent ahead of his arrival. He seemed tall. He already had one wife, I knew. We sat in chairs facing one another. I said little. Later that day I starred in the school play as the king's wife.

For a long time I wished my father would die, and I refused to pray to Allah. I defied Baba. I washed one hand, but not the other. One foot, not the other. I prayed to Allah, my God, to save me from my despair, to kill me if He had to. I prayed for him to forgive me for my bad thoughts. I did not want to get married. I prayed in my room, on a bedcover my mother had made. It smelled of mangos from the yard. With all my strength, I wanted to die there.

The next week I lay in my grandmother's darkened hut, my body sheathed in white linen, over my face and over my feet, covering my arms, which could not move from my sides. My grandmother and many other women chanted over me. I felt more like a mummy than a bride.

Above all, my feet were not permitted to touch the ground. A man whose name I don't recall carried me over his shoulder, while around me people sang and danced, rejoicing in my virginity. If I had tried to speak just then, I do not know that my voice held the power to be heard. As it was, I was commanded to keep silent, and I did.

I was placed in the back of a truck and driven five hours to the village where my husband had been a boy. I lay there on a rug in the middle of the road. It was still rainy season. The people in the village streamed by. They were curious about me, but my face remained covered. For the ceremony, my sister and my aunt spoke for me. I stayed voiceless, on the ground.

Later I learned that I was not supposed to speak or shed my veil for a full week, but no one had told me this. When my husband's neighbors came to see me, I poked out and said, "Hi, I'm Kadi."

The women laughed. "She's from the city," they said. "She doesn't know better."

Soon my husband took me to Liberia, to the bush country in the southeast, and there he left me. My baby began to push out late in the summer. I had no husband with me. My mother and sisters were not there. I had not been able to get word to my family I was pregnant. I turned to the doctor, a woman, who I pretended was my mother.

"Oh my God," I cried. "Women have work to do."

The doctor cried, too. She touched her cheek to mine, and I felt her tears. She kissed me. "Yes, child, it is hard to be a woman," she said, "but don't worry, you'll be fine."

When the baby came out, the doctor held it by the feet upside down, and I felt strange because the baby did not cry. The baby came out in a light coating, as if in water and cotton. At first I thought my baby was transparent, but then I strained my eyes to look harder, and I realized my baby had come out in a bag. A very rare thing, I discovered.

"When angels come back, they appear this way," my mother told me later.

The doctor rubbed the bag away from my baby, and that is when my son Amadou gave out his first cry.

He was a gentle boy. My son Amadou could not swim and feared water altogether. As a child, and even as he grew, he bathed so as to avoid showers. Water running over him made him anxious. I would take him to Sugar Beach, where the sand really looked and felt like sugar. It was fine and white, and it made you feel rich just to rest on it. The water was calm; I do not recall many waves. His friends played freely in the ocean, while Amadou went with me to the other side of the sandbar where there was a small tide pool. He showed no fear there, but no mischief either. He liked to stand with his arms folded and look out. Separated from the sea by the dunes, he could pretend that he, Amadou, water up to his calves, was the king of all that surrounded him. Remembering him now, I can still sense the serenity he commanded.

He was a boy of unusual beauty. This did not come from one place, nor did it overpower you. I can tell you he was small. He had small hands, slight shoulders, a face that did not impose itself on you. His eyes were kind, and they were still for a boy. Settled, I think. His eyes were settled in his face in a way you don't often find with a child. He did not take on the world so much as he consented for the world to come to him. He had kind, merciful eyes, and yet, what they saw I really do not know.

When he was very young and I was away from him, he had a bad time with chicken pox. His teeth turned black, and I was still a girl myself and I didn't understand and I thought he was going to die because I had left him alone, and so I cried while praying. He was just a baby going through what he had to go through, but I thought he would leave me right then. I was sure I had returned too late, but he improved within a day of seeing me, and after that he never got sick. At least, he never had the sore throat or the fever to worry anyone too much.

He found sleep easily, but nightmares would encircle him. He might not wake, but almost every night, I heard him and came to him.

"Amadou, why are you talking in your sleep? What are you saying? What do you want to tell your mom?"

I'd rub his hand, and, in a while, his breathing would settle down until I could hear it only a little.

I was a child myself, barely *sixteen* when he was born. I could not have told you what I was doing, married with a baby, could not have told you who I was. But I knew how to console Amadou. I would rub his hands, smooth the bridge of his nose. I would put a fingertip to his lips to let his jumbled dream-talk flow through my arms and my chest and my aching heart. That's what I told him. *"It's your Mom. I am here. Give your troubles to me."*

When a young person leaves home from Guinea, he becomes the *setté*. He is the explorer and the envoy, carrying the family name to unseen places. In the villages, towns, and cities, too, they will talk about him, imagining his triumphs and new riches. On his return, they will gauge his manner of speaking or of entering a room, the ease of his walk, perhaps a satisfaction that shows in his eyes, to determine if his travels have given him the bearing of a successful man. Beyond his conquests, they wait for the tales he will carry back. Even the man who has not filled his pockets with gold can still be a witness. For years he can tell people what happened when finally he stepped onto strange land, what surprised or scared him, lifted or saddened him, what he has discovered for *them*. Amadou was the *setté* for his brothers, sisters, cousins, friends, and for me, who anticipated a magnificent return.

He returned, a silent body with a tale untold. If there is anything as cruel as the taking of a man's life, it is the taking away of his story, the particulars that make him holy. The mother who dreams that she can undo any harm that comes to her child, dreams fruitlessly. The one last thing she can do is to try to give her child back his story, the greatest and least obligation she can fulfill.

Part One

✈

The Age of
Untold Knowing

CHAPTER ONE

DISCOVERING WATER

*A*gainst all reason, I see him gliding in the forest. He taps lightly on the barks of the nehri trees to wake them. He curls worms with the end of a stick, drops a rock in the water to watch the reflection of the sun break up into a thousand pieces. Sometimes he just stands on a hilltop, squeezes his eyes closed, and makes an extra effort to feel the wind, bounding along the Fouta Djallon, brush against his cheeks.

What a fancy dream I have. There is no sense to this vision, no reason to believe he would have behaved this way.

First of all, the country rolls strangely here. The mountain paths may turn left while the mountain itself slopes right. The horizon reveals whole plains and valleys rising and falling at opposing angles. The way God arranged the land is still visible: sudden ridges, odd crisscrosses of rivers and red rock, great movements toward the sky. A man not careful to keep his head down could suffer illusions in a place like this, become dizzy and fall down.

He had no time to fall down. He had to get to school.

On dry days, he left Diontou at six in the morning. He set out when the forest was still drawn in night shadow, still filled with the phantom shapes of prowling monsters. Most times he took an orange, two bananas, a mango, a long twist of bread, two small bags of red goro nuts, and pieces of cassava shredded by his mother's fingers. He also brought a mathematics book, a reading book and a book of someone else's history, two shirts, his prayer robe, called a boubou, and a prayer mat. The load was bound in a sack that he balanced on his head. The food held him for five hours, the entire journey between villages. On arriving in Diari, he gave his hosts the second bag of goro nuts in gratitude for allowing him to stay with them. They sat on the floor together in shared blessings for his studies. They ate the nuts and talked excitedly with their mouths full and their tongues red.

Over the school year, he came this way a dozen times or more, thirty kilometers each way. He would remain in Diari for three weeks, sometimes longer, before returning home. He was eight years old the first year, twelve the last. He did not own shoes. He pulled down the large pohpoh leaves, thick as lily pads, and tied them to the bottoms of his feet. In this way he avoided the worst of the blisters that came from the hard, wind-burnt open spaces, and the leaves helped him keep pushing in the rainy season, kept him from dropping in the mud.

There were brilliant days, too. He walked through long, yellow grass and swelled banana groves. The bananas hung in plump, satisfied bunches. The mountains were free of mosquitoes, which were not interested in clean, light air such as this. Mischievous monkeys sometimes stared after his slight figure appearing in one opening in the bushes, departing through another. Entire hillsides smelled of nothing but oranges.

In the vision I wish, he lingers, makes faces at the monkeys, finds whole stories in the rivers and roads. And I am holding his hand. I know him well. He tells me we will be home soon.

He set out at six in the morning, earlier in the rain and mud season. There in the murky morning, in the near dark and the not-quite light, is the rightful place for this story to begin.

He pushed past the mirages. He was my father, son of a wise man, grandson of a king, and he was Amadou first.

Great imagination swept through Guinea in this time. The other families in Diontou noticed my father's long absences and whispered that the French had stolen him in the middle of the night. The women in the village visited with my grandmother and told her a plot was afoot to control their minds. The kidnapping of her Amadou was just the beginning. The French knew that the children were the wealth of the families. They would come for all their sons, and without them, the women would not have the help they needed in the fields. The rice and maize crops would surely die out. The other mothers watched over their own children nervously, brought them together under blankets at night.

The women of the village were only partly right. The French had announced that each family must choose one son to go to the government's European school, and this worried the men, too. It was one thing for the French to hold sway over the banks and far-off houses of government in the big cities, but the men's voices took on great dread when they talked about their traditions, their language, their children. These, the men said, were beyond trespass.

On their way to prayer the men stopped to see Alfa Oumar Diallo, my grandfather. Diallo, pronounced "Djallo," was a name shared by descendants of one of the four original families of the Fouta Djallon, the mountain region in the north. To the men of Diontou, he was Karamoko Alfa, the title given to the teacher and spiritual leader of the village. At his house, down a small hill, below the two yellow spires of the mosque, the men could be sure to hear the high summoning cry of the *salee*. It came to them like a melody. With water my grandfather gave to them in clay jugs, the men of Diontou squatted on my grandfather's land and performed the *saliqui*, the ritual washing of their hands, mouth, nose, face, ears, and feet. Then they walked in a single quiet line up the hill to the mosque. When prayer was over, they returned to eat my grandmother's yogurt and to share their worries.

I do not want my son to be taught by white men. We have a good school here. My son is learning the Koran and we all write in the same alphabet. We are organized. I do not want him to speak French or read books from Europe. The chiefs do not favor this. How will that help him when he returns to Diontou? How can he teach his brothers and sisters what they need to know?

The men turned to Karamoko Alfa. Many times before, they had dispatched their sons and daughters to him for a deeper reading of the Koran. My grandfather calmed jealousies and spites between neighbors and listened to their longings and private misgivings. Husbands and wives came to him to trade accusations. He passed no gossip. He was the teacher of the village, the most righteous man anyone knew.

But the question of whether to send a son away was too personal for him to settle. Every other family in the village ignored the government's decree. My grandfather considered his riches—three wives and thirteen children—and decided that his eldest son, my father, the one with the sober eyes, would go to the school. Perhaps, my grandfather believed, it was not a bad idea for just one of them to know what was happening in the school, to see life in another village. His Amadou might discover an unheard-of history from across the ocean, or ride a bicycle, or sleep under a zinc roof.

One morning, in the late summer of 1936, my father started out from Diontou with a sack on his head, and was not seen again for some time.

The way life happened here was slow, with the feeling of something drooping for a long time and then changing with the suddenness of a heavy curtain collapsing.

Four years at the European school led to a promotion test, which led to four years at a high school even farther away. After graduation, my father strode into the village, and everyone gaped at him in his dark suit and white colonial hat with a wide brim like the French business-men in the city wore. He also wore a belt. No one in Diontou owned a belt. He was given his own *caz*, or hut, separate from the main hut and away from the younger children, and the message went out that Karamoko Alfa's oldest son was eyeing for a wife.

My grandfather had already seen the girl, Diaraye. She was from nearby, in the village of Tinkin, set on another hill. She had been perched on the bare back of a pony, wearing a white dress and a gold necklace, when he spotted her. This was at the celebration after Ramadan a few years before. She rode into a great open field covered in gifts her father had brought her from Senegal. My grandfather was surely struck by her long back, the long youthful neck, and by her eyes, which held just enough mystery. My grandfather grabbed hard on her wrist.

"I want her for my son who is away at school," he told her father.

And when it came time to tell his Amadou, he said, "I know of a girl who is interesting to look at."

Of course, my father wore the suit the first time he and my mother talked. The suit fit well on his narrow waist. My mother wore a chain with a pin in the center, and my father watched it nervously, thinking it might cut her, just at the soft cleft above the breastbone.

"May I hold it?" he asked.

She hesitated before she understood, and then she laughed to think he was worried about her this way. She laughed again, though in a different pitch, when she understood that he had noticed her skin where the pin rested. She felt him look down her body.

"Give me your ankle bracelet, too," he said. And they laughed more.

She was a girl who had been well tended by her father, Thierno Mamadou Bobo Diallo. He had brought socks, shoes, and watches from abroad into Tinkin. This had given him the status of something like a discoverer and her the aura of a little princess. Soon after that day in the field with the pony, her father died while off in Guinea-Bissau. He was found holding a Koran and poems he had written exalting God and nature. Dying away from her, he left her with wonder about how he could have died at all.

The family went to Guinea-Bissau to bury him, and on their way back, walking in the lowlands on an especially hot day, they ran out of water and fell ill with thirst. My mother saved them by scratching the ground with a stick. Finding the ground softer than expected, she scratched and dug some more. The more she scratched, the wetter the earth became until she, her mother, and her two brothers were able to cup their hands full with water.

Quickly, the family descended from a life of abundance to one of hardship. Her mother, my grandmother, was named Kadiatou Diallo.

She, with the help of her children, had to grow her own crops. The others in the village saw their struggles and came to help. Diaraye was sent to stay for a while with her aunt, who happened to live in Diontou. On the day she met my father, at the moment he realized he could not turn away, my mother was beauty and entitlement mixed with a question.

Tenderness and rapture had merged with pain and pity, sorrow and puzzlement, and all of it showed on her face. She wore sandals, and her toes were lovely. My father only knew he did not want to live without her.

As for her, she admired my father's thinness. His fingers were long, like hers. His body had a wiriness, suggesting someone who could slice through anything, as though his time in the bushes had brought upon him actual physical change, his adaptation to the wild terrain leaving him with new contours conferring upon him strength and ingenuity.

She had been promised to another boy, whose mother was practicing to be a witch. On learning of their marriage, the boy went to my mother's family and demanded her return. My uncle, my mother's brother, now the head of his family after his father's death, carried the message to my father in desperation. His village was talking about the broken contract.

"Give me back my sister because I can't go back without her," he said. "There was a commitment."

My father, it turns out, was brave. Karamoko Alfa had told him to never give up on his love.

"You have to take care of that business alone," he responded. "I have my wife. I will not give her up."

It's not clear what happened after that. The spurned boy undoubtedly went back to tell his own mother what had happened. My mother and father left for Boké, far west and beyond the Fouta Djallon, where my father hoped to become a doctor. Moving forward, they never learned—it is not certain they ever wondered—if the spurned boy's mother had reached full witchhood and placed a curse on their young marriage.

They began having babies with funny feet and uncommon hands. A daughter, Halimatou, was born early in the morning on January 1, 1952, with six toes on each foot, six fingers on each hand. A son, Alfaoumar, was born two years later with eleven fingers in all. To each other and to all the brothers and sisters to come, she would be Diadia because that is what the eldest sister in Fulah families are called, and to the younger ones he would be Koto. My father was disappointed in Diadia for being a girl when he wanted a boy first, and disappointed in Koto for not coming before Diadia. But he saw a star quality in Diadia. Her eyes twinkled a deep purple. He called her his New Year's Day Miracle.

And my father needed to have Koto close to him. He carried Koto constantly, told him stories about the bushes before Koto could understand, and in time, when he began to toddle, Koto would follow my father everywhere.

My mother and father, who now were Néné and Baba to their children, also had Abdoulaye, one of my father's brothers, living with them in Boké. It was customary for new husbands and wives to take care of other members of the family, and Abdoulaye demanded attention. He had a small, thick body, liked to wrestle other children, laughed boisterously, and had a shyness revealed by a persistent stammer. His presence gave my parents' union the kind of dignity that can come only from honoring obligations and fulfilling tradition. Baba made sure his younger brother went to the big school in town. Abdoulaye's being there gave their lives the fullness of responsibility, so it can also be said that my mother and father never had a young marriage. There were always children to care for.

In the deep, dark tender part of the night, they were never far from a child's breathing.

In Boké, Baba worked in the public hospital, which had one examination room and a dozen beds divided into two rooms. He administered shots, wrapped legs in splints, pushed patients in their wheelchairs, dampened the foreheads of children with high fever. Most of the patients he saw were either victims of malaria or road accidents, the maimed and handicapped who needed pills for their pain. He made sure the hospital had enough bandages and the few medicines that were necessary to treat yellow fever and malaria. Whenever his duties quieted, he read through books on biology. He had the semblance of an idea he would end up in medical school in Nairobi or even Paris.

In the meantime Baba bought rice and maize in the high season, stored them until the low season, and sold them at a premium. At home, he was able to pay a young girl to cook. Néné stayed with the babies and with the other women and their babies, and she learned to sew. Abdoulaye returned in the afternoon with tales from the classroom. Néné had never gone to school, so as different mysteries of growing up fell away, the mystery of school remained. What did they talk about? What did they see? What did it feel like to hold a book in your hands and know what the writing said? Abdoulaye ran Néné's fingers over the big black letters from the writing books he took home, and tore pages from the back of his notebook for her to use. He read to her, and she began to recognize words.

My mother sat against a tree with a book. I have heard that this happened.

Then Baba got into a bad mood. I heard about this, too. He would walk fast or pace or find fault in others. Weariness rolled over him, a fatigue so overpowering that it was best to just let him sleep. Even then, he might awaken more disturbed than he had been or happy, but in a way no one had ever seen in him. He yelled a lot. He wanted to roll in the grass with the babies or he didn't want to see them at all. His hands became tense and twitchy. The first time Néné had gazed at his long fingers, she had not foreseen this possibility. He gave money away to passersby or threw coins in the air. The more depressed he was, the more money he gave away. Once he gave away his most ornate embroidered robe. Néné, always following Baba's tracks, later bought back the robe.

The day Baba came home and saw Abdoulaye helping Néné with a book did not improve his mood. They were outside the hut, not expecting him for a while.

"What is happening here?"

"I am teaching her to read."

"My wife?" He looked at his brother. "You will never do this again. If I wanted an educated wife, I would marry one from the city. I married a girl from the village on purpose." His eyes burned Abdoulaye. "You are a man. Keep your books to yourself."

A fever in the family, and Néné would go straight to the bushes as she had watched her mother do and bring back the kasia leaves for boiling into tea or for bathing. These were small, fine leaves with a bitter taste that could be felt from throat to nose. Drink three from the left hand, three from the right, Néné ordered. It could wipe out the fever and nearly everything else in its path. Néné could fix a cold with kenkeliba leaves and cilantro. For the bad headaches that stole from behind the eyes, she boiled pelitoro leaves. But Baba dumbfounded her. She knew of no plants or oils to calm his fitful energy, and she could not be certain that something was wrong. Most people found him reasonable during this time. He gave away food and clothing at whim and lent advice more freely than ever. He was tirelessly accessible, suddenly talking a lot. When he slept or sulked or when he took away her book, Néné could not be sure which conduct came from a sickness and which from manly behavior.

Men have their states, she thought, so do as he says. Baba says be quiet. Be quiet. Baba says the rain will end soon. It will. Baba throws money into the stream. Smile for him. Baba wants you, too, to throw money away, do it without questions.

It was Baba who declared himself sick. He said he had Agitation.

He was unable to focus at the hospital. He left patients unattended, drifted in conversation, forgot the hour. His supervisors decided to treat him the French way, which granted him a full escape, a trip to Dakar in Senegal, but they told him a man with his condition could never to be a doctor. Most people saw Dakar as the hub of the French colony in West

Africa, which in some ways made it a symbol of the region's dependency on outsiders, and of the changes the outsiders had wrought. But it was indisputable: In Dakar, the best of everything was available. The treatment of choice for Baba was pills. He slept sixteen hours a day and was otherwise not disturbed. Solitude gave him new clearness of mind.

For a month Baba dreamed.

He dreamed about the forest, dreamed that his feet were scorched, that the animals were after him. He dreamed about steps. He saw steps for his two children and his children still to come. The steps spiraled up from a center space where they were knotted and rooted into the ground. This was Baba's mental pinwheel. Through his confusion, he saw his children and knew if he stayed well, his children would be well, too. It was then he began to sense himself as a builder.

Another baby came in 1956, Hadiatou. She had twelve fingers and twelve toes.

Shortly after her birth, an older man named Ibrahim Diallo, a relative of Néné's, on his way to the hajj in Mecca, stayed in their house. Baba gave him food and water and anything he needed. The man was so taken with the respect Baba had shown that he blessed Baba, and said, "You have respected me like a father. May God give you someone to respect you in your lifetime."

Because he was known as clever with money, and because he could write in both Fulah and French, and because he could type, Baba was given a job as a tax accountant for the government. He worked in an office in Conakry, the capital that sits on the Atlantic Ocean, far removed from the Fouta Djallon. He inspected the records of businesses and collected their taxes. As a bureaucrat he was considered privileged. He was paid enough to live in a cement house. He hired two girls, one to cook and wash, the other to mind the children. He bought a piece of land north of the city that was wooded with thin-trunked nehri trees, and he tested the market in palm oil and rice. On Fridays, he went to the weekly market in Boké and bought barrels of the oil, which he turned around and sold for double the price he paid.

Conakry was an odd, swirling place that brought out Baba's expansive side. Each morning, overfilled buses left for the diamond pits in the countryside. The miners sipped air from the tiny window slats or hung loosely from the rear running board. The country's one rail line chugged into the center of the city every day, coming from as far east as Kankan, loaded with cigarette cartons, canned foods, aspirin, metal scraps, boxes of tissue paper, ink drums, Fruit of the Loom underwear, and a hodge-podge of other products, some ridiculously unneeded or unusable. One day, a cache of used tires might arrive, another day sunglasses. Once, reams of telephone cords came in, enough to outfit a quarter of the city—this in a place where only government officials owned phones. No one knew who sent them or why, but sure enough, someone snatched them up.

That is the way business was done. Get your hands on whatever you can, make yourself an owner, worry later about the selling.

Change was happening. There was a boom in Conakry at the time, but it was evolving unevenly. Three times a week a big ship arrived from Paris or Morocco with a payload of Coca-Cola or cornflakes or women's cosmetics, or large equipment. Conakry stretches like a long pinky finger into the Atlantic, and in the late afternoon you could always spot men tugging a loaded-down crate up from the pier over the broken, knuckling road. You could see a man carrying a discarded, rusted icebox on his back next to another man heaving a shiny just-manufactured Frigidaire into a city where maybe a dozen homes had electrical wiring. At five o'clock the canoes, called *kunki*, came into the fishing port, and a line of women formed, first to buy the catfish, tuna, conque, and soy soy, and then to sell. Behind them, the sun, a burnt orange ball, slouched low on their backs.

This place, smelling of dead fish and cardboard boxes, belonged to no time exactly, but at least people would be ready when the time came.

Baba wanted to be first in line.

He bought and sold gold and began to build a house. He told his mother in Diontou that he had money now, and he offered to give her gold nuggets. But his mother was concerned that her husband's two other wives would be jealous if they saw her with jewelry. They would want jewels of their own, and she did not want to put her husband in that position. She refused the gold and told Baba to give her cows. The other women, she reasoned, would appreciate the cows and share the milk, but a woman is not going to fight over another woman's cow.

Conakry would have been a perfect place for Baba and Néné, except for maybe a thousand reasons. The ocean itself had a sluggish way. It was crazy hot there. The air crept reluctantly off the ocean, stinging with bugs, dirt, and dust.

The dust, rising off the earth, was red, which was a good thing, because it meant the land was rich, and more important, it made everyone feel richer for just living on it. Many people, Baba, too, felt proud. When talking about his country, he talked about the rich dirt often. It would have been better, of course, if the government had extracted the iron and bauxite that made it red. The air would have been lighter and the people cleaner and richer. Instead, the people were tired and dirty. Even Baba and Néné, whose floors were made of cool concrete, resented the government for allowing the iron to seep under their skin and into their lungs. There was one paved road in the city. There were no maps because few roads had a name. When it was not hot, June through August, it rained. The rain carved out craters and gullies in the dirt. Trips into town or just to visit a neighbor turned into tricky, tiptoed adventures over flowing, runaway garbage and drowned mice.

Nothing much worked well, which was acceptable in the villages where people lived off the land and relied on one another, but in Conakry people had to rely on systems and faceless ministries to keep things going. The dirt and the heat and the garbage made everyone angry at someone or some thing. Many people were angry at the French, who owned most of everything, or they blamed the Guinea administrators, who took directions, slashing budgets and rerouting goods.

Anyway, no one was tender with Conakry. No one gave it special care. A place without a map or names for its streets feels like it is dying all the time. A pinky stretching into the ocean. It was more like one of those extra dangling pinkies that Néné's and Baba's babies were born with. When they were old enough, Baba and Néné brought the babies to the hospital to have the extra fingers and toes taken off. This was done with a tightly knotted bandage that cut off the circulation. In a few days the unneeded toes and fingers fell off. Perhaps that would have been the kinder way to treat Conakry, rather than let it wearily hang on.

The people had been mad at each other for some time. Few roads in the country were tarred. The coffee was contaminated, and a country that grew maybe more rice than any place in the world was importing rice, not exporting it. The city people, mostly the Soussou, were angry at the Fulah who had come from the mountains, people like Baba and Néné. They had crowded Conakry, they thought, and taken away work. The Soussou and Fulah fought and killed each other in the streets. Baba, worried for his family's safety, bought a rifle.

Even by 1958, when tensions had calmed, the country worked only in fits and starts. In May 1958 the railroad between Kankan and Conakry stopped running altogether. Guinea sits near the bottom of Africa's left shoulder. It is roughly the shape of a rounded fist, bordering six countries and embracing nearly all of Sierra Leone, which sits right in its palm. Conakry is the big city in the west and Kankan is the big city in the east. Shutting down the railroad was like cutting the country in half.

General de Gaulle distracted everyone from all that. He offered Guinea and all the French colonies a kind of independence, a halfway standing between country and protectorate. Sékou Touré, the new Guinea president, preached "ethnic integration," which had a promising ring. The different groups turned their anger against the French instead of one another.

"We have a first and indispensable need of our dignity," Sékou Touré declared in 1958. "Now, there is no dignity without freedom. We prefer freedom in poverty to riches in slavery."

De Gaulle took him at his word, making sure that Guinea was poor.

Before the French left, they emptied everything—from bank accounts to file cabinets. They burned records, and took nearly all the country's engineers and agriculture experts. Every bit of gold they could get, they jammed into suitcases and into their pockets. The last of their planes flew out over crops still burning from the fires they had started. When they were done, there were maybe a dozen people in all of Conakry who had gone to college.

The government radio called itself the Voice of the Revolution. And people paraded and sang triumphantly:

> *Good-bye, Europeans*
> *Good-bye, Europeans*
> *And without a grudge*
> *I, myself am not offended*
> *Good-bye everyone to his own home ruthless*
> *Without any fuss*
> *Good-bye provided you disturb us no more*
> *Let him follow you*
> *He who believes you indispensable*

Baba admired Sékou Touré, but he thought independence had come too soon. After all, the French had treated him well when he was in Senegal. Though he had given money to the government's party, no one from the party had come to help his family when he was away. Baba could not always be sure who his friends were. He sat on the step in front of his house with the rifle. No one bothered him—and he demanded much respect this way.

The rifle wasn't far away when Néné told him another baby was coming.

Nothing finishes as it begins.

Before the scholars entered Guinea with the word of Mohammed, the Fulah women picked their husbands. If this is surprising to you, it was not to me. My father told me so when I was only a young girl, no more than six or seven, and early on I firmly understood the natural order.

The men of that time, seven hundred years ago, arranged elaborate dances, a kind of competition that required the men to preen. They painted their chests and colored their cheekbones and eyelids bright reds and yellows, and they gave special attention to their teeth, cleaning them, and shaping them, too, against the smooth edges of river rocks, until their smile had just the glint of the devil.

Each man held a spear and made a whooping warrior dance over each woman, but when a woman held up her palms, they stopped and slumped off. If the woman nodded, the man approached her and went to his knees for the woman's closer consideration. In the end, the women surrounded the men and made their choices.

Soon came the weddings. The whole village turned out, the women were regaled with music and poetry, and the men swore their faith to their new wives. Then, after days or even months had gone by, should a woman look at her man and see too much of the devil in him or not think his teeth fascinating or his unpainted physique tempting, or had she discovered him to be unwise, she could declare a change of heart. With that, the woman would move on, not to scorn but to even more fervent wooing by a string of suitors who saw in her now something they had missed before—the aura of true independence and elusiveness.

So nothing remains as it begins. We followed the cattle through the bushes, building our huts around the spot where the animals found water. There we lived for a hundred years before the springs dried or the animals finally grew restless. The women grew their gardens, or *suntoureé*. The men were responsible for the fence around the gardens. The men and the women grew old and died in the same huts where they were born. We believed in the old ways, and still the old ways evaporated. In time, the children left the villages before the animals did. The men told the women what to think and then thought little of what the women said. The men preached the Koran to the women but did not let

23

them read it, and when it was time, the men left, to explore, make money, to satisfy an itch.

The women waited for their men to return, or they waited for something to happen. When nothing happened, they waited for nothing. They only waited, their babies growing heavier on their backs.

Questions: Did my father tell my mother about the way it was in the beginning? Did he dare? Would it have changed anything?

A detail: The deep well my mother discovered as a young girl swelled quickly from below and in a single season became a spring. It has helped many villages survive, and because some people in the villages knew my mother, they named it after her. It's called the Bhundhu Diaraye. People traveling between Tinkin and Guinea-Bissau drink from it. It is the place where my mother scratched at the dirt and discovered water.

CHAPTER TWO

WAITING FOR BABA

Early in the summer of my fifth year, the bees came back. We were living then in the town of Labé, back in the light air of the Fouta Djallon. The bees entered the yard unhurried, like family visiting for the season. I know they had been there before because Néné said, "Can you believe it? Here they are again, like last year and the year before. They must think this is their house." One bee came first and dispatched word that everything had been left the same, and the rest of the clan followed in a noisy, spinning bundle, excited as we were.

Diadia whirled. Koto's eyes became big and round and interested. Hadiatou's eyes darted, but her face and her body otherwise froze on the spot. Mamadou, two years old, sitting on the ground, didn't react to the bees, but he shrieked at the sudden commotion. We called him Bobo. And Néné, whose belly was round in another summer, laughed in a way the bees must have taken as a blessing. They paused by her at the open doorway and with a last grateful curtsy, zipped into the house.

I clapped and danced. "Good afternoon, bees," I shouted. Then I ran as fast as I could away from them. It was possible to like the bees and be frightened by them, too.

They hovered just inside the door in the center of the big room where Baba liked to greet guests, before descending behind the big table, through a hidden opening, I guessed, and into the single drawer that held forks and spoons. The table was an important place, because

Néné kept a great pot of rice on it. With the bees inside, the table vibrated with strange busyness. Happy, happy bees.

It was a good day. Néné told us that Baba had asked the griot to come that night, promising there would be music and we would all sit together late. Néné sang to herself that day, and we children found one place or another, bouncing a ball, talking to the goats and mutton, drifting on the road to another house. We lived on a square piece of land surrounded by other squares. No one strayed far, in case Bobo needed watching, or better, if the sauces needed tasting. I was fast for that. Néné held up a long spoon, and one, two, my fat face beamed from Néné's knees. She guided the spoon, thick with yogurt, into my mouth, turned it once, and just like that, the spoon came out shiny clean. "My Mama," Néné laughed. "I always count on you."

They called me Mama. I was not as dark as my mother. I had more honey in me. Baby fat stuck to me. My cheeks were a newborn's, swelled with gladness or pouty soft with worry. My eyes were my mother's, full planets that pleased the grown-ups who reminded me constantly that my eyes resembled windows flung open. I heard "Mama's happy today" or "something's bothering Mama" when I had not said a word. I showed everything, hid nothing. My cheeks and eyes and arms and legs popped with information.

Optimistic, I danced, I flew. Doubtful, I shrank. My arms hugged my legs, my legs against my chest, my arms and legs guarding all of me. It depended.

It depended on thunder. A safe off-in-the-distance rumble gave me warm chills. That storm was another village's worry. I was safe in my house. But one up-close, earth-cracking bang, and I was convinced that the storm had been sent for us. The thunder would flash the lightning on a targeted zigzag to the bed I shared with my sisters. Maybe God had singled out our house, or maybe it was Sékou Touré. He was powerful enough.

God or Sékou Touré, at thunder, I ran to Néné.

It depended on the glow of the moon—the whiter the better. And on rain—it quieted me. It turned to hail in the evening, and I grabbed the rain. I placed it on the center of my tongue and swallowed it whole.

It depended on day and night. Either was fine, but the in-between time frightened me. It depended on my sisters and brothers. Were they playing or were they fighting? It depended on the sounds of their sleep, Diadia and Hadiatou with me in our bed, Koto in his bed across the room. On their coughs and wheezings; one or the other of us was always coming down with a cold or fever. It depended on mango trees and avocado trees, and wind, voices, other sounds, rocks from the yard, the comings and goings of neighbors, the happiness of bees.

I didn't belong to myself. I belonged to the elements that buzzed through our house and visited our yard. It was a cement house with a zinc roof. It had four rooms, one for Baba, one for Néné, one for the children, and the big room in the middle. There was a much smaller cement house where the food was cooked, and another even smaller house, also made of cement, where we sat on a hole chiseled out of concrete to go to the bathroom, except for Baba, who had his own bathroom inside. I belonged to a lot of cement. We had a well that we used for cooking, washing, and bathing. For drinking water we used the nearby well of a friend of our mother's. We had no glass windows, only wooden shutters.

I belonged to Néné's garden. I'd sit on the ground using my shoes as a cushion in order to keep my bottom clean from dirt. "Don't take your shoes off like that," Néné said. "If you do, it means you will have a life of travel."

Mostly, I belonged to Néné. Sing the song about *kankalabé*, the village where everyone is beautiful. Why was Néné crying? I heard something. Be happy, Néné. Tell the story about the girl who sang to her magic chicken, who then granted the girl's every wish. Please laugh, Néné. Laugh the whole day long, because your laughing always feels like a surprise.

As I belonged to her, so she belonged to me, for I was the measure of the house, the measure of herself, her Mama. Mama sensed things, saw signs, expertly read the faces of grown people. Mama felt the earth tremble before the thunder burst. Mama confirmed Néné's dread, emboldened her hopes. Mama was Néné's own surest reflection, gave her permission to laugh.

"Look at you eat," Néné said. "Mama's excited today. I don't blame you. I'm excited, too."

"When's he coming, Néné?"

"Tonight, for dinner, after dark."

"Will he play his guitar?"

"You know he always does."

Diadia began singing *"Djarabi,"* a love song.

"Will he let us touch the strings?" she asked. "Will he stay late?"

Néné laughed. "When he gets here, you will ask him, and he will tell you.

"But first," she said. She pointed to the large bowl of vegetables at her feet. The carrots and tomatoes were a sweet orange and yellow. "I must prepare. So be good."

Néné's lap disappeared. I watched her move in serious strokes across the yard. This was a yard without grass, laid unevenly with silver and gray stones. Mango, avocado, guava, and orange trees gave depth and shading to the yard. Greenish, silvery geckos slid over the stones and up the trees. The ground jutted with pointy rocks and other odd, camouflaged objects like bottle caps, the missing wheels of a toy, and thrown-away, fallen-away baby pins. Néné's feet padded over them, but Néné did not wince. The bottoms of Néné's feet surely felt nothing.

Into the main house with one bowl, out with another, retrieving spoons and chopping knives and many wooden trays. She stirred cow's milk hard until it became stringy, then mixed harder to give it the creamy firmness of yogurt. Sitting on the ground, she held a calabash bowl in her crossed legs and ground couscous with the end of a smooth *bingawal* stirring stick. She shaved the sweetest pieces of cassava into a bowl. It fell away in slender, white arcs. She whipped the root again to make it firm.

Rising, she laid a rubbery slab of beef on a wood plank and pounded it with her fists. Her arms flew lightly and landed smartly. The meat puckered, absorbing each blow with a small, surrendering noise, what sounded like a gasp. She lifted the meat itself, held it above her head, and brought it down with a full thwack. And another, and another. She smacked the meat with open hands. Finally, she leaned into it with her palms pressed flat, and I noticed the blue muscle lines in her arms, the blood running down her fingers.

She held the meat out across her arms. It lay there, defeated.

"This will cook well," she said.

Néné carried the meat into the kitchen house, through a long, narrow space, and she disappeared into black. It was dark in the kitchen house, just light from the sparks popping from the pots on the ground, where everything got cooked with Néné's oil. There were turtle-shaped cooking stones, stored firewood, a small rusting water pump, several jugs of the oil, the pot, and the sparks, which floated out through the opening, and up into the sky, where later, in the evening, they came back as stars.

"Néné," called my sister, Hadiatou, running to the kitchen house, but stopping many steps from the opening. Hadiatou seemed to know what was coming.

A yellow flame leaped through the opening, felt the air for a long second, and withdrew with a whoosh back into the dark.

"Néné!" This time Hadiatou ran up to the entrance, crying. "Néné, Néné, where are you?"

Fire hurt Néné? Never. She appeared out of black smoke, laughing.

"Look, look, Hadiatou. It was the pot, the oil, the meat. Every time I do this, and every time the fire comes, and every time you cry."

Hadiatou was a worrier. Her eyes were thinner than the rest of us, the bones in her face sharper. She held suspicion in her face in the way of a grown-up, the way Néné or Baba did. Her trust was something to be won. She had to be convinced.

"See my arms, my legs," Néné said. Shiny globes of sweat sat cheerfully on Néné's face. "Nothing. Just cooking fat. It's good when it burns. It means the meat is good and rich. It means the cow had a good life."

Another face appeared in the opening of the kitchen house, the darker, slighter twin to Néné's face. This was Idrissa, Néné's cousin, who lived with us. She slept in Néné's room. She was not as tall as Néné, but her legs and her arms were thin to where she often appeared the longer of the two.

When Néné's father died, Idrissa's mother cared for Néné, and the two girls had grown close. Even as young women, it was not uncommon for them to hold hands and talk in a whisper. Idrissa often appeared without a word, alongside Néné or behind her, a hushed partner. With Néné expecting, Idrissa was nothing so much as her shadow. Because Néné was often expecting, you could say that Idrissa, now a young woman, thin as a leaf, was the not-pregnant picture of Néné. We called her Néné Idrissa.

They both stared down at Hadiatou, and it was something in the companionship of their eyes that gave Hadiatou ease. Hadiatou backed away with half acceptance, and Néné and Idrissa retreated again to the bubbling pots.

Once the meat and the oil and fat calmed, the smoke rising from the kitchen house changed its look. It lost its blackness, accepting more red and brown from the meat, the orange of the peanut, and a lighter hint of red from the tomato sauce. The smoke did not lift away, but became a cloud in a blue sky. Our cloud, for me and Diadia, Koto, Hadiatou and Bobo, and the unseen baby, too, tucked away in God's most luscious place.

I lifted my face to the smell and knew right then, with the wisdom of a child, that this smell would never escape me beyond retrieval. It was mine as if I had invented it, which in a way I had. Peanuts and honey, sweet potato and sizzling sauce, fried dough, boiling new potatoes and eggs cooking inside of meatballs. It was the smell of the inside and the outside, of Néné and Idrissa. The smell was curled and soft, and hollow. At the center it held our impatience and our anticipation. And if I had not been there, if somehow thieves had grabbed me or if the earth had swallowed me, if for some reason I had never lived in that space, there never would have been such a smell, so great a wonder.

"Mama loves food," they would say.

I did. When I was three, my mother had sent me back to the village to live with my grandmother in Tinkin, the one I was named for. I was fed bananas and pudding every day. Uncle Sharif gave me red-and-green sucking candies, which I bit into pieces. I swallowed them fast that way, and the faster I swallowed, the faster my uncle refilled the supply. Aunt Djengui carried me on her back and fed me over her shoulder. I would eat gobs of yogurt from a large bowl, and then, what harm could it do, I jumped in the bowl.

Plop!

No one rushed to take me out. They liked seeing me creamy in the bowl, blinking, eating yogurt from my arms and knees, the fat, honey-colored baby in the white sea.

Months later, when Néné came to bring me home, she found a roly-poly child with enormous cheeks. The word for it in Fulah is *woufindho*. "I will have to do something about this," Néné said.

She couldn't do much. She made yogurt that was extra creamy. She added salt or sugar. I swam in her yogurt, too.

Finally, I grew too big for that, but food always gave my arms and legs ideas of freedom. That day, waiting for the griot, my favorite smells milling in heaven's haze, I ran in circles, and laughed for its own sake. If I were a grown-up, they would have called me a laughing fool, maybe even if I were a boy, but a girl could get away with a laugh like that, a high laugh, a laugh for the birds.

Koto loved my laugh, not that I knew this from anything he said aloud. When I laughed, he noticed me as if recognizing an old friend from across the way. His eyes narrowed, but in a pleased way. It was not the look of a brother who had always been near, as Koto had. It was the look of someone who had left and come back, and was pleased to find I was still there.

Koto was ten that summer. He looked at me from one knee, from the corner of the yard he preferred, where he had cleared the rocks away and smoothed the red dirt for a tidy playing surface, no wider than his hips, maybe as long as both his arms together. At either end of the space, he had scooped out dirt for two small holes, and what he had then was a football field in miniature.

From his pocket, Koto took out three small rounded stones that had been hollowed in the center and each filled with a pristine marble, one green, one red, one yellow, that gave the stones rotation and speed and surprising spin. You can find these stones sold everywhere. We called the game *bille*, and it was simple. Propel the little ball into the goal by pinching it between two fingers. Even a near miss could get you points.

Koto leaned forward, our brother the general, and Diadia, Hadiatou, and I closed in around him in that little space. Koto could maneuver a stone with mastery by slight adjustments of his thumb and pointing finger. Somehow he could make the stone change direction twice on a single roll. He could make it skip, which was useful for getting past a pebble blocking the way. He knew his sisters liked the trick shots, so he paused, weighed the stone in the center of his hand, rubbed it between his palms, and discharged the rock when he was ready, but only after he had scanned the terrain. A stray weed called for more backspin. A divot required more skip, more downward thrust.

"Go, Koto. You can do it, Koto."

That was my voice. Koto was playing for Guinea against invisible French defenders.

Koto! Koto! Koto!

We clapped and chanted, gaining a bigger crowd. Koto's friends, Aliou, Meka, and Papa, floated over from next door. Our houses were attached and we shared the yard with them.

"Koto has thirty-three!"

"Isn't forty-five the record?"

"Yeah!"

Koto! Koto! Koto!

Koto stayed on one knee and kept his head down. He could have told us to run and leave him alone, that if we kept at it, the commotion would obscure the sound of Baba's arrival, that Baba might suddenly be standing in back of us, staring down on Koto's football game. Were that to happen, our fun would become Koto's loss, and that would be a terrible thing.

Koto said nothing, but the thought was now in my mind. I made my best effort to see through the back of my head. *Cheer Koto. But don't forget about Baba.* Baba has his way of being there, when a moment before there was open space.

I loved Baba, but I did not like how he closed off open space.

I listened for the tires of his Land Rover coming to a rest on the road, alert to the whiny surge of the engine before it coughed to a dead stop, the certain tempo of his stepping from the car, closing the door, his footsteps on cracked pavement.

I allowed myself a look. No Baba.

Go, Koto!

You just knew that Baba would appear at any second, his face turned to stone, that this grand afternoon would end with Koto dragged from the yard by his ears. That's what I was thinking when I just stopped thinking, when Koto made forty-one, then forty-two, then forty-three, then . . .

I was smart enough to know that the physical body of Baba came from work each day at half past three o'clock, but that the rest of him did not arrive until after lunch, way after lunch, after he had changed into his white boubou without sleeves, after he had washed his hands and feet and nose and bent over in front of the house for the afternoon *Alansara* prayer, after he had lain on his bedcovers, holding his transistor radio on his stomach, listening to the news.

Have faith in the path we have chosen. The price for freedom is never greater than the price for no freedom.

Remember, we are free when we have our honor.

The deep Fulah voices preaching an age of liberty for all Guineans was certain notice to the children in the yard that the hour of our liberties was over. Baba's disappearance into his room signaled the older children to open up their Koran lessons, and me to keep my games quiet. While Baba's rest made us still, the radio voices, rising in a drum song, muffled on Baba's belly, made us tired. That was the hour when, if it were a practice, we might have all have lain down beside Baba for a good nap.

Every day it happened this way. Baba came home. Baba got mad at Koto. Baba changed clothes. Baba prayed. Baba ate. Baba listened to the radio. Baba drifted off without us. These were the probabilities.

So I turned again, and there was Baba.

In one hand he held a bag overstuffed with skinny loaves of French bread. In the other he held a slim briefcase. No free hands. That was good. He was dressed in the business suit he usually wore for the office.

I shuffled backward, pulled by Diadia and Hadiatou. Koto's friends ran. Koto, without turning or standing or so much as taking a breath, clasped his hands behind his head, using his elbows as shields for his ears.

Baba looked at Koto, but it is another thing to say that he saw Koto. He just stared. Baba had above-average powers of staring, and Koto, on his side, could remain frozen with his arms around his head for just as long. They would become two yard lizards squaring up, throats pulsing, but otherwise petrified until a hint of a move by one or the other and then the thrashing and chasing, dust lifting, Baba swinging, Koto running, falling, arms still folded, small eyes peering out from between two pointy elbows.

This time Baba was past staring. His eyes were dots. And then, he smiled, just like that.

"The griot is coming," he said. "And the air. Néné has made wonderful food for us, I can tell."

We looked up. The sky surrounded our father and held his smile.

"It's going to be beautiful in Labé tonight," he said.

Probabilities were only that.

Soon Néné made the baths. She took the bark from the mango trees and dried leaves from the papaya trees and placed them in boiling water. To fight the coughing germs that jumped from one child to the other, she sprinkled the water with small leaves of the kasia bush, and she waited for the water to turn red. She poured the water into a metal tub outside and surrounded the tub with a wall of hourgou, or dried grass, for privacy from the yard.

Stepping in, I felt the odd chill in my jaw that came from hot bathwater and a shrinking in my stomach from getting used to it. I scraped Néné's soap onto a sponge, which I slowly rubbed over my skin. The soap was black and made from the kidi tree. The sponge was splintery in its touch, scratching as it cleaned. I found the harder and faster I scrubbed, the less the sponge hurt.

"Néné, I saw, she didn't wash enough," Hadiatou announced, busy watching like always.

I washed my shoulders until they were red and sore. That was fine, because soon Néné stood me between her knees, and with the hands that had conquered a wall of beef, she rubbed me with karitè butter. Only now the hands held kisses.

She turned me by my melted shoulders and whispered, "Mama is good."

It was getting to that time. Past day, not yet night, no sun, a low, weak moon. I could feel myself tipping on the edge of something drawing near. The oil lamps set out in the big room looked like strangers to each other, their tiny flames not up to the job. In dusk, their meager light only hurt our eyes and shrunk the house in fluttering shadow. Waiting for stars scared me. Other houses vanished and all that was left was this red landscape, darkened and naked. At that time, you could sense the curve of the planet, and you knew we were alone.

Dark, this crawling, grainy dark, had powers to take away faces. I could see the shape of Néné in her boubou, but not her. Baba became smaller. The outlines of my mother and father shifted to the ground. They hunched over for the evening *Foutoro* prayer, Néné behind Baba,

Baba saying the prayer, and in this dark, I believed they prayed to keep away the dying of something. I ran to Néné, to be near her breath, and I imagined that all the little girls of the Fouta Djallon were running to their mothers at that moment.

Not much time passed before the dread began to lift. The covers came off the bowls of food, and the moon rose swiftly to light our garden of riches. We sat on a mat, all of us together, eating out of one big bowl with our hands, and we looked up, and there he was in the doorway, a small man holding a guitar, smiling to wish us a kind evening, a man conjured by the moon itself.

His name was Mangua Sarra. He was a man my father knew from long ago. He sang about Samory Touré, the great-grandfather of Sékou Touré, and he sang about Alfa Yaya. He sang in a strong voice, and his voice sweetened when he sang about the beauty of the Fulah people. My father closed his eyes. Mangua Sarra sang of heroes.

Hours went by. "Is there anything else?" the griot asked. My father pulled more money out from under his boubou.

"Sing more about the Fulah people. Sing the song about our ancestors."

The griot went on, past midnight and one in the morning. When we were taken in to our bedroom the griot still sat with my father. He read poems to him and sang more, and the day ended only when our burning eyes gave up and consented finally to Néné's pledge that another day would come tomorrow.

We were asleep when my father came back into the big room with a burning stick. All we knew is that the next morning the bees were gone. Néné told us later that Baba shook the table to wake the bees and chased them from the house with the stick.

By now you know that Baba and Néné left Conakry.

In 1956, the year Hadiatou was born, people were stabbed in their sleep or poisoned or stoned to death. Homes were stampeded and ravaged, farm animals slaughtered. People were strung up in their yards and their bodies dumped in the wells behind their houses.

Unlike the Mandingos, who could be distinguished by their dark skin, the Soussou and Fulah shared similar brown tones, meaning it was difficult to systematically kill each other, meaning they had to devise ways to ferret the other out. One method was the word test. Soussou foot soldiers entered the homes of strangers and asked them to repeat a few words. If the words were said properly in the clipped Soussou style, the visit ended with a handshake and a bowl of goro nuts or yogurt for the intruder.

Any faltering or the wrong inflection meant a knife to the throat. Fathers, sometimes with their families, were wiped out. Longtime friends became enemies when they discovered who the other really was, or they took their friendship underground. Everyone slept lightly, alert to sounds of a trespasser in the middle of the night.

Néné was in the kitchen house making dinner when a neighbor ran in to say that a truck would be coming through to rescue families and carry them out of Conakry and into the mountains. *Get out now. They're coming to your house. It's the word test.*

Néné grabbed Diadia, Hadiatou, and Koto, and an armful of chickens. She left oil burning on the fire and rice boiling. Baba pulled his rifle from the closet. We huddled in the truck with neighbors and old friends, knees to knees. Baba and the other men took turns driving and placating Guinea soldiers at the roped-off checkpoints on the road. *We're visiting family. We're not selling anything. Look, you can see, just women and children.* If that didn't work, they gave the soldiers money, and the rope lifted. The men directed their guns at the dark, on guard for an ambush while the children slept in a corner. The chickens, stowed below, their legs tied, cried through the night. Néné alone thought of the burning oil and fretted that the house had burned down by now. She imagined that all of Conakry was burning. They arrived in the mountains at sunrise, the children leaping out with so much joy, the adults deciding that the Fouta Djallon was their only true home, where one day they would return permanently.

They say that when the French airlifted themselves out of Guinea, the country was left without an immediate way to harvest the rich, dormant rice fields or to transport the rice that was being grown. There may not have been a better place for growing rice in all the world, but with so much land forsaken, the fields brown and fallow, Guinea had to turn outside for rice shipments, by the tons. What's more, mountainsides bursting with gold and bauxite and diamonds retreated into quiet. Gone was the sound of hammer drills sinking into an obedient earth. Missing were the men at the top end of the drills, exercising their muscle and pouring out their sweat.

People say that without enough rice to grow and sell, and with precious stones lying tantalizingly out of reach, it was natural for the Soussou and Fulah to turn on each other. There's nothing more dangerous than unused muscle and unspent sweat, and they owned knives.

Years later Néné and Baba told me about all the troubles, about that night on the truck when no one could scarcely breathe, about the families up the road who did not get on the truck, never seen again, and the ones killed for sure in their yards for a misspoken word. Néné and Baba told me about that night once, around the time the griot sang for us, when I was five and quickly growing older, and it is my memory now.

The next day Baba got hold of Koto and didn't let go. First he beat him with a thin stick, then a fat one. We did not know if it was for yesterday's game of Bille or for the time Koto slept late or spoke over an elder or did not speak enough or had not prayed or appeared lazed or dreamy or watchful or had eaten too much or not enough or because Koto was small for his age. It was always this way. Baba had every reason and no reason.

"Focus! Focus!" Baba screamed. "I didn't have any of this when I was a child. I'm trying to make things better for you. Why don't you focus?"

The stick fell on Koto's arms and his back and his legs. The more Baba hit Koto, the angrier Baba grew. "I expect more. I expect better," Baba boomed.

Words gurgled out of Koto. If he pleaded for mercy, the words were drowned in his whimpering sobs. Maybe it was Koto's crying that Baba did not like. Baba boiled like the oil in Néné's pot. He tossed the stick aside and hit Koto with his hands, and when Koto cringed in the dirt, Baba kicked him until Koto lost the strength to hold up his elbows. Baba stood over him then, waiting for a response that Koto would not give.

Poor Koto. It was hard to watch this, again and again, so many times. Hadiatou and I cried, "Baba is hurting Koto. Stop it. Stop it."

Baba did not hear us. He finally withdrew to his room and his radio while my sisters and I approached Koto, cubs gingerly circling a wounded member of the pack. If Baba ever yelled at Diadia or Hadiatou or me, or if he struck one of us, or Néné, he would come back in a little asking our forgiveness, as gentle as he had been ferocious. Baba would cry and say he cherished us. First came angry Baba, then rueful Baba, followed by a prayerful Baba. More than anything we wanted one Baba.

With Koto, Baba's rage trailed on. We heard him bellowing from the house. "My oldest son! You! You cannot disappoint me!"

I ached for my Koto. Hadiatou put her arm around me and held my face. She was eight but acted like someone much older. Néné had gone into the house.

"Do not cry, Mama," Hadiatou said. "I think there is a reason Baba is always so angry with Koto."

Hadiatou was always trying to solve things, always constructing reasons for the way things were.

"It must be that Koto is from another family," she said. "Why else would Baba be so mad at him all the time? It's like Koto doesn't have a chance."

I stared at her, knowing she was wrong.

"I think Baba hits Koto," I said, "because Koto is his son."

We thought on this for a while, and finally I moved away, into the house. I stood behind a fold in the curtain that swung in the entrance to Baba's room, separating Baba from the rest of the house. In Baba's room was a bed and a dark, wooden wardrobe closet holding both his suit and his boubous. A photograph of Baba's mother was nailed high on one wall, a photograph of his brothers high on another. I remembered these from the few times I had been permitted in Baba's room, but I could not see them then from where I stood. His room was the mystery place. Through the pale fabric of the curtain, I could not see Baba's face or much of his body, but I could see his shoes resting on his bed. They were brown, not too large, and I was thankful for their stillness. I guessed that Baba was sleeping. Like always, and for the longest while, I stood in the curl of the curtain and watched my father's shoes.

Sounds in Labé dropped in on a ribbon. The roosters exchanged throaty good mornings, the goats kissed with their heads, and soon came the chatter of older children, mostly boys and some girls off to the school, named Kourould for a section of Labé. Other girls passed by later, singly, on the way to sewing lessons, hardly noticed. The children sang the national anthem in the yards, some loud and mournful. Baba prayed. Such care Baba had with the words. Not a shout, or a whisper, but the tenor of the shepherd, gently escorting each word along. God would listen to a man with this voice.

Before the hot middle time of day, the mothers worked in their gardens, *suntouré* in Fulah, picking the best of their taro or cabbage for dinner. Later, the mothers sat beside the houses and talked. A car passed by, banging noisily over the rutted road, and the mothers looked up. If they recognized someone in the car, they waved with a stiff arm. If the faces were strange, they looked after the car, not unkindly, as it rattled along. The children returned in the early afternoon, and the mothers looked at their faces to know what had happened that day, what was learned. There was the noise of families getting to know each other again, and the noise of people paying visits. *"Onjaramaa. Onjaramaa,"* they said in greeting. In the late afternoon and into the evening, visits were welcome events in any house.

News traveled in our neighborhood. Someone was getting married. Someone's mother was having a baby. Someone bought a new dress in a new fashion. We could tell if something important had happened, if someone was angry or sick or happy, if a son or daughter had misbehaved or shamed a parent. Murmurs were everywhere. We heard the murmur of gossip. Someone is moving back to the village. Someone's daughter is wild. These murmurs brought excitement, but unease, too. I liked the murmur of prayer better.

At news of a marriage or engagement in someone's house, whoops of celebration went up. The father stood in his doorway, and everyone ran over with rice and nuts and money. The women hollered and laughed. When someone died or word of a death came from the village, we ran over again, the children trailing the mothers, and the mothers wept loudly, falling on the ground from stabs of shared grief. Finally, the grown-ups covered their faces. They offered Koranic verses to bless the family and pray for the deceased. Everyone offered food to the grieving family. The children sat on the floor. The prayer was a murmur, and the murmur knitted us in a strange happiness that can rise through sorrow. Sorrow cutting through happiness plowing through heartache.

The grown-ups fought a lot. Husbands fought with wives. Screaming, then quiet, then a new outburst. Diadia and Hadiatou, Koto and me, listened to the volley of pans flying and tables slamming, and we were held by the lulls that often signaled not a truce but the building up of strength for a new battle.

Across the road, Mr. Kamara and his wife, Aissatou, carried on every day. First Mr. Kamara yelled. Not an ordinary yell, not even the yell of a man, more like an angry child's, high and stubborn, a yell to get his way no matter what. He was an airplane pilot for the government, and he was tall. I imagined him looming over his wife, shaking his fist, screaming his high scream. Néné would run over to find Mr. Kamara stomping away and Aissatou crouched in a ball, crying he had hurt her and pointing her finger after him. "It's his second wife," Aissatou told Néné. "He wants to be with her."

Néné's best friend was Maimouna. She and her husband, Saidou, lived in a small house that was set at the bottom of a sloping yard. The house smelled like smoke and sour, like alcohol. Light bugs crawled on the floors and walls, along cement pocked with tiny holes. Maimouna was a short woman with a quick stride, who, Néné said, owned God's grace to accept hardship. Saidou fixed radios out the front window of the house, and when he finished a job, he made his own celebration. He turned up the music and handed away money his family needed. He had a special place for me. He gave me candies and told me he would marry me in a distant day when I was older, which always made me laugh. Maimouna would take him by the hand and walk him to his bed.

"Lie down and sleep," Maimouna would say. She never yelled.

Maimouna would sit with Néné. Each was a comfort for the other.

"Saidou is sleeping again," Maimouna would say. Néné held her friend's hands calmly in her own.

"It's better this way," Maimouna would say. "He'll be better when he wakes. He's always better after a good rest." They would lower their heads and pray for this to be so.

Whole afternoons passed this way, Néné and Maimouna vowing to see a better day.

One day Maimouna told Néné, "You look tired."

"Yes," Néné said. "The children are all sick."

"I will bring soup for all of you," Maimouna said. "I will make your dinner. I will bring you medicine for the babies. This is a hard time."

"Yes," said Néné. "Sometimes it is this way."

Maimouna smiled, and she said, "I heard Mangua Sarra again." She could not pay for a griot, but she could listen to his voice sailing from our house. "So beautiful, when he sings. Many of us heard him."

Few people we knew had the things we had. Néné often hired a cook. This cost about five hundred Guinean francs a month, about seventy-five cents. Baba sometimes had a driver, paying him about ten thousand Guinean francs a month, or about fifteen dollars. When Diadia needed a new school uniform, Baba bought one. We owned forks and spoons and a set of plates. And Baba still owned the house in Conakry. These things separated us from our neighbors.

But when the griot sang for us, he sang for everybody. I liked thinking about our friends, sitting in their yards at night, the children and the grown-ups listening to music from our house.

I grew to understand that as the sounds of other houses belonged to us, the sounds of our house were not ours alone. It was an equal transaction. We heard them. They heard us.

They heard the serenading of Baba and Baba's own laugh rising above the griot's voice.

They heard the fighting, too, the small and medium fights and the big ones, when Baba warned Néné not to correct him when he told a story. Néné would say she could not change the truth. And Baba would explode. Sometimes he hit her with his open hand until she cried.

"Thanks to you, man, you did a good job," she yelled.

Away from Baba, Néné never spoke badly of him, and Maimouna, in her grace, knew this, for she never brought the conversation that way.

"So many children," she said. "You are tired. Maimouna will cook for you. You will feel better."

Maimouna brought rice and sauce prepared at her house. We rarely ate earlier than nine, and Maimouna's small, bowed figure moved in the moonlight through the yards. She wore soft shoes, open at the toes, which she slipped off at the entrance to the house, and she pattered in near silence, bare feet swooshing on the floor.

I think this was the main thing that happened in Labé when I was young. People like Néné and Maimouna came together, made small sounds and held each other up, and were barely noticed.

CHAPTER THREE

POINTING TO AMERICA

*S*oon came the grand day when I began first grade. I followed Diadia and Koto and Hadiatou out of the house with the bearing of a chosen one. I wore my uniform skirt, the color of light chocolate, proudly. My shoes, while stiff, helped me feel upright and fancy. They were shoes Néné had found in a secondhand shop. They were shiny brown, with a brown, silk bow in the center, their bottoms slippery against the flat rocks. The best part, they were from Paris, wherever that was. I carried a bag with bread and a thick slab of cheese.

Baba wore a special boubou, the prayer robe, to see me out. It was deep lavender with gold threads on the sleeves. He was proudest of all. He reminded me that I already knew my numbers and that I spoke more clearly than any child of six he knew. He told me I would be the smartest student in the class.

"All my girls are smart," he said. He smiled. "Mama will let everyone know."

From the start, Mrs. Aicha promised to be demanding. She called for rigid penmanship, never to leap sloppily over lines or into the margins, and insisted we practice at home. One letter at a time, twenty times over for each page. She had a way of holding up her hands, or folding them at her chest, either gesture lowering silence on the room. She never called on you to speak without making it an occasion. She pointed with a long, elegant finger.

"Yaye Kesso? Do you know the answer? Then tell us."

"Buntu Touré, allow us your best ideas."

"Kadiatou Diallo? It is your time to speak."

She taught in both Fulah and French. I wanted to know her. She wore softly pleated skirts that stopped above her knees, and jackets that turned her shoulders into squared corners. She was young and from Labé, but she could have been from somewhere else. One day she rolled a map of the world down from the ceiling, across the blackboard. She tapped continents with the end of a steel pointer.

"This is our land," she said with a tap. Africa was large and plump.

"France is here," she said with another tap. That was not so far away, just up from us.

"The big city is Paris." I rubbed my new shoes together.

"America is there. The big city is New York." She reached to touch it. America looked over at us from the other side of the map.

I liked her, but I thought she cared more for the boys. The right answer from a boy endowed her praise with extra sweetness.

"Suleiman, you are doing so well."

"Aliou Touré, this is magnificent work."

It made no sense that the boys received the best marks when I scored highest on the tests. I might have been the single student who did not mind tests, especially the ones with numbers. I had a method. I shared a small bench with my friend, Safiatou.

I traced each problem with the point of a pencil, gazing off to study the walls in the classroom. It was an old room in an old single-story building. I would make out the shapes of continents in paint that was chipped and peeling, and soon I found my comfort.

My teacher noticed only sometimes, not often compared to Aliou Touré or Suleiman. My report cards put me third or fourth in the class when I deserved to be first.

At home, I told Baba.

"It is not right," he said. He reviewed my homework each night, finishing with a long, satisfied look at me.

"I know you are the smartest," he liked to say.

I told Yaye Kesso I would talk to the teacher. Yaye Kesso was small like me, and thin. She had a bold side, and she gave me the encouragement I sought, but I held my thoughts for many more days. Then I received another perfect score. My face was surely beaming when I noticed the boys pointing at me.

"Look at smarty," my friend Omou said.

That's all it took. I stepped toward the teacher.

"I would like to talk about my grades."

"You have the best test results in the class," she said. That sounded like the sentence I wanted to hear.

"Mrs. Aicha, thank you." I nearly turned away.

"Kadiatou?"

"My report cards do not show that."

She looked down at me as if a bird had landed on my head, and I instantly felt wrong about complaining. Many other students required her attention, and really, in a way, I didn't care, and I didn't want her to think I cared. I liked school, and the last thing I wanted was for Mrs. Aicha to feel bad. It was her firm teaching that had helped me in the first place.

"Kadiatou, you are so smart, and this is what you think about."

I could not tell if this was a statement or a question.

"My advice is simple," she said. "Look not left nor right. Look only at your own footsteps."

Instantly, I felt better. *Look at your own footsteps.* A beautiful thought. If I just looked down at my feet wearing the shoes from Paris, I could think of Néné going to the store in the main market, looking seriously at many different shoes and not leaving until she had found the shoes that she knew would make Mama happy. I liked my own footsteps. I liked my feet and my legs and I liked how I walked into a room, expecting to find people who would be glad to see me.

For a time, Mrs. Aicha's words kept away busy, unkind thoughts like jealousy and resentment. Then the girls started giving me trouble.

It started with the bigger girls who watched me at lunchtime. We ate in the schoolyard, and they eyed me digging into my bag and bringing out a good-sized piece of bread.

"Give me the bread," one girl said.

I looked at her.

"Your family has everything. You don't need such a big piece. Give me your bread." I handed it over.

This happened day after day, the same girls also taking Yaye Kesso's food. We gave them our bread and fruit and cheese, fraught with guilt that we had more than they did, and by the end of the day our stomachs clamped with hunger. We had our mothers prepare bigger lunches, but the girls just took whatever we had, their requests turning to commands. Yaye Kesso and I teamed up, resolved to ward off their ambushes, but that did little. Yaye Kesso hardly weighed anything. They shoved her aside, then me, and bore into our paper bags.

One girl was bigger than the rest. She was bigger than any of the boys, too. She had great, round shoulders and a large neck, thickened by extra rolls of skin, that sat atop one another like folded cloth. Any exquisiteness to her features was overwhelmed by her size. Her puffed cheeks stretched her lips thin and hid her ears from easy view. Her name was Aissata. She was fat and used her fatness so meanly, we called her Pumpatonn, Fatty, to be mean back, though never for her hearing.

On those days when Yaye Kesso and I decided to stand firm, her deputies called for Pumpatonn. She clomped over and thrust out a fist. "Now," she would say. And that was that. Shrinking beneath her, we slipped the cheese between her blunt fingers.

I tried to think about my footsteps, but it was not easy. At school, each of us was responsible for little gardens where we grew tomatoes. Every Monday, we had to bring the dried manure of a goat or a cow to use for the gardens. Pumpatonn told me to bring extra for her, that her family could not spare manure they needed for their own garden. Néné had two goats, and for many weeks I took extra manure without her noticing, carrying it away in an old tomato can. Néné finally wondered where the manure had gone, and she said that the manure was too valuable to share. One Sunday, Pumpatonn came to our house to collect the manure.

"Why must you give it to her," my mother asked. I stiffened with the dread of confronting Pumpatonn without the manure.

"Because she is my friend," I told Néné.

Pumpatonn was not smart. She failed the tests, and was constantly required to sweep the classroom as punishment. Pumpatonn wearied of this and ordered me to sweep for her. In exasperation, I told my sister Hadiatou about the girl who was ruining my life.

"Do not worry," my sister said, laughing. "Tomorrow, I am going to see this girl who is giving you all this trouble, and I am going to deal with her."

That night I dreamed that Pumpatonn shrunk. Faced with the power of my sister and my giant family, she shriveled into almost nothing. In my dream, she offered to do anything for me. I woke happy.

Late the next afternoon, the classroom nearly emptied, and it was sweeping time. My sister arrived as scheduled. She was pleased, nearly skipping for the chance to perform this service for her sister. "Okay, where is this girl?" she said eagerly.

Pumpatonn was standing in the middle of the room. "Over there." I pointed.

"She is the one?" my sister said.

"Yes." My sister looked at Pumpatonn. Pumpatonn looked straight back at her, and my sister turned to me.

"You better do what she says."

Those were Hadiatou's only words. She wheeled around and left for home. I swept up again.

That night I yelled at Hadiatou. "How can you humiliate me?" I asked.

"If I had fought with her, you would be more humiliated," Hadiatou said, "because this girl would have killed me in front of everybody."

I put my head in my hands.

"I will say it another way," Hadiatou said. "It is better to negotiate than to bury me."

The truth of things was showing itself hard to know. Néné had the right to the manure in her own garden, but the goats were always making more, and anyway, it could not be wrong to help someone who had less. My sister was right and wrong. In search of honor, she chose safety. I was weak. I turned to others, my mother, my sister, and my teacher, to show me the proud way because alone, I did not know which was which.

I was coming to the age of remembering. A disappointed look, words of reproach or a tale from an elder about something recalled from the village days, these gained a shape and held fast in my mind where earlier they had merely grazed me and passed by. With memory comes the knowing of sorrow. The people I knew, even the people I loved, did not always get things right, and they accumulated acts and omissions that lessened their sense of sureness. Realizing this instantly made me older.

I was seven and zigzagging through Labé, through dirt alleys and in cement corridors created by houses nearly atop one another. Just when you thought you had reached a dead end, and were out of breath, you would come to a street or a field you hadn't expected and a neighbor would wonder why you were so many streets from home.

One path always brought me to the red walls of a thin, low building, the Center for the Promotion of Women. I imagined the inside of the building as a hollow log or a tunnel. It clattered and clacked with noises sent and answered. *Tat-a-tat-tat-tat* calling *chu-chu-chu-chu-chu,* then a sudden, heavy *GaDunk-GaDunk.* One day I stood on my toes to peek through the shutters, and, placing my palms on the wall, I felt the school shake and pass something almost electrical into my fingers. It was not unpleasant, but it did not remind me of Néné when she sewed Koto's pants or a dress for me, sitting in a stuffed chair in the big room. That sewing was sleepy and soft. This sewing hummed and roused the lizards crawling on the trees.

Looking in, I found a dark room with two rows of dull silver machines. Over each machine, seated on a round stool, was a girl who could have been an older sister, maybe the age of Diadia, neck bent, fingers stiffly spread, keeping a slender piece of fabric moving on a tiny toothed track. I did not notice any girl looking at another or talking to another. It was noisy, but the commotion felt lonely and private. The girls' feet moved on big pedals, like birds' feet, and I watched the girls rise slightly, then sink back with drooping shoulders. Just silent girls with obedient hands. Only the machines talked.

In that time, I had a friend named Saran. She lived near the hospital, near my house. Her mother, having ideas that troubled her, stayed at the health clinic. The doctors thought it best that Saran's mother stay very still and sleep away from her children, where they would not hear her wake screaming from nightmares. Saran developed a way of being by herself. She was quiet. She did not make jokes easily. She found methods, I thought, to contain her energy. I walked with her many times to visit her mother, and on these walks we held hands.

Her mother, sitting on clean sheets on a soft bed, said, "Nice to see you, Kadiatou." I could not see what was wrong with her at all.

There was a field outside the health ward and in this field were strewn the discarded utensils and supplies from the ward—small needles, bandages, cups, tubes with blood, plastic bags, pillows, bigger needles, a couple of file cabinets, and mostly, old bottles of penicillin. At certain hours, the sun struck the aluminum rings wrapped around the necks of the old medicine bottles, and the field shimmied and shook, something like the River Sassè glittering with whitecaps. On each visit to the ward, Saran and I waded into the field, foraging for the aluminum rings. Sometimes we picked them from the ground, pushing aside rubbery bags filled with unpleasant liquids. Other times we found it necessary to smash the bottles against rocks to loosen the rings.

We put the rings in a bag and went to the market in town. Everything was sold at market, out of tiny zinc shacks, standing in a long, low row, really one long shack thinly separated into dozens of cubicles on a bumpy dirt road. The cigarette and toilet paper shack became the shack where sunglasses and hats were sold, which became the place where a tall man traded French francs or even American dollars for Guinean francs.

The biggest of the shacks belonged to the owner of an open-air butchery, where sides of beef rested on slats of wood. People driving jeeps would stop at the stand, briefly negotiate with the merchant, unfold several bills into his open hand, and then, with the merchant's help, heave the beef onto the front hood of the jeep, before driving away.

Among the spectators were two or three old bulls. It might have been their street once, but now the beef merchant swatted the backs of the bulls hard, screaming at them to get away or else he would slice them and sell them. The bulls slung their heads and moved off, not wanting to get into an argument.

A family of vultures sat in a row on the roof of the shack, their black heads hanging from ugly hooked necks. They always looked as if they were about to say something but never did. Occasionally they dropped down for gristle tossed by the merchant especially for them. Saran and I walked among the vultures and the bulls, eager to find customers. We sold our aluminum rings to people at the market who found them useful for making tins and other containers.

We would return home almost at dark with perhaps fifty Guinean francs, equal to about two and a half cents. I gave most of it to Saran, whose mother slept in fits in a room at the hospital. The coins could help her family buy rice and potatoes. I went off to bed thinking about other trails in Labé not yet discovered. Days finding metal scraps with Saran were the best, I would think, as I nodded away.

I told Diadia about the dark tunnel where girls learned how to sew. She said she knew about the school, and had gone to sixth grade with some of the girls before their fathers removed them from regular school. "They like it fine," Diadia said. "They are learning to help their families. It's not so bad. After they learn how to sew they can start a business and bring money home. They have something to help their marriage."

Diadia was a special one, the oldest, and she spoke about the center with the assuredness of someone who would never have to go there. The center was for the *other girls*, girls with worries about money and marriage. Given their giant burden, sewing for eight hours a day in a dark, clanking tunnel wasn't at all bad. Diadia owned the first and only requirement for reaching judgments as surely as this—she was sure. She was sure about everything.

Born on the first of January, the first grandchild of Karamoko Alfa, she enjoyed a holy person's privilege. On Sundays, Néné became annoyed with any of us who slept past nine. She might rattle the pots or bring a pot to our ears and bang it to wake us, but she protected Diadia's sleep. She would tell us to go outside or push us off to the mosque or clean the yard. A word too loud, even at noon, and she would puff out her cheeks and whisper harshly, "Shh, your sister is sleeping." Even Diadia's friends knew not to come by until afternoon on Sunday. They waited outside, sometimes looking in, with more than a bit of envy in their eyes.

When the seams on Diadia's school uniform wore out, Baba drove to Pita to buy her a brand-new one. Baba preferred to greet Diadia as he might a royal, not with an embrace but with a long arm and a cupped hand. If Koto's mere appearance angered my father, Diadia's return from even a short trip away could lighten his mood. Taking her by the fingers, he kissed the back of her hand, his head tilting in reverence. He would hold one arm against his chest and say, "Hello, my dear."

He would sometimes say, "Hadiatou and Kadi will do great things, but Diadia will be famous."

Baba forbade Diadia from cooking or from going into the kitchen house. Smoke, he said, would damage her eyes.

Boys at the high school never approached her in a straight line, but instead circled toward her. They were glad when she was sick for exams because it meant they would not have to compete with her for the high score. And their friends told them that if they had any plans to court her, they should be prepared to treat her like a princess.

One minute she was a princess, the next a star athlete bearing down on them at recreation. Diadia was not big, but she had strong calves, and during football games, the boys backed away as she set to kick. She beat everyone in footraces, too. But Diadia showed her best skills with a basketball. She practiced alone for hours and then she made baskets from points all around the schoolyard.

I watched Diadia, the way she walked past a boy after scoring a basket over his head, the way she walked by everyone, head up, eyes fixed on something high and in the distance. "That's Amadou Diallo's oldest," fathers said with a smile, imagining her for their sons. If she knew she was gaining a trail of admirers, she never said so.

Koto and Hadiatou and I liked watching Diadia play on the high school team. We cheered her and called her *Bien champion*. She dressed in green and white and wore the number 10. Her poise earned her the job of delivering the ball from one end of the court to the other and she was the best scorer on the team. The opponent was usually forewarned, "Watch out for the short, light-skinned girl."

Nyssss. And again, *Nyss*. That's the sound we heard each time Diadia sent the ball up and through the basket. Diadia once scored all the way from the center of the court, and Koto, Hadiatou, and I hugged madly.

Naturally, her coach favored her. He called her Allumette because, he said, she lit up the world. Diadia decided that the coach liked her too much. One day he called her to his office to praise her and soon became angry when she said it was time for her to leave. He came close. He told her that she had no guarantee to play. She left the office anyway and stayed in her star position.

Baba did not like hearing what the coach had done. He told Diadia, loud enough for all of us to hear, "This is a different time for girls. You have school ahead of you and a modern way. That's what I want for you, like my father did for me."

CHAPTER FOUR

SLEEPING IN THE VILLAGE

One day in spring, Baba awakened us with excitement in his voice. "Today we will go to Diontou," he announced. I had been there before when I was smaller, too young to remember.

All the children went, and Néné Idrissa, too. We traveled uphill all the way, or it felt that way, although the road took a few turns. Straight into the Fouta Djallon, over rocks and dirt, the road barely found passages between the trees. The trees were different higher in the mountains. Giant trees held long, spectacular branches that spread in jagged streaks. I imagined an old woman's hands reaching to the sky in prayer, her fingers gnarled, and still she pleaded. These trees loomed over much smaller trees with glowing violet and pink leaves, bunched like children.

"The big trees are called coura," Néné said. "The smaller ones are sungala. The red grain from the sungala makes very good drinks."

In the village of Popodara, the air became quickly cooler, and we stopped for Baba and Néné to pray. We bought kula nuts, peanuts, bananas, and oranges from women sitting on the ground amid piles of food. Everything was familiar, and different, too. We passed a road that led to another village, and Baba stopped to point.

"That is the way to Diari where I went to school as a boy," he said.

As we neared Diontou, it became even rockier and harder to tell that a road was there at all. The whole family bounced and slid on our seats. I shuddered thinking the car might tip over and roll off the mountain.

Baba stopped the car.

"Everyone out," he said. We looked at him.

"I want you to know this road." We walked.

We walked over earth that had turned the color of peach, by mango trees that were opening with new fruit, and past strange trees with wild, twisted roots. Every so often, we passed a man sitting on a rock, and we saw families of mutton and goats, and every so often the lone bull. We fell into shadows and walked into bright sunlight. We passed fields of dead, yellow grass. Baba said the villagers would burn the fields soon to allow new grass.

We walked through whole crowds of the brilliant sungala trees that were only slightly taller than Diadia and Koto. Baba said that there was a joke often told about what happened to people who drank the juice that comes from the sungala seeds. The seeds are healthy but can also cause difficult growling of the stomach, he said.

One day, Baba said, the chief of the village gathered many of his faithful in his hut for a meeting, but soon the chief detected an unpleasant odor. The chief thought to himself, I must find the person who drank the sungala.

The chief was smart, and he told his people that his supply of sungala seeds had run out and he needed some. He asked if anyone had any stock in his house. One old man stood up.

"I have sungala. I just drank some this morning. I will bring it to you," the old man said.

"No, do not bother," replied the chief. "Just go outside. You are giving us all a very uncomfortable time in here. Please go."

Then, Baba said, everyone in the hut realized what the chief had done and they said, "Oh!"

"And they all laughed their heads off," Baba said. We were getting closer to the home of my grandparents, and we all laughed, too, heading up Baba's road.

"Stay alert," Baba said.

That's when we met the monkeys. They shuffled onto the road and tagged along, keeping a distance, until Hadiatou yelled, "Look at what I can do." She tucked her thumbs into hiding and held out four fingers on each hand and made monkey noises. "Choo, choo," she cried. The monkeys only looked bored. They turned their mopey eyes from us, tucked in their long chins, and let us walk on.

In all, we probably walked for about eight kilometers, about five miles, and by the time we came to Diontou, we were breathless, our legs dragging. Baba, though, had gained breath. We followed him to the crest of a small hill and looked down on groups of huts that covered a slice of lowland and crept up another small hill a short distance away. We could see that the huts were brown, made of mud, but mostly we saw yellow, the color of the dried grass roofs that covered each hut and of the mosque that stood in the foreground.

My father motioned for his children to stand at his side.

"This is Diontou," he said. "The home of your father, the home of your grandfather, the home of your great-grandfather."

He pointed down to a small cluster of huts to the side of the mosque. "And there is where your father was a boy," he said.

The whole village seemed to have heard him, because no sooner did we start down the hill than people streamed out of their homes to greet him, some dressed in what must have been their best boubous, as if they had expected him. Everyone knew Baba. Many were his cousins. His brothers and sisters were there, my aunts and uncles, and their children, my cousins, and other men and women he must have known well, their faces smiling with devotion. There was much shaking of hands and small blessings and the giving over of goro nuts and bananas.

The welcoming carried us down a path flowered with pink buds, straight and then to the right, bringing us to three huts, one larger than the others, sitting on a square of land perhaps three times the size of our yard in Labé. The home of my father's parents was big, surrounded by orange trees and encircled by clean, smallish white stones that doubtless attracted the sun to stay. Never before I had seen a place with so much light.

My grandfather and grandmother stood in the center of their land.

My grandmother had thin arms. She had a fine chin.

My grandfather was tall, much taller than my father. He had big feet.

My grandmother kissed me. My grandfather put his hand on my head and left it there for many moments. His hand covered my whole head, and his fingers felt my brow.

Joined by all the villagers who could possibly squeeze in, we sat on the floor of the largest hut in our bare feet and prayed. Others crammed their heads at the opening. Baba told us that we were in the place where his father counseled the villagers on their problems, where his grandfather had reigned as king.

"Onjaramaa," my grandfather said softly, and everyone lowered their heads. *"Onjaramaa."* It is the word for greeting and for thank you. Rows of naked toes stayed absolutely still. My grandfather's Fulah accent and his language were pure, not like Labé, where the Fulah tongue was mixed with French. He thanked Allah for our safe arrival and for the health of the family, and he praised Allah for allowing him to be surrounded by so many children.

My grandfather looked around and said *"Bisimila."* It was time to eat.

Food came from everywhere. Meats and sauces, yogurt, steamed maize and mounds of rice. The whole village ate, heartily, stooped over shared bowls, their fingers full and sticky. Many people stayed until long after dark. Some left for the evening prayer at the mosque and returned. More food arrived from other families, and the eating went on, even after my grandmother had taken Diadia, Koto, Hadiatou, and me into the middle hut to sleep.

This hut glowed, lit by embers nestled in a hole between three large stones, surrounded by blocks of firewood. We set down with Néné on a bed on one side of the hut and stared at the light. Néné told us that her mother cooked meals with the light, using the wood to create an ample fire. I supposed that the light would die off soon, but in the middle of the night I woke and saw that it was flickering. In the morning, the stones were still lit. In the afternoon they cooked our food, and the light lingered into the night and again the next morning.

We stayed a few days in Diontou. My grandmother, I discovered, was an orderly woman. We called her Néné Diontou. She liked creatures. She fed ants, chickens, lizards, and birds from a line of bowls she kept in back of the house. She kept all the rice and cereals and other food stock in neat rows high in the hut where I slept, in a storage space near the roof. Many times a day, she climbed up and down a ladder to retrieve what she needed. The white rocks surrounding the huts had been arranged by her in careful sequence. The smallest pebbles created one tier at the edge of the land, and evolved into a tier of slightly larger pebbles, and then slightly larger until the rocks were the size of mango pits. My grandmother was afraid the children would run and play and spoil her creation.

"Walk slow," she told us over and over.

Most important we were not to step on a wide, flat rock in the middle of the yard. This was my grandfather's rock. No one had the right to sit there but him or to stomp on it. It is where he studied the Koran and where he gave his blessings.

He blessed me. He wore a large robe, a round prayer hat, holding a bracelet of pale beads. Placing his hand on my hair, he closed his eyes, and then came a voice that was strong, mellow, too. His voice was musical, like Baba's.

"You pray to honor Allah," he told me. I nodded and stared up at him. I wondered what it would be like to hug him.

On our last night I fixed my eyes on the light. It was a forever light. I would go home to Labé, return in another season, and the light would last. I thought it almost as a wish. It would keep for my grandfather and grandmother and for my father and mother. I knew that it burned even as I slept, but I told my eyes not to close. Someone, just once, should watch the light all night through.

Morning came and Néné woke us for the trip home. I had missed the vigil. I looked to the stones, and seeing that the light had not weakened, had not been disturbed at all, I left Diontou sure my wish would come true.

⤤⤦

Another baby came. There were now six of us, Diadia, Koto, Hadiatou, Kadi (me), Bobo, and the new one, Pathé, a boy.

Néné seemed tired and slept more. She did not make conversation easily. She traveled often by herself, to the villages and to Conakry to visit with friends and family. Néné Idrissa watched over us and this meant we could sleep late and play football instead of doing our homework. She never interrupted our games. If we left a mess at the table or in the yard, Idrissa cleaned it away without fuss. I became accustomed to a new system in the house, with fewer rules but a greater sense of unease. Néné not being there, Néné weary without expression to her face when she was there, put the house at an odd angle.

"Kadi, I need your help with the meat," Idrissa said. She lugged a chunk of beef on her shoulder. My knees were needed to clamp the beef in place as she sliced the other end.

"No," I answered. "I have other things to do." Baba, I realized too late, stood behind me.

"Mama, sit down, I want to talk to you."

He put a hand on my shoulder.

"You cannot talk that way to Idrissa. She is part of the family. You must respect her."

Baba spoke as gently as I had ever heard him, no scolding in his eyes, but I detected a sudden shift in the ground. My belly rose, then fell with a thump. I felt the whole house turning on its side.

Sooner than I thought it could happen, there was another new baby, this one a girl they called Fatima. It was not Néné who went into the pains this time, but Néné Idrissa. They brought her to the clinic one afternoon, and a few days later she came home cradling the baby and making a place for her in the room she shared with Néné and little Pathé.

I still slept with Diadia and Hadiatou, and Bobo, too. Space was cleared in a small shed in the yard for Koto, as the eldest son, to have his own room. Néné and Idrissa tended to both babies, and they held hands again. Baba went to work and listened to the broadcasts in his room.

I washed Fatima and held her. I kissed her a lot. Such a beautiful baby, a girl in the house who was younger than I. Small breezes told me the house was returning to some balance.

No one said anything to me or asked if I had questions. My brothers and sisters, if they were confused, offered nothing. I thought about Mr. Kamara across the road, the one whose arguments with his wife always ended with his squealing cry and his wife accusing him of loving his second wife more than her. Other fathers, too, I knew, left for days, even weeks at a time. Yaye Kesso's father had two wives, and Buntu Touré's father also. There was a girl who spelled her name almost like mine, Kadiata. Her father was married to two women. Now my father had two wives.

It was all right if no one wanted to tell me what happened. I reasoned I was old enough to know some things because I had been told, and to know other things from footsteps, tiny vibrations, conversation stopped with my entering the room. Grown-ups, I concluded, reaching their own age of silence, counted on their children to reach an age of knowing without being told. I had gotten to my time of untold knowing.

My mind was busy. I wanted Baba to tell me one more thing. I wanted him to tell me he would never leave this house.

Baba appeared in a window at school. I looked up and saw him and knew he admired me. He bowed his head in a small way. He watched me with one ear turned to the classroom, and he was gone. For many moments, his eyes still filled the space where he had been, and I think this was his intention.

He showed up that way, in the back of the room, for the school plays, the dances, and the recitals. Néné did not often go, not that Baba told her to stay home. She said it was Baba's place and that if he alone saw me, this was good with her. She counted on me to rehearse for her and to give a repeat performance as soon as I returned with Baba. They sat together on the couch, and I went word by word and step by step through my part, singing and dancing, and at the end, I curtsied to their hoorays.

In third grade, just before Ramadan, the teacher told me I had a nice voice and picked me to lead all the children in a song. I would begin the song and they would join in. Better, we would appear at the high school auditorium, near Diadia's basketball court, next to Labé's football stadium on Tiendel Road. The auditorium was not fancy. Rows of long wooden benches sat on a cement floor. Lamps hung on long cords stretching from a high metal ceiling. But to sing on the big round stage at the high school planted me right in the center of town.

Many afternoons I practiced for Néné. I sang a patriotic song. On the day, just before my solo, I looked out and found Baba off on the side.

"Kadiatou Diallo will now sing," the teacher announced.

I stepped forward, saw my teacher's hands go up, and in that moment, my throat made a decision to shut tight. She raised her hands again and I felt my cheeks heating up to five hundred degrees. My classmates moved around nervously. They needed me to begin the song.

Once more my teacher tried, but my head was emptied of verses and melodies and all ideas of stardom I had envisioned while rehearsing in front of Néné. The voices of the other children filled the giant room, and I backstepped to my place in line. My head throbbed. I had done something terribly wrong.

"I was not surprised because I know," Baba said when I came home. "You feel somehow this is your father and you couldn't sing in front of me."

Baba looked at me for a long time.

"It's okay. Don't worry, I feel proud. I feel proud of you."

Baba had a rifle. Néné said he had owned it for many years.

He brought it with him on a Sunday when we all went to the market in Popodara, an hour away. On other trips like this we stopped in the middle of the bush country. Baba took the rifle from the back of the Land Rover, marched straight into a thicket of branches. He always came out with one or two scrawny bush chickens.

This time, from the road, he caught sight of a bigger prize, a deer. Baba held his rifle high and still. I had never seen Baba stand so straight.

He looked like a soldier. The rifle was long and black. The bottom of his boubou fluttered. He shot the deer and brought it home on the hood of the car.

The deer—legs, hoofs, and all—went into the kitchen house. The rifle went with Baba into his room and, I imagined, into a hiding place. It would stay there, as usual, until the next trip into the bushlands, but I heard Baba talking about the rifle to Néné. He said he would use it if pushed. "I will protect my family," he said.

Something Baba had heard on the radio had made him unhappy. I heard him telling Néné that Sékou Touré had broken his promise, that the program called "ethnic integration" did not honor the qualities that made each tribe special. Instead, Baba said, it sought to blend everyone in obedience to the state party.

"What the president wants, the president gets. Anyone who disagrees is sent to jail," Baba said.

A large portrait of Sékou Touré hung at school. He had very white teeth and very shiny skin. I had never seen a picture of him not smiling, and I did not remember Baba speaking in a sharp way about him before. Sékou Touré also had a strong voice. I heard him many times on Baba's radio saying *"Victoire! Gloire!"* Sometimes he began talking in the afternoon and was still talking in the night.

Men in town had told him, Baba said to Néné, that village leaders, teachers, businessmen, and students had been arrested, members of the Peace Corps thrown out of the country and the American ambassador told not to leave his house. The radio said that the French were trying to get back into Guinea and that the country needed to stand as one.

"The president should let people live as they want," Baba said. I did not think Baba would ever say another approving word about Sékou Touré. His voice went low. Life might change overnight in Guinea, he said, and he would have the rifle ready.

Men from down the road came to our yard to talk about Sékou Touré with my father. Their voices possessed the same sharp tone I had heard from Baba. Baba sat in a chair in the yard listening, and when he rose, he had this to say:

"Sékou Touré is a great man. Without him, we would not have our independence. There is no Guinea without Sékou Touré. We must honor him. Sékou Touré will be known as the first liberator of black people."

Néné Idrissa dropped her baby in a pot of boiling peanut sauce.

Idrissa exploded from the dark of the kitchen house, Fatima lifted over her, mother and daughter both wailing for help. The women ran from all the houses, yelling and crying.

"Put her in butter."

"No, in yogurt."

"Get blankets. We need blankets."

"What happened? The baby's eyes. Take care of the baby's eyes."

"It was for dinner," Idrissa cried. "Oh God. Her head, my baby's head." Fatima had slipped from Idrissa's arms into the peanut sauce face first. The baby's face was orange and seemed not damaged, but waxed and glowing, my baby sister turned peanut. Idrissa grabbed Fatima's head tight and began lifting a film of sauce as if unrolling a bedsheet.

"Allah, oh Allah," screamed Idrissa. Her startled eyes looked at her own hand, which held a hot layer of her baby's skin.

Néné took the baby from Idrissa, who was trembling and falling to the gravel. Someone brought Néné a bowl of eggs. Néné broke them over Fatima. Now Fatima turned yellow and clear, and Néné broke more eggs on her. Fatima's shrieks turned to whimpers.

Néné brought a bottle of milk to the baby's mouth, and she rocked her while others continued to crack the eggs. In a little, everyone became quiet, including Fatima, and Idrissa, too, who had taken her sobs inside her chest.

"It's all right, nothing bad will happen," Néné whispered. The women watched my mother, and as my mother rocked the baby, the women themselves swayed, rocking also, the women embracing my mother and the baby from steps away.

"Idrissa," Néné said softly. Her cousin, the second wife, lifted her chin. "She will be all right. This happens. Now we have to take care of her. Do not worry. I have seen her eyes, and her eyes are fine. Allah is watching over us. Your baby closed her eyes. She knew to close her eyes and they are not burned."

Néné watched Fatima all that night. She used eggs and honey, yogurt, and anything that spread like cream. In the morning, Néné and Idrissa brought the baby to the hospital, and Fatima came home with her face and one hand wrapped in white bandages and cotton, my baby sister from outer space. Her cries came from a dark hole where her mouth should be. Her eyes peered out from two slits, moving inside her white cocoon.

The doctors told Néné and Idrissa that the baby's burnt face would grow new skin. I thought of the yellow fields near Diontou, set on fire each year so as to spawn healthy, new grass. The doctors said to keep her warm until the new skin came because her body was prone to the shivers. Strange to think, hot fire had made her cold.

Not crying, Fatima became a quiet presence. Her eyes, I thought, did not look like a baby's. They beamed with an intelligence that I reasoned must come with the freedom to spy.

Idrissa could not help her own crying. She cried in the house and in the yard, sitting low to the ground on a *joulerra*, a tiny, three-legged wooden stool, under the branches of an avocado tree. Baba finally waved his arms.

"If I see you crying, I'm going to hit you," he screamed. Little green avocados bobbed around Idrissa's collapsed shoulders. "You did this thing. Why are you crying like you don't know how it happened? Why are you pretending to cry?" I wished Baba would not be angry. I wished he would leave Idrissa to Néné, who tended to the baby inside, but Baba's temper usually magnified before it dwindled, and that's how it was this time.

Baby Fatima was hot and cool and swaddled in cotton. The peanut sauce had burned her ears, and they were covered, too. Her eyes looked out. I could even make her eyes smile with a funny face or a silly noise, but I felt pretty sure that way in there, beneath the wrapping, she couldn't hear much else that was going on.

CHAPTER FIVE

SAVING KADI

*T*he older I became, the deeper I fell in love with the moonlight. At night we gathered, Yaye Kesso and I, Buntu Touré, and a girl named Yallean, and we danced in our yards and on the broken road in front of our houses. We held hands and sang songs about cows and girlish romance. We giggled and howled, and not a living thing seemed to mind. Focused brilliantly on us alone, the moon's rays zipped down to us a strange, new feeling of authority.

I could feel this in myself and see it in my friends. We were larger in the moonlight. A new daring inspired us. We decided to steal chickens.

Our scheme was simple but demanded exact timing. We picked the house of a neighbor we knew had lots of chickens in back. I was considered the best talker, so my job was to go to the door and ask if the people were well, and, if necessary, tell them something about Néné or Baba or Diadia, Koto, Hadiatou, Bobo, Pathé, or Fifi, the seventh child. If that did not take up enough time, Yaye Kesso or Buntu Touré, beside me, would chime in.

This usually gave Yallean the minutes she needed to sneak in back and grab one of the chickens. The chickens of Labé were well fed and stronger than they looked, and it was important that Yallean be the one to do the actual stealing. She was the biggest of all of us, and knew how to grab the chicken by its legs with one hand and keep it quiet with the other. Later, we fried the chicken, mixed it with onions and tomatoes, and made ourselves a party.

Our plan always worked, until the night I came to the door of Mrs. Kamara. For one, she was not in the mood for much conversation. She looked down at us, and before I could even get to Diadia, she stopped me short.

"Don't you girls need to be getting home?" Mrs. Kamara said.

"Yes, but we wanted to see you and ask about your family."

"Everyone is well."

I said that was nice. I said it was much better to have everyone well. Mrs. Kamara said nothing, and I sensed she was about to move away from the door.

"If one of us in my house catches cold, we all get it. My mother sometimes gives us medicines before we catch cold. She says it's the best way to keep sickness out of the house. She can't keep up if we all get sick at one time. I don't know why it works that way. I guess the cold just jumps from one child to another child. Glad to hear that everyone is well in your house."

I looked up into flat, gray, blank eyes, chilled specks.

Goodness! Then we heard the chicken. No ordinary squawker, it let out a piercing cry.

ACAAAAAAW! ACAAAAAW! ACAAAAAAAAAW!

"I wonder what that could be," I said.

Mrs. Kamara took a step into the night, neck craned, her head sideways.

"Maybe a couple of animals got into a fight. That happens sometimes," I tried.

It came again. *ACAAAAAW! ACAAAAAW!* Only this was worse. It was followed by a thrashing, kicking, yelping, barking, snarling noise, half chicken and half human.

"What! Someone's at my chickens," Mrs. Kamara yelled. And she started past us.

"You want to be careful. You shouldn't go there alone." With that, she gave us a look back, and was gone, a blur around the corner of her house.

I looked at Yaye Kesso and Buntu Touré. They looked at me. It was time to run. We shot through the moonlight, as far down the road as we could, stumbling and lurching over rocks and crevices, through the alleys, cutting between houses, until we fell into a dark spot in back of a bush, against a fence.

Our bodies froze, not daring to twitch. We listened, but heard nothing. Suddenly, not a soul or anything in all of Labé was making a sound, only crazy, thumping hearts. We stayed against the fence for a good while before figuring enough time had passed. The moon was dropping fast, and sounds were rising, of unknown creatures moving in the bushes. We went back up the road in darkness, slowly now, in careful silence. In a few minutes, I recognized the front of my house and I realized we had not run far at all.

We were near our homes, practically safe in our beds when a hazy figure emerged up the way. This someone was large, a grown-up, probably Mrs. Kamara looking for us, set to deliver us right to our parents. I was in for a terrible punishment. Baba did not like to hit me, but Néné might, and they would be very angry. Baba would ask how I could possibly shame him in front of a neighbor. They would tell me, no more moonlight for you.

Yaye Kesso let out a short breath and stopped.

"It's Yallean," she said. It was. She walked up to us with her palms up.

"Where were you?" she said.

We didn't know what to say.

"What happened? What did Mrs. Kamara do to you?" I asked.

"Nothing. She never saw me. I heard her saying, Who's there, who's there, who's bothering my chickens. But I was already out of there. If she saw me, she saw only the back of me."

We could now see feathers on her hair and arms.

"That was the biggest chicken ever. That chicken was biting and kicking. Big as a goat. Nobody I know can steal a chicken big as that."

Once our laughing began, it did not stop until our mouths and our chests hurt. It was a new laugh for me, coming from a new place that squeezed out tears, a laugh I recognized as the laugh I had seen from Néné on occasion and the other women when they sat together in the yard.

Néné wanted me near in the kitchen. She taught me to wash the lettuce thoroughly and to help her slice the vegetables from her garden. I held and Néné cut. She taught me how to mince onions with a small piece of carved wood we called a *mortier*, and how to cook rice, how to fry a piece of meat in a pan and simple dishes like a plate of green beans. The most delicious way, Néné taught me, was to boil them in cow butter. In time, I knew how to mash potatoes and how to make sauces from spinach, cassava leaves, okra. Néné said I was very good in the kitchen.

Baba did not say much about my cooking lessons. He thought it was good for me to spend time with Néné so long as I paid attention to my homework. He checked it from time to time and sometimes asked to see the notebook I kept for school lessons, just as he did for the older ones. I was eight, getting close to nine, and I felt much older.

Getting older had many meanings. I was already helping to care for the smaller ones in the house. I especially liked sitting with Fifi, the first girl born after me, and braiding her hair. I would be starting Koranic school soon. Baba let me stay up a little later with him when the griot came to sing, and a few times I sensed Baba looking at me with a measure of sadness. The look on his face was windswept, an odd withdrawal just as my eyes met his, so fleeting I was not sure of my sense at all.

Many girls I knew had already gone for their female circumcision. I did not know what it was, but those girls who had it spoke proudly about it, or their mothers did. They said they now had girls who were clean, girls they could bring back to the villages without shame.

Yaye Kesso said that it was a cut and that girls who had the cut were more desirable for the fathers who sought pure wives for their sons.

"I am not getting married," I said.

"Not now, but someday. You don't want to be the only girl who doesn't have the cut."

I asked Yaye Kesso if she wanted the cut and she said she didn't know what it was either.

Baba and Néné had a hushed discussion. Baba said he knew it was almost that time, but he told Néné that he did not want me to have a circumcision. There were other fathers who thought like him, but on this matter they bowed to their wives, who saw it as a communion between mother and daughter. Néné's mother had taken her. Néné took Diadia and Hadiatou, and now it was my turn to be proud like my sisters, even if I still didn't know what a circumcision was. Baba said it was fine for other families still stuck in customs of the village, but not for him and definitely not for his Mama. He said that I was already pure. Néné nodded and said she would obey his wishes.

Sometimes I did not understand the Néné who held her tongue, and Baba confused me, too. He desired one set of ways for me and another set for Néné. Quiet Néné nodded a lot.

Restless ways crept into my body, a protest finding root in aching bones. I would have to choose sides, but who for and over what? I became aware of an invisible rope running through the center of our house, in the front doorway and out the back. Néné tells Baba that Koto missed Koran studies, and the rope tenses. Baba bites into a rich mango, and the rope relaxes.

Back and forth. Sékou Touré rampages. Good school report. Bad Sunday, we oversleep. News from Diontou, lots of excitement. No talking in house. Singing all night. I'm too young. I'm old enough. Baba welcomes friends, wears best boubou. Stay outside with Koto, no place inside.

Baba and Néné and brothers and sisters in one house. Sound sleep. Sweetest dreams. One way and the other. I do not think Baba and Néné knew about the rope, but I did, and I refused to let go.

I knew a girl in third grade, Oumou Keita, who was the daughter of the governor of Labé. She was calm and polite and never bothered anyone, never asked to join in games, but she wanted to be friends with me.

"Every day you must bring me a gift," I told her.

"Why?" Oumou asked.

"Because your father is a governor and your family is richer than my family, so I need something from you."

Each morning she brought me coconuts, oranges, mangoes, cheese, milk, yogurt. And each time I turned to share the gifts with my friends. I remembered Pumpatonn, the fat girl who took my food in the first grade, and I enjoyed the power of getting even.

Finally Oumou came to me. "Please, tomorrow, I will not bring anything. I want you to forgive me for tomorrow."

"No, you must bring it."

"Tomorrow is too much. Please give me some time, maybe after tomorrow," she begged.

"No."

She showed up the next day with nothing for me. My friends looked at me.

"Today you shouldn't go home," I told her. "You have to stay with me in the class until everybody is gone. Then you and I will have our own account to handle."

After school, the classroom emptied but for Oumou and me.

"Okay," I said. "Come here." I was going to beat her.

She came toward me, very close. Our lips could almost touch. Her lips quivered, her arms shook, and she half closed her eyes. Whatever I was going to do to her, she would take it without resistance. She might pray, and what if she did? I would not weaken, unless God came to help her and saw the angry glare on my face and told me, Kadiatou, this is not just. She is not Pumpatonn. If, after that, I still decided to beat her, God would think me foolish or mean. God would say to me, *Let go of the rope.*

I looked at the girl. She was frail, also pretty, in a way I hadn't noticed. Up close she had a faraway look.

"No, no, no," I said. "I will not hurt you. I forgive you. No more presents. Nothing. Don't give me anything else." Giant tears appeared on her face.

"We are friends now. I want to be your friend."

With the discovery of my own cruelty, greed, and vanity, shame hung over me for many weeks, until Baba declared my time had come to study the Koran. Instantly, I lifted.

"Great!" I said. "I can hardly wait."

We gathered in a neighbor's yard, all the children I knew and played with, sitting under a mango tree. We met for two hours every day after school except Thursday and Sunday.

The imam was a short man without upper front teeth. He loved to chew the red goro nuts, and he smiled a lot, and when he smiled, we plainly saw the red of the nuts stuck to the roof of his mouth. He was an older man, who rode in from another part of Labé on a skinny red bicycle. His name was Karamoko.

At the first lesson he held up a big sheet of characters. He said these were Arabic characters and made up the alphabet of the Koran—aliph, mim, bah . . . Some had curves and some looked like little houses. All together, he said, there were hundreds of these shapes to learn, and after many years of study we would know all of them and their meaning and be ready for the Tabarah. The Tabarah, he explained, was the ceremony for children of thirteen or fourteen who had learned their Koran.

In the meantime we wrote the letters in black ink on small white wooden boards called *planchards* that we held on our laps. The *planchards* were curved at the top and bottom, and they were very difficult to clean. After a lesson, we used rough leaves, almost like sandpaper, to scrub the boards clean.

Every day we recited the letters as a chorus, adding maybe five letters or more each lesson to the ones we already knew. He called out the letters and we repeated them many times over, *aliph, mim, bah* . . . until our tongues hurt.

When my father and other men prayed, it sounded like a deep rumbling to me, like a language without any words, a long, deep *mummmmm*. When I became too tired, I said, *blubba blubba blubba*, bringing the sounds up as though I meant it, with a heaving chest. One day I said *blubba blubba blubba*, attracting Karamoko to my side.

"I can see you are an intelligent girl," he said. "That was a beautiful recitation."

At home, Baba would ask me if I had cleaned the *planchard*, and he always insisted I say the alphabet for him. "Come, I want to listen," he would say, and call my brothers and sisters to sit with us. My father could not be fooled by my *blubba blubba blubba*, and so I forced myself to improve. Another thought encouraged me. I pictured my Tabarah, when my mother and father would sit under the same mango tree and watch me receive the commendation for truly knowing the Koran. I did not want my friends to reach that day first.

I recited letters and words, strings of words and a few short prayers, with no idea what they meant. Baba had told me that the Koran was filled with stories, and when I had studied them long enough, I might achieve a state of *taqwa*, the awareness that everything in life existed before the eyes of God. The stories demonstrated that God knows everything we do and all that runs through our hearts.

Karamoko did not tell stories. He remained steadfast with his ritual. He pointed to the board, said the words, and listened to the pleasing ring of our voices. I did not know what I was saying, but at home, Baba invited me to pray with him in the front yard.

I sat on a mat beside Néné, facing the back of Baba, the man in front facing Allah, the women in back, because that's the way it was.

Then one day, when my father was away, my mother took me for the circumcision. I did not expect it to hurt so much. It made me faint, and I lost a lot of blood. For two weeks, Néné, my sisters, Idrissa, and the women neighbors cooked and sang and danced for me until my father returned home. Until I was healed, I was not permitted to eat with a man, which made Baba suspicious after I had not come to the dinner table for many nights.

"What has happened here?" he said.

Néné told him the truth. Baba did not yell or respond really in any way at first. He asked to see me, and he told Néné and me that if this is what we wanted, he could accept it and be happy for me. "It is a woman's affair," he said.

Not having to hide from Baba, the women returned to celebrating over me, and not wishing to be left out of the party, Baba joined them in the yard, dancing and singing, the loudest one of all.

If God really knew the inside of my heart, did he know how much I loved Baba and Néné? Did he watch them stand together? Baba kissed Néné's hand, and she put a hand on his arm, and they let no words be said. At good news, Néné laughed and Baba brought his hands together. They shared bowls of rice, and sometimes they washed for prayer side by side. If Baba's prayer robe was folded wrong, Néné straightened it and patted it down. When the neighbors came for visits, Baba changed into another boubou and insisted everybody sit and be comfortable. He opened oranges, and Néné brought water and sodas, and the stories they shared about their children, they told together. Baba began, maybe about Hadiatou's trick on April Fool's Day.

Néné said, "Hadiatou made a big fancy envelope and wrote, Special Delivery."

"I thought it came from Paris," Baba said.

"And you should have seen the look on Hadiatou's face," Néné said.

"And Mama's, too. She was right there watching."

"They dropped it by the door," said Néné. The girls were watching Koto, too.

"You know what it was? It was a rock. A big white rock. Right from the garden."

"And he came out and said, 'Look what I just got in the mail from Paris,'" said Néné.

"And all the children laughed," Baba said, "because they wanted to fool their father."

Could God know my happiness to hear my mother and father tell a story?

Did God know Koto watched me, on the road, across a lot and the small side paths? Did he know that I sometimes looked over my shoulder, sensing Koto was there, and if it happened he was not, I felt a twinge of missing him. Koto would do anything for me.

Did God know the life of my house, and did he know I always slept well? Did he know they called me Mama? Could he see Néné come into our room at night to make sure we were quiet?

And what of Baba's prayers? I watched Baba, legs folded beneath him, on his prayer mat, swaying, hands covering his face, Néné always on a mat behind him, Baba in front, alone. Please do not let Baba be alone.

Once I noticed a bee circling Baba as he chanted the Maghrib, the prayer at seven in the evening. The bee flew by, returned, and settled on Baba's shoulder. Baba did not notice. The bee crawled to the back of Baba and, reaching the collar of Baba's robe, plopped on Baba's neck. Baba remained in prayer, and the bee stayed in the center of Baba's neck, and I wanted to rush to Baba and warn him or grab a stick and chase away the bee, but I knew that it was not right to move while praying, but then, the bee might be preparing its sting. I watched the bee until Baba was done. Baba rose and swatted the bee away.

Had God seen the workings of my heart? Could he tell I was afraid and unsure, not knowing which was best, to run and save Baba from the bee or to hold my breath and stay in my place, still as my grandfather's rock?

Koto still suffered in ways only the elder son could know. One day he decided to surprise Baba at work, but found Baba deep in discussion. Without looking up, not knowing he was greeting his own son, Baba reached to shake his hand. "Welcome," Baba said and lifted his head. A thick scowl came over him.

"Why are you here?" he demanded. "Why are you not doing your studies?"

Baba bought Koto a bright blue bicycle. It was a special bicycle with a new invention for a braking device. To brake, the rider had to pedal backwards. Baba promised Koto he would teach him how to ride if

Koto did his penmanship perfectly. Otherwise, he would take the bicycle away. Koto told us he planned to find new trails and race with his friends. He wanted to bring the bicycle to school and park it alongside the others outside his classroom. But Baba gave new orders. He allowed Koto only brief rides and only if Koto had done something worthwhile. The bicycle stayed in Baba's room, and Koto could look at it only from outside the curtain.

I was almost ten on the day Koto told me his secret wish. Baba was away in Conakry.

"Sometimes I pray he doesn't come back," Koto said. "I pray he has an accident and we get the news he is dead. But then he always comes back. The car pulls up, everyone says 'Baba's here.' And I say 'Oh no, he's back again.' "

Then I learned that the girl Oumou Keita died. She had been ill for a while and may have been dying when I played the dictator over her in school. I did not know much else. I had never met her mother or father. I did not know if she had begun her Koran lessons or if she danced. I remembered that she was lonely, and thinking about that especially bothered me. I might have told her that things get jumbled sometimes, and you can't think too hard about all of that, and you can't be smart and good all the time. That is that. They would have a funeral for Oumou Keita just like they did for old people.

I once heard Baba say that when a person dies, angels appear on the person's shoulders. One is the bad angel who knows all your sins, all your shows of arrogance or jealousy or hatred. The other is a good angel who knows all your good deeds and if you have atoned for your wrongdoing.

The most pious, he said, die young.

Yallean's battle with the giant chicken had brought forth my mother's laugh, and now with the death of a girl I knew only by her faraway eyes, I heard myself crying like a woman. Poor Oumou Keita with angels on her shoulders. Look what she got for never doing a wrong thing in her life.

Baba decided to build a new house. He found a space not far from where we lived on land rougher than what we had known. Half the road that ran in front was collapsed and there were wide patches of bent weeds and tracts where people had brought their garbage and set it on fire. Charred rubbish blackened much of the ground.

Labé was a hodgepodge, and there were also full mango and avocado trees and even blueberry bushes. Thankfully, Baba was not the only one who saw lush promise in this area. He and many other fathers, with men they had hired, set about to smooth and clear the area. They built houses the color of peaches and grapefruits, and set the houses in from the road and created huge front yards with small round gravel brought in from the nearby mines. Unlike most of the houses in Labé, they were not closed off to the road by cement walls, and this meant one man could see another man's front door. There was a lot more space, but the families and their children could still be together just by stepping outside.

With all this land, Néné wanted a much bigger house. Cousins from Tinkin, where Néné grew up, had come to live with us for a while, and there were now ten children who needed places to sleep.

Baba said he feared that a big house would make other people envious, and a righteous man did not show off to his neighbors. When people came to visit or to share in prayer, he did not want them to feel uncomfortable and outsized in a big house. I heard Néné say to Baba that for once, he should listen to her advice. "We need room for the children," she said.

The house Baba built had a room for him, a room for Néné, a room for Idrissa, two rooms for the children, two storage rooms, and a central room for eating and sitting, where our one lightbulb shone dimly from the ceiling. In back, there was a small cement room, big enough for two or even three boys, a new kitchen house, and two tall sheds, one for washing ourselves with pails of water taken from the pump, and another with a paved hole for going to the bathroom. The house was painted yellow and framed by mango trees, and in the center of the yard, in back, a small iron door opened to a well used for washing clothes.

When the project was complete, Néné had a bigger house, but only slightly. This house had just one more room than the old one. I shared a room with two others and longed to get one of the storage rooms that had been turned into a room for Hadiatou. When we moved in, there were still buckets of unused cement and leftover zinc and sand. Baba said that anyone in the neighborhood who needed the materials could come and take them.

An evening arrived in September, just after my tenth birthday, when we were sitting at the table for dinner, brothers and sisters close, Néné drifting off into houses she had known, places she had lived. Baba was already finished and resting in his room.

Growing up in a hut in Tinkin, Néné said, she always believed she was the wealthiest girl in the world. She ate bananas right off the tree and bathed in the spring water. The hut was as solid as any house, and her father always filled it with colorful objects and cloths he had found in Senegal. With his death, the hut lost its color and her mother, Néné Tinkin, lost hope for a while and sent her off to stay with her aunt. "You can't always see change before it happens, but the way it is with God's plan, everything can change in a day, anytime," Néné said.

"The house Baba and I had in Conakry when you were babies was small, but we were well. We welcomed the future. When Baba got sick with the agitation, everything changed, just the way it happened when my father died and nobody knew which way to go. I didn't know what to do, except I knew I had to take care of my children while Baba got well. When I thought Baba was better, everybody was fighting, the Soussou and the Fulah, and no one trusted each other, and really, Baba was still sick.

"Mama, you were born in the middle of everything mixed up, and right then, Baba was very depressed, and maybe this was God's plan that everything should change right then, with you."

Néné, tell me the story of Mama the baby. You wrapped me in a blanket and brought me to Tinkin for everyone to see. Néné Tinkin said I was the most beautiful baby she had ever seen, said she had never seen a baby so perfectly round as me. Right? You carried me on your back and felt my heart beating through you. You never knew a baby to love food so, you watched me in the yard rubbing bananas and mangoes on my face. I know this story, tell it again.

"Mama," Néné said. "We almost lost you."

I watched Néné's lips.

"You were three weeks old. I went with Baba to the hospital in Conakry, the big one, Balle Hospital, to see Baba's doctor. It was the same hospital where I gave birth to you. The French doctor thought you were beautiful, and she put you in a crib.

"I don't know what happened after that. I know Baba's mind was very bad. He grabbed you. He was holding you like this."

Néné raised both hands to the ceiling.

"He brought you to the balcony and he said, 'I will drop this baby.' And I thought you will be dead. We were far up on the fourth floor, and I told him not to do a thing like this. You were wrapped in a blanket and you wore a little hat. The hat fell and the blanket fell and it was only you. You kicked and fought. You hung on to Baba's thumbs.

"Baba smiled and said, 'I'm going to drop this baby.' He said, 'If you touch me, I will let her go.' "

Listening, I wanted to laugh. I saw a baby in midair, and I was not scared. I knew the hospital stood on Cameroon Road, which was ordinarily filled with street merchants, and people walking and people on bicycles. I imagined the people looking up to see a baby in the sky and wondering if a miracle had occurred.

Baba came out of his room. Baba's cheeks were wet. "We almost lost you," he said.

He said that Néné ran to get the French woman doctor. Baba said he liked her. Néné said that the woman was the last hope. "I thought he would listen to her," Néné said. "I left them alone."

Baba nodded. "She was a good woman. I said, 'Do you want this baby girl? I cannot take care of her. If you want her, I will give her to you and you can keep her for your own. She said, 'Yes, I will take the baby.' She took you in her arms and carried you away. A little while later Néné came back."

Néné spoke, her breath nearly gone.

"I said, 'Where's the baby? What did you do with the baby?' He said he gave you away to the doctor, and I screamed. I ran through the hospital. Where is the doctor, where is the doctor? I found her. She held you, and she said she saved the baby and it was all right, and I had nothing to worry about, she would keep you for her own. She said that she would take you to France. She said she already loved you."

"If it wasn't for your mother," Baba said, "we would have lost you."

"I begged her," Néné said. " 'Please, give me back my baby. You do not need this baby.' She said Baba was ill and this was the right thing, and France was a calm place for a child, but I was the mother and she knew this, and finally she gave you back to us."

"It didn't stop there," Néné said. "You were home for a few days, and you were lying on your back and Baba came over to you holding a big knife. He looked at me crazy and said, 'Why don't we cut the throat of this baby?' "

Sitting at the table, I knew I liked our new house. The dimensions were right. The people I loved could never be far from one another so long as they were in the house. We sat at the table, our legs touching, Diadia, our star, serious Koto, worried Hadiatou, Bobo with a brilliant smile, long and gentle Pathè, sweet Fifi, humble Idrissa, too, and Fatima with the big eyes. I was Mama, who giggled and sensed things. Néné had great strength and endurance. Baba built solid houses and divined houses that we might yet build.

Baba cried. "I do not like to think what might have been."

I do not know why my father and mother told me about the day Baba hung me in suspense. I slept without bad dreams of falling from the sky.

I dreamt about a woman I did not know who took me to France and treated me well and taught me many things. I saw a garden. When it came time for her to tell me who I was and where I came from and who else knew me, she refused to say. I dreamt I had been erased, and woke up trembling.

Part Two

❧

Things
That Happen
to You

CHAPTER SIX

LEARNING TO HIDE

*I*deas came to me about candy. I bought tins of condensed milk, emptied the milk, and heated it over a small flame until it took on the texture of caramel. One spoonful at a time, I lifted little balls from the pot and wrapped them in notebook paper. I took the candy to school and to market and sold them for one franc each.

Success meant greater expectations. I bought ripe coconuts and took the flesh out to make coconut grounds. I punched holes in a tin to make a kind of grater, and I scraped the coconut against the tin until I had a mound of shredded coconut. I cooked the coconut until it turned brown, added sugar, and molded it into candies. These earned five francs apiece.

By age eleven, I was a familiar sight to people in the neighborhood, selling my bags of sweets. They told Baba and Néné that I was the child who had ideas. By twelve, I knew better ways to make money. I cooked the shavings from cassava, which made a kind of dough. I added tomato sauce and served it at market on a taro leaf. We called this dish *kouti*, and it became my best seller. With my profits I bought the nicest dress I had ever seen. It was purple with white polka dots and it was very short like a mini-dress. It was now 1972, and I was in fashion.

I wore the dress on Saturday nights. My friends and I came together, Yaye Kesso, Buntu Touré, and another girl from up the road, Oumou Bah, nicknamed LaFiesta, who loved to dance. We changed into our dance clothes and walked to Tiendel Road, by the stadium and across from the high school, to the Palais de Kolima. Inside, a vast round space waited, with small lights glittering on the walls and a strong white light puncturing the dark in rapid bursts. Everything swirled and flashed. Shadows bounced everywhere. A band of teenaged boys pushed out waves of Latino music that ricocheted off the domed ceiling. This was a room made for sound.

We danced madly with each other for maybe an hour at a time before we finally gave in to sweat and a need for air. Outside, in back, there was a counter with sandwiches and a small hut surrounded by flowers. We all brought cameras and posed in front of the flowers. Sometimes Koto stood off to the side, watching me. A young boy named Taliba often asked me to dance, and I sometimes called him my boyfriend.

My friends and I also went to the Cinema de Labé. It cost fifty francs, extra if you bought candy or gum or barbecued meat at the door. We saw cowboy movies and several showings of a movie called *Champion*. An actress named Dara sang songs about love.

"Dara, Dara, Dara," we called to the screen.

Indian movies played often. *Mangala* was about a wealthy woman who lived in a palace and was forced to choose between two men. *Cita and Gita* was the story of twin girls, separated as babies. There were no subtitles, but the action told the tale. One twin went to live with a poor family and another with a rich family, and somehow they met and arranged to switch. But the poor girl was terrorized by a wicked woman who beat her repeatedly with a belt when she refused to scrub the floor. Finally the girl managed to grab the belt and she took control, and she was the one who did the beating. In the end, the girls reunited, one of them put on roller skates and they swept down the street singing "la-la-la." We saw the movie many times, and each time, on leaving, we pretended to be skaters, gliding through the center of Labé.

At home, there were more babies. Néné had a boy, her eighth child. We called him Oury. And Idrissa had a girl. Baba had allowed Diadia to switch to a boarding school in Popodara, where she stayed much of the time. Even so, cousins from Diontou or Tinkin stayed for months at a time and there were normally about fifteen children in the house. Idrissa kept her children with her in her room. The other babies stayed with Néné. When it came to meals, the cousins were served first. If the food was rationed, I might not eat at all. The cousins were never told to do chores.

"It is important to care for the children that aren't yours," Néné said. "If you don't, people will look on you very poorly."

I was happy to now have one of the converted storage closets as my room, though Néné still kept sacks of grain and cereal there on a shelf. It had no windows, no light at all, so I did my homework in front of candles I placed around my bed. I thought about the movies. In the movies everything always ended well, but to get there, people had to spin and crawl and scratch and endure wretched, evil people. They were sad for three quarters of the movie. Misery first, then "la-la-la."

An interesting thing happened. Mr. Kamara, the airline pilot, and his wife had another fight, and just like always, Mr. Kamara unleashed a terrible high scream to scare the goats. Everyone in the neighborhood knew that yell. Néné ran over as always, expecting to find Mrs. Kamara wailing over the second wife, and her husband storming off. Néné must have arrived a few moments earlier than usual, because this time she did not find Mrs. Kamara cowering in the corner, but standing and with a tight hold on Mr. Kamara, in a place, Néné said later, "men don't like to be grabbed."

Néné laughed and said it was funny how things turned out. "Now we know what he was yelling about," she said.

On a hot school day afternoon, Sékou Touré came to Labé.

Baba was angrier than ever with him. The government had increased taxes on the village markets, taken all power away from the village councils, and worse, to Baba, the president had given speeches discouraging people from learning or focusing on their tribal heritage. The nation of Guinea demanded one hundred percent dedication, Sékou Touré said, but Baba had an answer. "Nothing can stop me from being Fulah."

All students were given white flags and positioned on the track encircling the stadium football field. We wore blue-and-white school uniforms, and when Sékou Touré appeared in an open white car, we raised our flags and chanted "Prez-zy Prez-zy." He was an impressive sight, standing, waving a white handkerchief slowly. He was in a white boubou and a white hat, and it was true, his teeth were pure white and his skin fantastically shiny. The sunlight nearly reflected from his skin, and maybe this is what excited the people to chant and stomp. It felt like all of Labé was at the stadium, maybe all of Guinea, bodies pressed together, sweat mixing, hoping maybe the president would get a glimpse of us, perhaps look into our eyes. In a place like this, with a man like this, a mind can get fuzzy. Perhaps the sun was just a thing in the sky and this man with light beams was the sun itself.

Whatever it was, I broke from the crowd. Other children followed and we grabbed on to the end of the car, and Sékou Touré turned with a smile and fluttered his handkerchief in our direction. "He smiled right at me," I told everyone later.

"Pour la révolution!" he began his speech.

And we roared *"Victoire!"* just like I heard on Baba's radio.

A few months later, they started hanging people on the football field.

The newspaper showed a picture of the bodies, limp rag dolls, noble, too, I thought, their heads bowed. Many people in Labé went to the stadium to see the hangings. Nobody held it against these people who had the urge to know if it was a real thing. Many brought their children.

I was kept away, but Baba welcomed all the children to listen to the radio. Sékou Touré announced that a group of conspirators was attempting to overthrow the government. He said that for the good of

Guinea, he had arrested the country's scholars and thinkers and put them in a military compound in the center of Conakry, Camp Boiro.

We listened to the playing of their confessions on the radio, scratchy voices saying *"Je suis je me nome."*

Baba spoke over them. He said the confessions were forced. He had heard that the jailers wrapped their prisoners with wire, sending electrical jolts through their bodies, enough to torture them or to kill them, depending on what they wanted. They had Barry Trois at Camp Boiro. He was one of the first party representatives of the opposition. The message was plain: No one is safe.

The government advised people to build pits to hide their families from the conspirators. People did not know what to believe. Baba built our pit among bushes only a minute's dash from the house. If we heard gunshots, we should be ready to run to the bushes and hide in the pit, he told us. Hadiatou said she would hide in her suitcase. One night she returned to the house expecting to see me, and when she didn't, she cried out, "Néné, Néné, someone has come to kill us and they have already killed Mama." Néné ran to her, clutching Baba's rifle, but I appeared and said, "No, look. I am here."

Néné put the baby Oury to her breast constantly, wishing him fed in case we found ourselves trapped in the pit. One night, we heard shots. Baba was not home. Néné and Idrissa snatched up the babies and we ran through the bushes and found Baba's pit. It was a shallow hole. We tucked our heads low for a little while, and Néné said maybe we didn't hear what we thought we heard, maybe someone was shooting at a rabbit. We walked in a long line back to the house. Baba said we had done the right thing and that he felt better knowing we had the pit.

Then girls in Labé began disappearing from their families. Word traveled that men from the government, sent by Sékou Touré, were buying the girls. They would offer money, and fathers, afraid not to accept the deals or out of greed, obliged by surrendering their daughters. Girls up the road were taken. We saw them crying as they were led away. Other fathers, hearing about this, hastily arranged marriages or sent their girls for refuge in the villages.

Baba was afraid for Diadia. A man named Emil Cissey had been assigned by Sékou Touré as principal of Diadia's school. Fearing nothing, he began boasting openly that he had special relationships with some of the girls at his school. Baba drove immediately to Popodara and discovered that Emil Cissey had barred Diadia from the classroom after she failed to do an errand for him.

"What did you say to my daughter?" Baba asked him.

"You are only the father. This does not concern you," Emil Cissey said. Disrespecting him this way, Baba thought this man had committed an unholy act on top of all his other sins. Baba slapped him hard on the face.

"Keep this old man away from me," Emil Cissey said. Baba was ready to fight.

"You will kill me or I will kill you," Baba said.

Baba came home and told the family to brace for his arrest. But no one came for him. In a few weeks, the worst of the crisis seemed to have passed. Sékou Touré went back on the radio and announced that the attempted overthrow of the government had been turned back and that the pure state of Guinea lived on.

CHAPTER SEVEN

DRESSING THE QUEEN

On New Year's morning 1973, joyous Baba waited until he was sure Diadia had opened her eyes. He tiptoed to her bed and knelt beside her, holding a box wrapped in flowered paper.

"Happy birthday, Halimatou. You are my New Year's Day Miracle, and your father, on this day when you are twenty-one, wants you to know this."

"Baba?"

"Always take good care of yourself because when you are in the world you are a piece of me. I tell all the people, these are my daughters and I am proud of them. And everyone smiles because they know Allah has blessed me. You are the eldest and I am proud of you."

Diadia began to cry. Baba held her hand in the gentle courtship of a father and his first child, the first grandchild of Karamoko Alfa.

"I have given you everything you need, and I always will. I want you always to be happy, and in return I want you to be careful. Please don't do anything to dishonor me. Carry yourself with dignity. And when, Halimatou, you choose your husband, whenever that is, I will bless the marriage because I know this is the thing that will make you happiest."

I am sure that no Fulah father ever said such words to a daughter. Diadia's friends were long married, matched with boys and men they did not know. Diadia had rubbed the hands of girls who cried they did not want to get married this way, without even a picture to go by, to a man only their fathers had met, who might even take them back to the village. And Diadia had followed many times in the procession behind the groom, the bride sitting bewildered on his back.

No, this is not what Baba wanted. Maybe Diadia wanted to be a doctor or a scientist. She could go to school in Guinea and then Paris or Budapest. He had heard about good medical schools in Hungary and other parts of Europe, places he had marked on maps when he was a young man bandaging bloody legs and giving people their medicines, before he had the agitation. He had told us many times, "Girls in France go to school and get married. They have babies, too. My father always said you must let your children be of their time, and so it will be for you."

Diadia was dating a very handsome boy, Telli, from a respected family, not wealthy but an educated family without pretensions. Like Baba, this boy was a grandson of a village king, his ancestors from the first royal family of the Fouta Djallon. Baba had told Diadia that if this is the boy she chose, he would bless the marriage, but if not, that is good, too.

A dozen times, maybe more, a young man had come with his father, a man Baba knew well and trusted, to ask for the hand of his oldest daughter. Baba was a sight, in his fancy robe, leaning back, nodding and tilting, a hand on his chin, legs crossed, appearing for all the world to be weighing their words with great seriousness. And each time, rising at the end with an outstretched hand to say, "I am honored, but I have decided not to give my daughter away for marriage." And then leading the confused father and son out the door.

Diadia did not feel well. When she was sixteen, she had awoken one day with an odd tingling feeling in her face, and for a brief period, one side of her mouth was paralyzed. The day after her twenty-first birthday she told Baba that the feeling had returned and that Néné Idrissa had agreed to accompany her to Conakry to see a special doctor.

A few weeks went by. Diadia sent a message that she was well but she wanted to enter college in Conakry to train to be a doctor. Baba told his friends and got word to Diontou about his brilliant daughter. Hadiatou told me she was scared about Diadia, and I said, silly Hadiatou, you're always scared about this thing or another.

In spring 1973, Hadi showed me a picture of a baby. "This is your niece," she said.

It was afternoon, I was just home from school, children in the yard, Oury beginning to walk, Bobo and Pathè kicking and chasing a ball, Fifi already with long legs, sitting elegantly, Koto, a man now, in the doorway, no fathers home yet, cool wind of May, a level time of day.

"Néné, I need to speak to you," Hadiatou said. They sat on *joulets* in front of the house. I heard the *hissss* of their whispers, their bodies close, their faces cheek to cheek. Néné's hands went up. More whispers. Néné shook her head. Hadiatou leaned in to Néné's ear. A short cry came out of Néné, and she covered her mouth. And Hadiatou stood.

"Néné wants everyone inside," Hadiatou said. "She wants you to go in the house." We passed in front of Néné, who stayed sitting in the yard.

"Hadiatou, what is wrong?" Koto asked.

"It is Diadia. She has a baby. She has given birth to a baby girl."

We heard then a deep moan and the long, low, howling cry of the cemetery. Néné was on her knees, on the soil, grabbing pebbles and twisting her hands in back of her head and heaving forward.

"My life is over," she cried. "I am ruined, I am humiliated."

I ran to her. "Please, Néné, don't cry."

"What can I do? Can I run away, not come back? . . . How can I tell your father . . . what will your father do? The mother. It is always the mother who is blamed, especially the mother of a girl."

Women from the other houses came running. The women always run. "Diaraye," they said to my mother. "Who died?"

"Nobody," she said. "It is worse." And she achingly lifted her head.

"Get your husbands. They must come and take the rifle from the house. I do not know what he will do. When he comes home, he will look for the gun."

Koto sat on a chair in the house and cried, too, with little squeaking noises. "I know what Baba will do," he said. "Baba will kill himself."

The men came and took the rifle. They huddled in our yard. A few men were dispatched to get Baba, to tell him he was needed at home. When the group returned, following Baba inside, Néné crept along the side of the house, wishing not to be seen. She began gathering food and clothing from the wash, preparing to leave.

I ran in circles. What is happening? My mother is running away.

The men told Baba. We heard him, too, cry out.

I looked at our house and I expected it to fall, one wall at a time, in silence and flying dust, leaving nothing except two big chairs where my mother and father always sat to greet visitors.

"Why are you here?" my father screamed. "Are you here to make fun of me? Are you here to see my humiliation? Why do you want to come to my house? Go away, I don't need to see you."

The men begged him to calm down. My father sat on his bed and sobbed. "She was my pride and she did this to me."

No one saw Baba for two days, except Koto. We heard his voice only once, saying, "I want Koto." Koto brought him food and slept in his bed with him. If Baba needed to say something to Néné, he sent Koto. Koto told Baba this was not a catastrophe. He pleaded with him not to break the heart of the family. Baba wanted Koto with him, but he shook his head at Koto's words. Baba ate and prayed and stayed cloistered in his room with the son who could never please him.

He was all action when he came out. He told Hadiatou she was no longer allowed at the dances and he did not want her to spend time with any boys. Hadiatou tried to sneak from the house, but my father saw her and pulled her in.

Word of Baba's unhappiness filtered through the family, and a letter soon arrived from a relation of Néné's who lived in Liberia and wanted one of Baba's daughters as a wife. Soon the suitor sent another envelope with a photograph and a promise to come to Labé as soon as possible.

Hadiatou showed me the picture of the man Baba had chosen for her, wearing a jungle safari outfit. His name was Saikou Diallo.

"Okay, if you want me to do the same thing my sister did, push me. If you push me, I'm going to do it," Hadiatou screamed.

Baba grabbed her by the hair and struck her. He beat her, a stick in each hand. Every day he beat her, in the yard, in the big room, wherever he found her. Hadiatou stumbled and crashed through the house trying to avoid the whack of the sticks across her back, her legs, her head. I stroked her hair, assured her that Baba's anger would soon ease, before I closed the door of my lightless room to weep alone. I was thirteen.

The next week, Baba delivered his decree to Hadiatou.

"I cannot take any more. You need to get married."

"I will do this," she said. "I have fallen in love with one of my cousins. I will get engaged to him." She had thought it out and decided that any fate was better than marrying the man in the safari costume.

"Good. Do you like this boy?"

Hadiatou was sixteen. She remembered the boy's name, Dourd, and that once or twice he had asked her for a date. He lived in Kirodia, to the east.

"I like him," she said.

"Good! Then you will be married." And Baba clapped his hands in triumph.

"I need to know nothing more. I do not want a celebration. I will bless this marriage. If you need money I will help you to have a budget for a house, I will pay for the dowry. I don't want anything from him, but I don't need to keep a girl like you here who gives her father a hard time."

Saikou Diallo arrived at our house in the middle of the afternoon, late in June 1973. I opened the door and saw a tall man in a dark brown short-sleeve shirt, two pockets on the chest, and matching pants, a safari suit, but I did not recognize him as the man in Hadiatou's picture. I noticed a motorbike behind him and I sensed that he had come from far away. He seemed foreign.

"I am here to see your father," he said.

"My father is in town," I said. I was dressed in a short denim skirt. LaFiesta, Yaye Kesso, and I had been dancing in the house, my legs happy and cool. We had a small stereo. James Brown was singing "I Feel Good." The man's gaze fell to my legs, and I shied back and ran to find Néné. Quickly then, I wrapped a wide cloth over my skirt.

"My cousin, Diarama," Néné said, and she held out a hand for him. Her mother and Saikou's mother were first cousins, meaning Néné and Saikou were second cousins. I stood behind her, covered up, all the way to my toes.

"My husband is not here, but if you come back later, he will be happy to speak with you."

"I will come back." He must have been busy or had much to think about, because he came back two days later. Baba put on a fine robe and they spoke in private.

"I think I knew your father," Baba said.

"My father's name was Ibrahim. He was a scholar of Islam, and like my grandfather before him, he taught the Koran to children."

"This is like my father," Baba said.

"He was a herder, and he also traded cattle for goods like salt and wood, but the Koran was his life."

"Yes, that is right," Baba said. "I remember now, I met him once when I was a young man, married with young children. It has stayed with me. He came to Conakry for the airplane. He was on his way to Mecca for the hajj. Relatives arranged that he would stay with my family. I gave him water and food, and your father blessed me for giving him respect as I would my own father. And he wished for me, I have never forgotten this, he wished that God grant me someone who would respect me in the same way.

"Did you also know," Baba said, "your father, when he was a young man, picked out my own wife's mother to be his bride. But she had already been promised to another family. Your father told me this."

Baba smiled over the notion that many years later, *hodoriye,* destiny, or God's wishes, had brought him together with Ibrahim's son. But Baba had bad news for Saikou.

"Like your father, you are too late. I am sorry. I have already given my daughter for marriage, just two weeks now."

"No," said Saikou. "I saw one girl in your house. I believe she is the one that I want."

"Do not tell me that. She is a baby. She is the sister of the girl I told you about."

"But even if I meet her sister, I think I like this girl very much," Saikou said. "If it is all right with you, I will come back and see you."

"You are welcome in my house anytime you want, but unfortunately, there is no chance for you."

Saikou came back after two days. He had been to Tinkin to meet with my uncle Sharif, the brother of Néné. Sharif was regarded as a wise interpreter of the Koran, a learned man. And he had advised Saikou to speak honestly with my father.

"I am miserable with my first wife," Saikou said to Baba. "The first marriage was imposed on me. It was not my choice. I need a wife who is my own choice, then I can be happy."

"Why this girl?" my father asked.

"It has stayed in my mind how, on the day I saw her, she wrapped another piece of cloth on her legs." This was his reason.

These were troubled days. Baba sent Koto to Conakry with money for Diadia, but he did not want to see her or the new baby girl. The grandfather of the baby's father, the chief of the large village of Dalaba, to the south, sent a delegation to meet with Baba, to persuade him to bless the marriage of Diadia to Telli. Baba refused to let anyone in the house. Then, Néné, now stooped and tired, eyes reddened from crying, told us she was expecting a baby, her ninth.

Baba thought about Saikou's father, Ibrahim. They had prayed together fourteen years before. The older man had washed himself with water Baba carried to him. He had looked at Baba with stone-serious eyes when he asked God to send someone to return for Baba the respect Baba had given him. I have remembered this after all these years, Baba thought. I have never forgotten this man. He almost married the mother of my wife, the one who bore the name Kadiatou like my daughter. Now his son is knocking on the door of my family.

Baba had a revelation.

It is Kadi. She is the one who has respected me. Never a bad day from her. She is the one the father of Saikou Diallo prayed for, the one God sent to me.

The next day he met Saikou in town.

"It is my intention to marry your daughter," Saikou said.

Baba replied, "Her age has not yet arrived, but if you ask her, and she says yes, I will bless the marriage."

Baba added a condition.

"She is smart. You must agree that she maintains her schooling."

"I promise to educate her and make her happy," said Saikou.

This was the summer of 1973. I had just completed eighth grade. In four weeks I would be fourteen, and the bees would be returning soon.

Even in the age of advanced untold knowing, I had no idea what was happening. I only knew that Baba went back to his room. For three days he did not go to work. Whenever he pulled back his curtain and saw me, tears came to his eyes. He seemed tired. I thought Baba was not sleeping well these days; perhaps he was sick, but no one said so.

Then, Néné Idrissa asked me to join her for a trip into town. She said she planned to meet some people and wanted to show off her cousin's pretty daughter. I was busy with a school play, I told her, and was due at a rehearsal later in the afternoon. "Come with me, and later, I will bring you to the school," she said.

She took me straight to another family's house and into a small room. Sitting there waiting for us was the man I first saw in Hadiatou's photograph, the man in a safari suit, who had been meeting with Baba, the man who had caused me to cover up my legs.

Now, he was wearing Chinese pajamas. It was a long red robe with a belt in the middle. He held a small canvas bag on his lap. Idrissa had me sit in a wooden chair. The man and I both sat in wooden chairs in the middle of the room, facing one another. Idrissa spoke first.

"I bring you here because I want you to meet with this man and because he has something to tell you. This is why I ask you to come with me today."

Then the man spoke.

"My name is Saikou. Amadou Saikou Diallo. And I am twenty-nine years old. I am a businessman. I met you in your house the other day. I am married. I have one wife and two children."

Why is this man dressed so strangely? I thought.

"The marriage was arranged by my family. I have decided I need to make my own choice because I am very sad, I am not happy. I need to get somebody, and I want you. And I ask your father because the tradition tells us this is the right way. I am glad because he said I should ask you myself. Now I want you to tell me what you think."

I looked at the ceiling for a long time, in deep study. I looked hard enough to nearly see through it. Néné Idrissa stayed within my hearing.

"Everyone calls her Mama because she was named after her grandmother, the cousin of your mother. Mama, we call her. She has always had a wonderful spirit.

"Okay, Mama," Néné Idrissa said. "Say something."

Why is Idrissa with me today? I wondered. Where is Baba? Where is Néné? So many troubles for my family. My father is thinking he is humiliated. He is angry at my sisters. They are angry with him. My mother is sad. My sister Fifi is sad, and my brothers are sad. Even the baby Oury, I think. My house is upside down.

"Mr. Diallo, I don't know what to say to you. I give respect to my parents. I want to tell you what they want. Whatever decision they make, I will agree to. If they say 'Yes,' then the answer is yes."

The man in red Chinese pajamas smiled. A nice, big smile.

"He wants to give you to me, but he wants me to ask you."

He reached into his bag and brought out a pair of sandals. "I want you to have this," he said.

He gave me a blouse, too, and many money bills. "Thank you," I said, and I handed everything to Néné Idrissa before the exchange of good-byes.

On the street I snarled at Néné Idrissa.

"I don't need this stuff. I don't want it. I give it to you. I am going to my play."

Rehearsal was in the high school auditorium, on the stage where I had performed many times before, the place where once, with my father watching, my voice went on strike. When I arrived, other students surrounded me to help me change into my costume. They twisted my hair into two large braids that sat on my head like a bow. They wrapped my head in lace, colored an unnatural gold, gaudy the way you need it for the theater. They threw over me a stiff dress that held little glittery pieces of silver. I reminded myself of tasseled lamp shades I had seen at the market in town.

With my big head and shimmering gown, I was the king's wife.

"You are the master of all that surrounds you," my co-star said.

"I will lead my people gently and serve my king wisely," I said.

"And you are my lady."

"Together we will bring peace and wealth to our people," I said.

The king's voice rang out over the vast, empty hall. My voice was holed up in a tight ball that fell out of me, airless, nearly dead. The long light cords that hung from the vaulted ceiling reminded me of the hangman's nooses I had seen in the news photographs. With the seats vacant, I noticed how gray a place this was. We danced and sang in a giant circle, my arms around Yaye Kesso and LaFiesta, before, finally, the circle fell around me and my king.

And the circle shouted,

Praise the king and queen. Bless them forever.

———

I left the school with Yaye Kesso and LaFiesta. We were the lucky ones. During the worst of the crisis a year earlier, when girls our age were pried from their mothers and fathers by Sékou Touré and his men, we were spared. I did not mention the meeting with Saikou Diallo or anything said there to my friends, because the words were still arranging themselves in my head.

He said that, and then I said this. Or did he say something else? Did he mean this or that? If you say yes, your father will say yes. If my father says yes, I will say yes. Have these shoes.

Daylight fled on the way home, and the sky was brushed with the blackish blue that always gave me goose bumps as a small girl tucked between Néné's knees, and it still startled me. Tonight, though, I saw Labé with new eyes. I noticed the concrete houses piled on hillsides, hillsides turning into dark lakes even as I looked. I could almost see the houses rocking, wash lines stretched between the houses and yard trees like rope twines to their anchors. It was still too early for candles or the lighting of kerosene lamps, and the hillsides were enlivened only by sparkled ash escaping from the tiny kitchen houses. If I headed straight into the hillside, into dark waters, I would be gobbled up, and no one would know.

I had raced, skipped, and jumped ten thousand times on Labé's hilly roads, but tonight the road left me winded. The farther I was from the auditorium and the nearer to home, the heavier my feet, until each step sank me deeper into the ground.

An hour after I reached home, Baba's dinner guest arrived. Saikou Diallo told my parents that he owned many houses. Baba said that I was very smart. The grown-ups talked for hours. I stayed in the room, but I didn't say a thing.

Néné called me into the kitchen house the next day. We settled onto a small bench, her belly large with another baby, our sides touching, which pleased her. "Okay," she said.

She opened her hand and showed me a pair of gold earrings. I knew they were a gift from her father. "I want to give you this because soon you will be getting married," she said. Even Mr. Diallo had not used those words, or said anything like "wife" or "wedding." Revived by Néné's words, my full voice rose up and out.

"Why am I to get married at this time?" I asked.

"Please do not give me a tough time. You know what happened to your sister. And you know your father decided he didn't want you to have the same trouble."

"Why can people not trust me? Do you think I will go with boys?"

Néné's whole body sagged against the cement wall. I was afraid she might slide off the bench in full surrender. I felt sorry for my mother, because I knew she was a helpless witness as sure as I was. The smoke from bubbling pots enveloped us, and long streams of water ran from her scalp to her chin. Néné did not mind the sweat, because the kitchen house provided her with something she could not find anyplace else—a retreat. Baba was sure not to poke his head in there.

"I have my conditions, too," I said. "From now on, I need to be left alone. I need to enjoy the rest of my life until I get married."

Salvation, at least for a time, I declared, would be the Palais de Kolima.

"I will go dancing. I will go out every night, and no one will tell me not to. I have some time left, and I will have fun. All right?"

For three nights I danced, with no thoughts about breaking for air. "Is it true?" my friends asked me. "We heard you are getting married."

"That is true. So what? Get out of my life."

The next night, I dressed up in my short dress, big earrings, and a braided wig. Baba stopped me at the door.

"No. You are not going out," he said. "You have gone out so much lately, and now, you ought to stop. Take off this stuff. Take it off, the makeup, everything. It is time to stop all this. I want you to learn how to pray. Go wash your hands and pray. Pray and then go to bed."

That is the night I wished my father would die. I know Koto had wished the same, and Diadia and Hadiatou. That made four.

I washed only one foot and just one hand. I closed the door of my room, inaccessible to the moon and the sun, but I was still sure I was within God's reach. I placed the bedcover on the floor and sank to my knees. I put my head down, and I whispered, "God, kill me. God, kill me."

And then a little louder, to be sure my own ears would hear my own wishes, I said it again.

"God, kill me. Why am I having this trouble? Why? Why? Why?"

Then I went to bed.

I woke the next morning and saw on my bedclothes the first menstruation.

I tried to run away. Three days later I told my mother and father that I wanted to do one thing more before the wedding. I wanted to go to Conakry to see Diadia. I said I needed to speak with her. Baba said he would allow this, and we agreed I would leave the next morning. Immediately I prepared my suitcase, happy for the first time in days. There would be no wedding because there would be no bride. Once in Conakry, I would stay, a runaway.

The plan did not go far, because that night Diadia appeared at the door, erasing my alibi. Baba turned away.

"How can you let her go to the city when she is soon to be a bride?" Diadia said. I looked at her with wild, volcanic eyes, she who could do no wrong, depended on by her brothers and sisters, the cause of my problems.

"Don't you ever talk about me like that again," I said. "Okay? Because you know what you did."

Diadia came at me to slap me.

"Try it. If you try, we will fight," I screamed. We swung at each other, and it was Koto who stepped between us. When we were spent, it was Koto we all turned to, Koto with the broken heart, sitting on the floor weeping for his family.

I met Saikou Diallo once more before I was married, two days later.

In the Fulah tradition, families prefer sons to daughters. When sons are married, they bring their wives to the village of their parents, perhaps to live with their parents. In this way, sons add to the legacy of the family. They make the family larger, with grandchildren, and preserve for the parents their house as the center of the universe.

Daughters leave. Duty-bound, they follow their husbands to distant towns and villages, becoming part of the husband's family. Everything revolves around the men and what honors them. For that reason, the wedding rituals begin in the village where the girl's father was a boy. And they end in the village of her husband. There is then for the girl the element of concession in her marriage. From everything she knows— her friends, shops, maybe her school desk, smells, certain footsteps, little house noises, a small rattling of the roof, a loosened window shutter, noises that pull her from the moment of still awake to the moment of just asleep—from all of this she must turn.

Before anything else, there was for me the sensation of having been dislodged. I can remember Néné yanking vegetables from the ground, never a neat process, roots tearing and a section of her garden left in up-heaval. It was not easy being taken from Néné's garden. Left to right, she grew sweet potatoes, spinach, tomatoes, onions, taro, green beans, sometimes carrots, and, in one corner, corn during rainy season. Two white, plastic chairs were stationed near the garden, one for Néné and one for Maimouna or whoever came by. I thought it reasonable to wonder if Néné would go on sitting there after I was gone.

The son leaves, and the family grows. The daughter leaves, and this makes her family smaller. I wondered if Baba thought about that.

CHAPTER EIGHT

EATEN BY WOLVES

I was brought to Diontou, Baba's village.

I lay in my grandmother's hut. Many women came to me, though not all at once, their tall shadows cast by the flame that still lasted. The women appeared at my shoulder with blessings and kind words.

"She is a pretty girl."

"An angel. So young and so beautiful."

"She is an honor to her Fulah mother."

I was told not to speak. The bride is the silent one.

A man came to the entrance, someone I did not know, a delegate from Saikou Diallo's family.

"Kadiatou Diallo? Kadiatou Diallo? Kadiatou Diallo? Your mother and your father and your whole family have decided to give you to Saikou Diallo. Your grandparents and the great-grandparents before them and all your descendants have blessed you with this marriage."

Both grandmothers, meticulous Néné Diontou and doting Néné Tinkin and Aunt Djengui shone down on me. They removed my clothes. They dabbed my face, my neck, my stomach, my legs, and my toes with a wet cloth. Then Néné Diontou brought out a cloth that seemed too small for a person to wear, but soon I knew this cloth held secrets. They called it a *selely*. My grandmother snapped it open, and before my eyes it expanded, resting on the air for a moment and then settling toward me in delicate ripples. It was soft, pure cotton, white. The women stood me up, their hands braced wide on my back to keep me from falling. They wrapped me, and I had the feeling of being sealed away, which was not all bad. I knew my grandmothers would never hurt me. The fine cloth kept me cool.

The women chanted and closed their eyes, and with that, my eyes lost their strength. For many days I had not slept long or peacefully. Certainly I had not felt that I, the offering, was at the center of events. Now I rested completely, content to believe that at least these women saw me as the irreplaceable piece. I was even grateful to be free of the obligation of speaking because it also relieved the burden of thinking. Let these women speak for me, and I will sleep. Baba had blessed the transaction. The women blessed me.

I was carried from the hut, away from the fire, and all other feelings fled, leaving only one in place, that marriage meant I would remain horizontal for the rest of my life. A man hauled me out on his shoulder. He had big shoulders and sure arms. It was perhaps early evening. The smell of the orange trees struck me all at once. I could not see them, but I knew where the orange trees were—behind the hut, halfway up the hill behind the main hut. I recognized Néné Diontou's pebbles, gruff beneath the man's feet. There were many people there, and they danced and made music until well after dark. Someone beat a drum, and they sang and clapped and danced old circular dances I did not recognize. They carried on for some time, a great party, them on the ground, me in the air. Finally, the man carried me up the hill, past the mosque, to Diontou's one dusty road, past the point where Baba had once introduced me to his village with arms broadly spread, all kinds of possibilities in those arms.

Next, I was lying in the open back of a truck. It was the kind I had seen in Labé bringing goods to the stores. I had seen them many times on trips to the villages, dragging and belching into the Fouta Djallon. There were always boys stuffed on and hanging from the edges. Men, too, shortened cigarettes stuck to their lips, giving hot, scowly looks at our windshield, first when we crawled behind them, then when Baba, trying to pass, shifted the motor into a higher gear and kicked out a strong cloud of exhaust. The men always thanked us with hard stares as we sluggishly beat them up the hill.

I had always imagined rides on those trucks as hard, crammed, sunburnt ordeals. This ride was not like that. I lay in the back, the cloth still around me. My head rested on the lap of Néné Tinkin. Starting out late, we had no worries about the sun. The breezes poked at us with playful fingers, and the women chattered like children. A caravan of cars and other trucks from Diontou followed us, and we were serenaded from behind. Crossing through the dark mountains, no one slept. Everyone talked and sang and laughed, but not me. I looked up into smiling stars held in place by a shy, hiding moon. Good thing it was hiding, too, because the moon always brought out the dance in me.

It took almost five hours to go from Diontou to Hollandé Bouru, the village of Saikou Diallo. At a certain point, I could hear in the gruffness of the tires that we had left the road. We were traveling over rocks and fallen branches. And then we came to level ground, probably grass, a field. We must be getting near. I heard tall grass welcoming us with swishing strokes against the sides of the truck, and then the truck stopped. Someone jumped from the truck. A gate whined open, and I heard men exchange greetings. The truck moved on, then stopped, and I heard the feet of many people from all the cars and trucks hitting the ground. I heard more voices and shouts of greeting, a bustling reception in the middle of night.

I was lifted up then, not only horizontal but weightless, a magician's trick. I floated through light air, the way it is in the highest reaches of the Fouta Djallon, the way it is in made-up stories. I floated above the tops of huts, and I could hear into the huts. *Jomba ari. Jomba ari. The bride has arrived.* I soared above the trees, above the top of a waterfall, and looking down, I saw a giant cluster of people, hundreds of people, maybe thousands, pointing to me in wonder. *Look. That's the girl. She can't talk, but she can fly.* High in a cloud, I heard them, but they could not hear me. "Mama," I said. "This is a very interesting thing that is happening to you."

I came to earth in the morning.

The white cloth was removed and became a veil for my head. I was put in a yellow dress, the material silkier than anything I had ever worn.

They laid me on a rug in a field of dirt and grass. Women and their children paraded past me. The men came separately. The women tended to smile at me, and they paid great attention to my face. The way they paused and held a finger to their lips, I thought they were discussing my face. Some of the women giggled. The men preferred a nod, more solemn this way.

Hours went by. Dozens of prayers and blessings were said over me. Aunt Djengui stood to one side, my grandmothers at the other side. And Diadia was there, smiling at me sometimes, silent like me. My sister, my sister, I was glad for her being there.

At last the men appeared. The imam stood at my feet, and Saikou Diallo stood by my head. To see him I had to turn my eyes up. He wore a royal blue boubou that stood out against the sky.

The white cloth was removed.

The imam asked my grandmothers if they blessed the marriage. "Yes," they said. "We bless the marriage."

To Saikou's family, the imam repeated the request and they said that they, too, blessed the marriage. Saikou stepped forward and gave each of my grandmothers money. This is called the "giving of the shoes," because tradition says the groom shall give the price of the grandmother's shoes.

For the dowry, the groom must give the bride's family a cow or the value of a cow in gold. And so Saikou presented a small pouch of gold coins, first to the members of his family and then down a line to my family, everyone smiling for being given the honor of holding the dowry. Finally, it stopped in the hands of my aunt Djengui.

"Have all the conditions been met?" said the imam.

Satisfied, he said, *"Sale Allah Muhammadin."*

With these final words, the entire village burst into singing and leaping, louder than anything that had happened at the celebration in Diontou, and even longer. They stopped only for praying, and the prayer, too, was exultant, the women and the men stealing kind glances at me.

They danced on, celebrating the purity of me. Some of the women performed dances I had never seen in Labé, heavy and thumping. The women pulled the cloth from my head and danced and ran with it, the cloth trailing after them. By tradition, the cloth is used by the bride on her wedding night as a marker. It will reveal the telltale sign of her innocence or proclaim her impurity. The women will fold it and carry it to the girl's mother, who, too anxious to see for herself, will hand it over to her own mother for inspection. The girl's mother will cry with relief at the sign of red upon the white cloth and otherwise wail from shame.

In nearly all regards, the marrying off of a daughter is the father's responsibility, but in this one regard all fingers will point to the mother. She is asked nothing, her opinion is not sought, but she is answerable to one charge: She must keep her daughter pure.

Because of my age, the delivery of the *selely* was not necessary. The women surrounded me, offered me food, and said that for the next week they would care for my every need and comfort. When finally I went to sleep, my aunt and my sister and other women slept with me or on the floor around me. In marriage, I had been given away to a man, but every way I turned, a woman clung to me.

Still, I knew not to look for Néné.

In the culture of the village, it is not uncommon for a girl to be given away as young as thirteen, but elsewhere it raises inquiries. People in Labé understood why Baba sent his second daughter away. But to give away the third daughter perplexed them and brought an odd tone to their voices. Sensing this, Baba decided to let the event pass with a muted response. He decided that Néné and he would not go to the wedding, better to stay than have their absence from Labé trigger more questions.

I looked for them everywhere. *Néné? Baba? Will you not want to see me anymore? I miss you. I don't know the people here. I don't understand this village life.* I begged Diadia to take me with her, to Labé or Conakry.

"I can't stay. Please don't make me stay."

"Please try," she said. "I will come back to see you."

Before leaving, Diadia told Mr. Diallo, "I make only one demand of you. Do not make her a young mother." My new husband promised he would wait.

An instinct for survival had given me the power to float over Hollandé Bouru. I already knew how to dangle and kick from memory, and when Baba let me go this time, I fell for a moment and then rose. I looked down on treetops, and still I lifted. I conquered gravity itself. I could see the Fouta Djallon stretched out before me, all the way to Labé. Chaperoned by the moon, I floated over my house, the house of Néné and Baba.

They told me later that while I was in the village getting married the house was very quiet, except for the crying, Koto's and Néné's and Baba's. Little was said.

Baba said often, "Oh my God, I have lost my daughter."

Little Oury grabbed everyone by the leg.

"I know where Mama is," he said. "Mama has been eaten by wolves."

The year I was born, Saikou Diallo was sixteen years old. He left the village of Hollandé Bouru with plans to make money, against his father's wishes.

His father had always nurtured the hope that Saikou would follow his example, and grow into a man of deep faith and pass on lessons from the Koran to the children of the nearby villages. He had chosen Saikou's name from the Arabic word *sheik*, or "holy person."

Growing up, Saikou studied the Koran with energy. His mother, Laouratou, died when he was nine, and his father explained that Islam promised he would see her again. Saikou would sit with his father under a plum tree, the holy book open across their laps. They sat in the center of a landscape that in a single generation had been transformed from scrubby brushwood to a small paradise. Perhaps fifty families lived in huts surrounded by plum trees, mango trees, and blueberry bushes. High in the mountains they lived off the land, churning sun-scorched fields into crops, growing corn and the tiny grain called fonio.

Saikou's grandfather built Hollandé Bouru with profits from cattle trading. At one point his grandfather owned five hundred head. He also counseled the villagers on Islam and matters of morality. No one else in Fouta Djallon moved as easily between the mosque and the marketplace. Saikou had the notion that he could cherish the Koran while taking on the life of the trader. When he and two of his brothers left for Casamance in southern Senegal, it was his grandfather's model that guided him.

First, they stood on a road and sold cigarettes and candy. Soon they opened a small grocery, with shelves of bread, sugar, vegetable, cereals and grains, kola nuts, and other staples. Knowing that other shops in town could not afford to send someone to Dakar for supplies, Saikou made the trip for them, bought up provisions and sold them to the stores. Saikou was now a middleman.

Saikou had a reserved way of being that served him well in business. He stood back in negotiations, listening mostly, talking only when necessary. He stayed clear of politics, a smart tactic in West Africa in the early part of the 1960s when disputes flared everywhere. City people fought with bush people. The loyalists to the French still clashed with the loyalists to a "new Africa," and border conflicts plagued countries whose lines had been drawn by outsiders. Saikou took ten thousand dollars' worth of goods to Koeda, a city in the center of Senegal's peanut belt, and stored them in a shed. One night, a dispute between two political parties ended with a fire that destroyed the main market but spared Saikou's shed.

For two weeks he waited, skirting conversations about who started the fire and who deserved to be hanged for the fire. Skillfully, he shrugged, vowed ignorance and withdrew from any conversation that got hot with politics. Then he started selling right out of the shed, one of the few places after the fire where people could find merchandise they needed. Saikou doubled and tripled the prices and left Korda with a suitcase filled with Guinean francs worth thirty thousand dollars.

Saikou dreamed of expanding in Guinea. But Sékou Touré mistrusted traders like Saikou, who in Sékou Touré's eyes would sooner turn the whole Guinea system over to capitalism. In 1965, many prominent traders were thrown in jail. With that, the economy of Guinea turned inward and Saikou turned elsewhere, to Liberia.

He was twenty-two, on his way to the Ivory Coast from Liberia to buy earrings for reselling, when he was stopped at the border. Ivory Coast police were routinely arresting Guinean traders who they thought had taken away business from their own traders. They put Saikou in the basement of a police station for three days and threatened to deport him to Guinea, where he knew soldiers allied with the Ivory Coast would execute him.

"You are from Guinea, I know this," a guard said.

"No, I am Senegalese," Saikou replied.

"Let's see." The guard put Saikou face-to-face with a woman from Senegal to see if he could converse in Wolof, Senegal's native language. Fresh from starting his fortune in Senegal, Saikou spoke fluently, surprising and satisfying the guard.

"God bless you, you are saved," the guard said. "You are from Guinea, but you are saved." The guard put him on a bus back to Liberia. That's where Saikou stayed, cured for a while of his desire to cross borders.

He decided on Greenville, a town in the southeast part of the country, Seino County, right on the Atlantic Ocean. In Greenville, his fortune multiplied. And Greenville is where he brought me in the summer of 1973.

We left on a motorbike from Hollandé Bouru. Hundreds of people came to say good-bye. Néné Tinkin worried that so many people would give us bad luck.

"Too many impure eyes, too much jealousy," she said.

We had a long journey ahead of us, south and east, a circling course around Sierra Leone. On the bending roads of the Fouta Djallon, I had no choice but to hold tight on to Saikou. Two hours after departing, we skidded and crashed near Mamou. Saikou went to search for someone to repair the motorbike while I waited. An hour passed, and then another. Cars went by, and a few trucks. It crossed my mind that the men on the trucks would not mind if I hopped aboard. I could escape. Imagine that, me swinging from the running boards, a runaway, just another face in the crowd.

But I didn't run. That was the first time I didn't run.

We spent a lot of time talking in the bushes.

We found small clearings. We sat facing one another. Our knees did not touch. No part of him touched any part of me. He asked me if I was scared, and I said I was. I told him the only times I had been out of Labé was to visit my grandparents. I told him I wasn't sure what was expected of me. I told him I was scared of tigers and lions. I told him I had seen vultures in Labé, but that they didn't bother you if you were alive. He told me there were no wild animals in this part of Africa. He asked me what I liked.

"I like singing and acting in the school play. I like my friends, Yaye Kesso and LaFiesta, also Buntou Touré, my brothers call her 'Untoo' for 'meatball.'

"I like dancing," I said, and I thought for a moment. "But you know that."

"Yes, of course. You were dancing the first day I came to the house." We laughed a little over this.

We sat through long silences. Other times he played music for me on a record player. We liked to listen to Cuban music, Marvin Gaye, and a Guinean musician named Kandia. Some days Saikou brought a mat for praying. His back was wider than my father's, and this made his praying different. His bending and lifting in prayer seemed stronger but more cumbersome. His voice was heavy, without my father's melancholy. I don't know if I had ever prayed with just one person before, and never in so secluded a place.

He was kind. He said he would give me whatever I wanted. He made no demands. He wished to make me comfortable.

Saikou owned three gas stations in Seino County, five markets and drugstores, and a lumber mill that employed fifty people. Nearly all the people who worked for him were his relatives. No fewer than three hundred members of his family had followed him to Greenville. Saikou loaned money to many of them, and to strangers, too, to help them open shops in town. With the help of his brothers, he had built an Islamic school and a mosque. He also owned three cars and a pickup truck. Saikou had other activities, but these I knew less about. He mentioned something about trading in gold, and I pictured Saran and myself in a jungle of jagged medicine bottles and poisoned needles, pioneering for our fortune. Maybe Saikou had adventure like that in his life. "Just business matters for me," he said.

Saikou also liked to say that Greenville was booming. I was not sure what he meant, but he usually said this at the end of the day after he had made the round of his businesses. "We are lucky to live in a booming place like this," he said.

"Booming" mostly lived in my imagination as a place with lots of dancing and cars and even televisions, but whatever it was, it couldn't be Greenville. The people there boasted that no other place in West Africa had as green a coastline, and this was probably so. This meant it had more bushlands. Greenville had a new road along the coast of the Atlantic linking it to the capital, Monrovia to the northwest, but this did not make Greenville a city. It still took twenty-four hours to drive to the capital. To me it was a large village with perhaps one advantage: Many Liberians spoke a fluent English, which at least gave me the feeling I was connected to something outside of this place.

Saikou built two spacious homes, and we lived in one of them behind the largest of his stores. The store and house were built not of grass and clay or cement, but of wood, which made them unusual. We were surrounded by a few other houses, huts, too, and beyond that, bushland. I had my own small room, but on the first night and every night after, families of rats came casually through holes in the floor. They had a routine. They stopped, sat up on their haunches, turned up their noses to me, and scurried merrily back and forth. I learned to sleep with the blanket drawn over my mouth.

I lived with Saikou's brother Abdoulaye and his wife Madinatou, and Aissata, Saikou's other wife, and the two children Saikou had mentioned to me, Alfa and Diaraye.

Saikou did give me one strict instruction, on the very first day, the day we arrived on the motorbike. "I don't want you talking to Aissata," he said.

Demands, I decided, were good for a person. You might just be going along waiting for something to happen, not noticing too much, and *Boom!* That's when a rocket fires off in your head, and you are woken from your sleepwalking, all because someone made a demand.

This man does not know me, I thought. "Don't talk to her" translated to "I'll talk to her any time I want."

"Why not," I said to Saikou. "She is a human being. I will talk to her."

Aissata was a thin girl, pretty, but by the way she moved, I knew she had no sense she was pretty. Her shoulders sagged, arms hanging with no expression, like heavy weights. She moved across a room or the yard, hardly lifting her feet. I could always tell she was around by the sound of her feet shuffling across the floor. She rarely looked directly at me or anyone else, except for Madinatou, who shared whispered conversations with her.

"Where are you from?" I asked.

"Near Hollandé Bouru."

"Do you see your family much?"

"Not often. When I have the chance."

"What school did you go to?"

"I didn't go to school."

"Do you like to dance?"

"I have the babies now."

So I wanted to talk with her, but she wanted nothing to do with me. Or she had nothing really to talk about. Or, and this took me time to consider, it troubled her to talk to me.

Saikou yelled at her a lot. He told her it was her responsibility to keep the house clean, to cook, and to mind the children. She was never to ask him anything about his business dealings. Sometimes she cried. Sometimes she straightened up and argued with him, but not for long. She would drop her shoulders, gather up the children, and hobble away. She was twenty-two. I asked her how old she was when she married. "Thirteen," she said.

The answer shook me. Saikou chose me not knowing my age, I believed. I had since learned about the time his father blessed Baba, and the idea had come to me that maybe fate had played a role. It was possible. Baba had told me that God knows everything we do and all that runs through our hearts, and that must mean God sees events before they happen. He must know things ahead of time. Had Saikou not known the age of Aissata? Had God foreseen their marriage, too?

"How come you went and got another wife?" Aissata cried at him one day after I had been there for about three months.

"She is my educated wife, and she is the one I love," he said. "It is good for a man to have more than one wife. You have no problems here."

Later I went to Aissata's room and said, "I am sorry."

She looked at me with a sunken face. "It was the same way with me," she said. "He told me he loved me and said I was special. This was my good time." Saikou came along and saw us side by side.

"I told you, I do not want you talking with Aissata." He meant, of course, talking with her *"this way."* He had no problems with Aissata asking me to watch Alfa, or asking for help finding the onions for a dinner stew. But when our voices fell soft, and if Aissata should rise out of her sad posture, if only for a moment, Saikou put his big foot down.

"You should not talk to her that way," I said.

"I am telling you when to talk. Do not tell me how to talk."

"I am allowed to say what I think," I said.

Saikou had married a young girl once before, but knowing Aissata as I did, I doubted he had ever argued with one.

"You are a child, and I must take care of you," he said.

Then it slipped out.

"I have my rights," I said.

A few days later, Saikou left for the capital. "To do business," he said. That left me with a listless first wife, two young children, and a band of Saikou's brothers and sisters, who had decided that something was not quite right about me.

I no longer danced, but I sang to myself. I rocked on a swing in the backyard. I sang in French about the girl walking along the river who catches the eye of a captain passing by.

> *Tout en me promenant le long de la rivière—*
> *Tick tin lálá—*

The air here did not own the lightness of the air in Labé or Diontou or Tinkin. The air was filled with hot breezes from the ocean that choked my songs.

One day I recalled a song from the school play, words that preached rebellion by the people.

> *Mawbhè bhèn no tanpudè—*
> *Duti dhin Fewtiké—*
> *Mobondiren, mobondiren—*
> *Wallè bhè.*

I bowed my head, performance over, and I cried. It was, finally, a selfish cry, just for me. Not for Diadia or Hadiatou, Néné or Baba, or even Koto. I took no pity on Saran's mother sitting in the clinic, or the dazed girls at the Center for the Promotion of Females sewing school. My heart was closed to Oumou Keita, the girl I tormented in third grade, whose death once tormented me. I didn't have a place for the men hanged in the football stadium in the name of Sékou Touré's pride.

Saikou's sister and brother-in-law never asked me questions about my family or asked if there were any special foods I wanted. I remembered how Néné always preached that it was important to give special treatment to newcomers in the house, but this house had no such code. No one listened to the radio or commented on the news. Besides me, no one in the house had gone to school. Their main concern was keeping the shelves stocked in the big store next to the house.

It was a community store. Tall shelves of grains, biscuits, rice, canned soups, Ragou macaroni, Nestlé's chocolate powder, Crest, Bufferin, batteries, and Palmolive and Lux soap lined one wall. Another wall displayed everything from plastic trains to sandals. The store carried Marlboros, Winstons, Camels, and loose tobacco, and anyone in search of charcoal or plastic plates stopped in. Not much *wasn't* sold in the store. A woman's shelf offered lipstick, hair weaves, and put-on fingernails. Assorted rugs and fabrics and yarn were stored in a small upstairs room. All around the store were jugs of kerosene that people bought for lamps. And around one corner, just outside, was a giant refrigerator where the sodas and juices were kept.

In October 1974, I had been there more than a year. In that time, I had given up dancing, Western clothes of any kind, certainly the short dresses, and I had not heard the singing of a griot or read a book. Saikou was away again, back in Guinea after all, for trading. With little else to do, I would spend time in the big store. I liked to stand behind the counter and play saleswoman, for the chance to see other people and to test out my latest business ideas. I got some eggs, butter, sugar, and flour and made a big batch of butter cookies. They went fast, but then Abdoulaye said, "No more of that. Saikou doesn't want you in the store."

I played a lot with Alfa. I talked to him about back home. If nothing else, Aissata came to trust me with Alfa. One evening I was cleaning a kerosene lantern when it slipped from my hands and crashed to pieces on the floor. "Alfa, let's run," I said. We hid in the bushes behind the house for half an hour before Aissata came looking for us. "You must not be serious," she said, and I laughed with her. Saikou was away, and we, the women of the house, could laugh that way. Things like lamps were women's business. A child would worry about a broken lamp, but not a wife.

About then, on a Sunday afternoon, the big refrigerator in the main store turned off. The store had no electricity and depended on kerosene for its energy. A cousin of Saikou's, Alguassimu, about thirty years old, was working in the store. I was standing near him when he removed a small cover and dropped to the ground for a closer assessment of the problem.

"The burner light is out," he said. "All I have to do is turn the refrigerator on, and the light will go on."

"No, don't do it," I said. "I don't think that's right. If you do it, there will be an accident." In my voice, Abdoulaye heard only a child. It had barely reached him.

"It's Sunday and we have many customers. I want to sell Coke and Sprite."

Alguassimu reached behind the refrigerator and found the switch. *Click.*

The next sound was unmistakably the short, steady building up of air sucked from the machine. *FffffwwwwwOOOOp!* Then a whistle, and then an alarming *POPPP!!*

We leaped back. A long tail of flame whipped out from below the refrigerator, and that's all it took. The flame rolled up the nearest wall, split and grew in two directions once it reached the roof. Within moments the roof wore a fiery orange hat, and then the fire made a small elegant jump across a small space to our house. People ran from all directions to see if they could help. It seemed that all three hundred of Saikou's relatives came running. A few of them rushed in with blankets over their heads and they came out within seconds dragging Saikou's cousin, screaming, his legs on fire. I ran to him and threw dirt and sand on him to stop him from burning. I picked at his pants, but they were made of polyester and they stuck to him.

For all that went on, the burning of the store and the house was quiet, except for the *Pop! Pop! Pop!* we heard, doubtless from the collection of kerosene containers, spread around the store like flowerpots, exploding. The fire raced through a hearty meal of wood, linens, wool, tobacco, rugs, gooey plastic dishes and used hair, mattresses, chairs, tables, and all of our clothes. It devoured everything. The only thing left standing was the blackened husk of the big refrigerator.

Immediately, the glare of Saikou's relatives fell on me.

"Why was she there that day?" Madinatou said.

"What is she doing here at all?" said Abdoulaye. "She's just around all the time. Saikou has to do something about this girl."

To me, Abdoulaye said, "You have brought something with you. I don't know what it is."

After that, and with Saikou still away, I found ways to avoid his relatives. We moved into Saikou's second house. In the mornings I left the house and walked into the bushes where Saikou and I had talked and prayed. I found a stream, and a splintery footbridge that I imagined had been there a hundred years. It became my new singing spot, my new thinking spot.

Néné has no idea I'm standing in the middle of the bushes. We don't have a phone in the house. I can't call her. She doesn't know what I'm doing or what is happening to me. Is the same thing happening to her? All along Baba knew it would work out, this way, me here, Hadiatou there, Diadia with her baby, Koto not able to keep an eye on any of us. We were always together, and he never told us the day would arrive when my brothers, sisters, and I would be scattered this way and that. He had to know, and he stayed quiet.

Saikou received the message in Conakry that the store and the house were destroyed. Upon his return, I pounced.

"Take me home," I said. "I don't want to be with you. I don't need you anymore. They think I bring bad luck to you, so I will leave. I don't want to bring bad luck."

"You are not serious," Saikou said.

"Yes, I am." Now I screamed. "You left me alone. Is this what it means to be a wife? To be alone? I want to leave this place. I want to leave you."

Saikou sat down heavily. He was in safari clothes, his usual business outfit.

"If you leave me now, it will bring shame to both of us," he said. "Everyone will know it is because I lost my money, I lost my store, I lost my house."

"So what? Your family won't think that. They will know," I said.

"And you, if you marry someone, you are expected to stay with them in good health and bad, in wealth or poverty," said Saikou. "You cannot leave when something bad happens."

"I am not from here. I do not care what anyone thinks. And Saikou . . ." I did not often say his name. "You don't care. Why do you want to keep me?"

His response must have been sitting inside him. I sensed no pause in him to construct an answer.

"Kadiatou, I know that in our culture, the first wife is usually the most special, the one who is the center for the man and his family. But not here. You are my true wife. You are beautiful and smart, and when I see you, I feel happy. If you were to go, if I lost you, I would never recover from the wound."

This was the first time a man had said words like these to me. I never heard Baba speak to Néné this way, and yet the ring of these words was familiar. I had heard something like them more than once, next to Yaye Kesso and LaFiesta in the darkened Cinema de Labé. The woman on the screen, her name was Mangala, was torn between two valiant suitors.

Choose me and I will cherish you forever.
Choose me or else I cannot live.

I always wanted to shout to Mangala, "Choose both." My friends always laughed later and told each other that nothing like that ever happens.

Saikou's words sounded like a proposal, and my anger fled.

"I know it has not been easy for you," he said. "I am here now, and I will take care of you, and you will never again have a reason to want to leave."

Saikou and I kissed. He said, "I love you."

I said, "I love you," as though I had said it before.

We left the house holding hands and drove in the pickup truck to an open space and watched the Atlantic. We talked more and held hands. We drove to the big store to watch workmen pulling up new beams and banging nails. "See," said Saikou. "We are already rebuilding."

In the following days, we returned to our walks in the bushes. We took rides in the truck. We drove through dense forests, not far from the ocean. It was true, Liberia did have the greenest seacoast in West Africa. We found small pebble beaches surrounded by woods. Once or twice, Saikou took me on appointments and let me stay while he discussed business.

I imagined that Abdoulaye and Madinatou were unhappy, but I didn't care what they thought. I was the center of Saikou's attention. His eyes looked for me only. I was not his curse. I felt amazingly, beautifully, like his wife.

By the end of 1974, fifteen-year-old Mama was pregnant.

Part Three

Days That
Will Never
Come Again

CHAPTER NINE

GIVING BIRTH TO AMADOU

I did not know at first. How could I know? My hips ached, the sides of my stomach swelled, and my insides felt bubbly, but not much, nothing to tell anyone about. It was February 1975. I slept a lot. I woke up, ate a plate of rice and sauce, then went back to sleep. Every day for two weeks I slept, ate, slept. One morning Saikou took me to the health clinic. The doctor who examined me was a Liberian man, graying, with a small belly that made him look as if he had just had a nice meal. He listened to my heartbeat, tapped my chest and back with a firm finger, moved his hand gently on my stomach, and removed blood from my arm into a clear tube. A little while later he gave us the news.

"There is a baby coming," he said.

Saikou smiled. Pins and needles raced over my body, and soon, with grace, dissolved away. I thought, *I am having a baby, just like Néné.* A smile came to me, only to fade. *Where is Néné? I want Néné.*

One worry tumbled into another. Mainly, I needed more information. I had seen many babies, but no one ever told me how they left the mother. Each time Néné came home with a new one I wondered how the baby had gotten so big so fast. I liked asking questions, but I had never asked that one.

"How is this baby going to come out?" I asked Saikou.

He laughed and said that when it was time I would know, and that nature would take care of everything. I lived restlessly with this answer for a few days, but really, I wanted to know what happened. How did the baby get from here to there? I should have asked the doctor when I had the chance.

It must be that they take the baby out of a small place in your body. But where? I'll figure that out later. When the baby comes out, it is tiny, weighs nothing, and then in a little while it grows. They feed the baby right away so by the time the mother brings it home, the baby is fat and jolly. But no, that can't be. A baby can't grow that fast just from food. Back to Saikou.

"What I'm thinking is the baby comes out, and it's so small it will be like a ball, the shape of a ball, and then the air comes into the baby, and the baby fills up, and then you can see it's not a ball, that it has legs and arms and it's a baby and it is really big."

I didn't know Saikou had such a loud laugh in him. "You are joking," he said.

"Please, Saikou, tell me what happens. If you know, please tell me."

He scrunched his nose. One, two, three seconds trudged by.

"The baby comes out the same way it goes in."

I walked away, the inside of my mouth dried to sand.

"Shocking," I mumbled. "I am completely shocked."

Quiet came over me and my belly. This was a quiet I could enter, like opening the door of a giant balloon, closing it behind me, and having the space to myself. I sensed the beat of my heart from behind my eyes and in my feet. My heart felt at home. If my bones ached, my heart calmed them. The inner space of me became my outer space, granting me the bliss of total insulation, the knowledge of peace in my own womb.

This baby was so quiet. I wondered sometimes if it was alive, but the baby heard me wondering and always gave me a soft kick to say, "Mama, you know better. I am doing what I have to do." I rubbed my belly in reply. "Yes, I know you are."

I became round as a ball, which suited me. I was not the type to grow just my belly out, pregnant in one place. All of me was pregnant. Néné Tinkin would have laughed to hold my chubby fingers, and Néné Diontou would have ordered me to sit down. But I did not suffer. I ate well and any sweeps of soreness or nausea came for a visit and never settled in. After that first examination, I went to the doctor for a checkup only once more. People pointed at me in the street and commented over the brilliant rays I gave out. Saikou said he never knew that a pregnant woman could be so beautiful.

Saikou worried I was too beautiful. He told me that the time had come for me to stay in the house. It was not right for a girl at this stage to be all around town, taking walks and stopping for conversation. But I liked the fawning I attracted, and I especially liked when the women fussed over me and ran to me with cups of tea and other small favors when I passed by. The bigger and more waddled my steps, the greater the attention.

Late in July, I went with Saikou to the naming of a baby. When it was over I told Saikou that I wanted to stay with the women, who were leaving arm in arm from the ceremony. He said this was fine, but I should be careful not to tire myself. The women took turns holding my arm, honored to be seen helping a beautiful, round girl. Constantly they asked me if I wanted to rest, but I liked walking with these women and I kept on. Eventually, a small car, a Peugeot, stopped on the road. The driver said he recognized me as the wife of Saikou Diallo. "Please let me drive you home," he said.

Gladly, I accepted the man's offer. He drove me to the house where Saikou was waiting. Handshakes were exchanged, the man drove away, and Saikou let not a second more go by.

"I tell you again, you are not to go all around town like this," he said.

"What do you think I will do outside?"

"This matter is settled," he said. And as if to prove the point, he bought the Peugeot from the man the next day.

August 3, 1975, came, my sixteenth birthday. A few days later, as a present to myself, I went to have my hair restyled with thick African braids. The procedure takes ten, maybe twelve hours, and by evening, I was still a work in progress in the salon chair. Saikou, meanwhile, ran the car all over town asking if anyone had seen me. I returned at ten o'clock to find Saikou stomping in front of the house, in front of Madinatou and Abdoulaye. He roared at me with a ferociousness I had never seen in him, chest out, fists shaking, pounding fist into hand, pointing skyward. He was suddenly gigantic, his body occupied by a god gone mad.

"If you feel bad or you want to really fight me, let's do it behind the closed door," I said. We walked past the narrowed eyes of his relatives into the house.

"Where did you go?" he asked.

"I went to do my hair," I said, keeping an eye on the fist resting on Saikou's hip. He was ready to sock me.

"Do you think I can take this big belly and go do things?" I said.

"I don't care. You have to tell me where you have been. We will get in the car and you will come with me to show me where you spend the day. I have to meet the people."

"No way for that," I said. "This is a lack of trust, and I will not do it."

"You will come with me and show me. You will come because this is the only way I can know."

It took a lot, but finally Saikou pierced my balloon. The quiet raced out of it, replaced by the sound of my screaming.

"Never talk this way to me, or else I will leave you. I will take my big belly and I will go away and have this baby, and you will never see me again." I am the one who is screaming now.

That ended the commotion. Saikou's chest fell in and he turned away, deciding it was better to leave me alone when I was in this state. By my count, this was the third time I almost but did not run away.

Saikou had business in Monrovia. I helped fold his clothes into a bag and escorted him to the car. We said good-bye and he drove off. Immediately, I felt my stomach seize into a tight ball and I nearly fell. I made tiny steps to get into the house, a hunchback now, nearly crawling to my bed. Aissata and Abdoulaye asked me if I needed anything, but I said no, I was just having back pain and I was okay. Aissata came to sit on my bed.

"I can stay with you, Kadi. I will talk to you and you will feel better," she said. She reached for my hand.

"No, I am all right. Please just let me be alone." No one had ever told me the date when the baby would come or what I would feel when it did. Now, when I really needed someone to come lift me on his shoulders and take me away, no one came.

I stayed curled on my bed, and I don't know what happened to the day. I closed my eyes and opened them, and it was night. My belly hardened, and I could feel the muscles in my back and in my hips pulled to this one hard place, and I knew through the pain that this was the center of me crying out. Over and over, I sensed the thing itself, the grip, rolling toward me, gaining strength, squeezing harder and then harder, before slinking menacingly away. By morning I was drenched, and I managed a small scream. "Somebody please take me."

I asked Abdoulaye to please go into town. There was a small store at the market with a phone that people paid the owner to use. Call Saikou and tell him what is happening. "Tell him to come fast," I said.

At the hospital, they put me in a bed in a room by myself. A woman doctor looked at my belly and felt inside me. She had strong, knowing hands, hands like Néné. She said the time was coming close but we would have to wait. Another night came, then another morning. The woman doctor came back and measured me again. I watched her face to see if there were any lines of worry. She smiled and said, "This baby has its own schedule. You will be fine." She held my hand. "You are so young. You are strong. You will be fine and soon you will hold your baby."

The woman doctor cared for me. Her name was Clarisse. She helped give me a hot bath. She worked lotions into my back with a touch that was Néné's. Her voice could have been Néné's. *Mama is good.* She dried me, and put me in fresh clothes and fed me with a spoon.

Still, another night came. *Where is Néné? She doesn't even know I'm pregnant. How could I be giving birth with no Néné? How, how, how is that possible? She should know. She always knows me. Where is Saikou? He should have gotten Abdoulaye's message. He should have arrived by now.*

Just before three in the afternoon, I was lifted from the bed and put on a metal table. I looked down to see Clarisse, and in fits, I thanked God for bringing this woman to me. It is then that I lifted my head and cried.

"Oh my God! Women have work to do!"

Clarisse brought her face to mine, and tears flowed from her to me.

"Yes, child, it is hard to be a woman," she said.

"Yes. Oh yes." And our tears joined as one river. "But you will be fine. I am with you."

When the baby came out, she held the baby by the legs. The baby was upside down. Still quiet. And I was sure that light passed through the baby.

"Look at your baby! Look at your baby." The doctor's face was filled with wonder. She put her fingers through the light sheet coating the baby from head to toe and pulled it apart as if drawing curtains open. *Ta-dah!*

"You have a boy," she said.

His cry was sharp and powerful, a little angry, I thought. I looked to the doctor.

"This is normal, this is good. It is the baby's way of telling the world he is here," she told me.

She laid him on my chest, and I felt the heat in him. My baby was warm. I felt his mouth on my chin, and my nose inhaled him. He quieted soon. I put my lips to his head and felt sleep fall over him with a light quiver that ran through his body. Sleep brought composure to his face. His lips formed a straight, peaceful line, and the eyelashes—my baby had eyelashes!—slept, too, in tiny curves. Was it odd for me to think that my baby's eyelids were contented, too? Such a loud cry had come from such a tranquil baby, and so small a baby, too.

The doctor put him on a shiny scale and told me he weighed two and half kilos, not even four pounds. "We will have to feed this baby up," she said. I didn't care. I was happy he was small, because there was less of him to catch cold or be hurt. A small baby was less complicated, more contained, his personal universe less vast.

"Please let him stay with me," I told the doctor, who read fear in my request. "Of course, dear," she said.

That night, my baby slept in a basket beside my bed. I smiled on him and told him not to be afraid, that I would stay up all night and make sure nothing happened to him. He seemed wiser than me, and I noticed that now and then in his sleep his mouth flinched and his lips pressed out together, as in a kiss. Or maybe it was small talk.

The baby was glad I requested he stay in my room. It was much quieter in here, and a baby should be with his mother, he knew. He wanted to be kept on his side so if he should wake, I would be the first one he saw. He noticed I was a child, but this did not bother him. He guessed this gave us more in common. He didn't think I should worry about Néné, because Néné was always with me wherever I was, just as it would be with him and me. He kissed me again and told me to get the sleep I badly needed.

Oh God, I was tired. Even the heels of my feet hurt with exhaustion, but I waged a mighty fight against sleep. It settled on me that Saikou had waited for this night before coming to the hospital. He would tread softly into the room, make sure I was soundly asleep, then tuck the baby into his arms and pad softly from the room. When I woke, he would explain to me that I was too young to care for a baby and that he had found someone to take him. The baby was already gone, he would say, whisked off on a jet plane to another country where he would be well. I dreamt that I was a sentry, guarding the baby from harm. My mission was to wait for Saikou to enter and to stop him at all costs. I woke with a start. *The baby! Where's the baby?* He had not moved. Don't be silly, I told myself, but the same dogged dream kept pulling me in and then jolting me awake.

The foreboding fell away as the first daylight trickled into the room. I gazed at the baby and felt happiness in a way that hurt my heart. In wonder of eyes and cheeks and toes and fingernails and ears, funny ears, oh dear God who made this creature, tell me that I am able. If this is mother love, assure me I am strong enough to carry it. Tell me that the burning in my chest will not melt me away. I am good. I believe I am good. God, tell me I am right to think this. Tell me I am good. Give me the same peace this baby has.

I came off the bed and placed a hand on my baby's chest. The baby stretched and shivered. I found comfort in putting my hand on his forehead. Lying here in this basket was a piece of me, same as if they had opened my chest during the birth and marked my heart with a hot iron.

"You will be Amadou," I told the baby. "You will have the name of your grandfather, Baba, who I have not told you about. He is not here and no one has told him you have come, but he already cares about you deeply, and I miss him with all that's left of my heart."

Saikou returned when Amadou was six days old, when I was a day out of the hospital. He had with him a high chair, a special baby walker, two cribs, a playpen, and several stuffed animals. My eyes held nothing but ice for him.

"I will never forgive my brother for not letting me know you were in labor," he said.

"He never called you?"

"No. On the street in Monrovia I met a man from Seino County and I asked him if everything was okay back here. He said, 'Yes, but I think one of the ladies, the pregnant woman in your house, has delivered.' " Saikou said that he grabbed the man by his collar and said, "What! Say that again! It is my wife." Fast as he could, he hired a small plane and rushed home.

Hearing this story cooled me down. Abdoulaye was to blame, not Saikou. Abdoulaye never went to town, never made the phone call. He told Saikou that he thought it was a woman thing and it was not necessary to contact him. I could not believe anyone could do such a thing, but it felt much better to be mad at Abdoulaye than at Saikou. It never occurred to me to ask Saikou why he had gone on a trip just when I was at my biggest or what would have happened if he had not run into the man from Seino County.

I liked seeing the baby swaddled in Saikou's arms, Saikou peering down, his chin pressed into his chest. Saikou liked to give the bottle to the baby. He even warmed the milk and stirred it, and he had a knack for burping the baby, too. He fed the baby at every chance until business intruded. The special baby contraptions flowed into the house, and Saikou gave me sufficient money for baby clothes, but steadily, he was not as available for holding the baby and he asked fewer questions about what the baby was eating or how much the baby weighed.

My arms told me that Amadou was not adding on weight. He felt as light as when I first brought him home, but none of the grown-ups in the house seemed especially concerned. They did not prepare special foods for the baby or for me, just the regular rice and meat dishes. I knew if Néné were here, she would follow the Fulah way, which means pampering the new mother for forty days. To help the body restore the blood lost during childbirth, she would boil chickens and mix them with clove and mint and maybe a dozen other herbs and spices. Just the good, thick steam would be enough to take care of Amadou and me, and the whole house would fall under Néné's spell. She would soak Amadou and me in bathwater enriched with boiled roots and leaves, and she would massage our bodies with karitè butter.

Nothing like that happened to me. Madinatou did not inquire if I needed anything. She certainly did not seem concerned about Amadou's weight, preferring to make fun. When she saw me carrying Amadou, wrapped on my back, she found the laugh in it. "Look at that little thing. What is that? That's not a baby. It's a mouse."

I put the baby to the breast many times a day, though often he cried and did not stay at it for too long, finding sleeping there instead. At ten weeks, he still felt the same in my arms. I brought him back to the hospital, where a doctor zeroed in on the soft spot on the head. Only with Amadou, the opening was much larger than normal. It extended toward the back of the head and was more a long crevice than a spot, nearly dividing the skull in two halves. This was responsible for the baby's undernourishment, the doctor explained. It was as if Amadou was born with a skull fracture, and his body was using every calorie to heal the break.

We turned to traditional methods. An elderly woman, Mama Tarissa, who lived in a house up the road, whipped up special medicines and broths for Amadou. She ground leaves into an ointment, which she spread directly to the tender line on his head. He gained a little weight, but not like other babies I saw in town. He lulled off at the breast, and I thought this was good because it showed he was contented.

A man we knew, traveling to Labé, carried the news about the birth of Amadou. He returned with news as well. Hadiatou had also given birth, to a boy, just days after my baby came. The man said that Hadiatou was in Labé, and I thought that she must have gone home to have Néné with her for the birth. Néné had been there for one of us. I thanked God. Néné could not have been in two places at the same time.

I did wish she could see Amadou now and how he was with me. When I put him down, he did not cry or clamor to be picked up, but he kept a watch on me. His eyes tracked me across a room or across the yard. Stretching to see me, he would lift his head and totter on his side, and then finally fall flat. It was his desire to see me that got him to turn completely over. The kisses kept coming, and he had a habit of smacking his lips together. He was saying, "Mama, you are doing a good job."

At six months, I still worried about his weight. He woke hungry three times a night. I did not understand how hours of breastfeeding had not given him nice, full baby thighs. Saikou told me that all mothers worry. I asked Aissata, and she shrugged. Madinatou laughed again and said it's good to have a small baby. This way, she said, he can fit in your pocket. I had not minded when he came out small, but I found

BABA AND NÉNÉ AS A YOUNG COUPLE

BABA'S MOTHER

NÉNÉ'S MOTHER, NÉNÉ TINKIN

BABA'S FATHER

BABA

BABA AND NÉNÉ.
CHILDREN, FROM LEFT: KOTO, BOBO, PATHÉ, HADI, AND ME

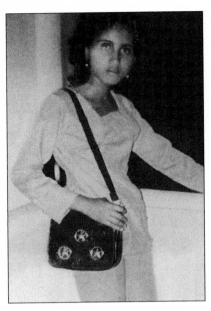

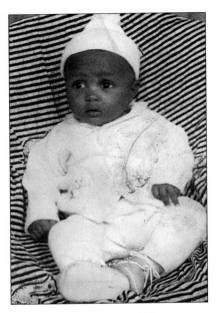

AT THIRTEEN, ONE WEEK
BEFORE MY MARRIAGE

BABY AMADOU

BANGKOK. FROM LEFT: ABDOUL, AMADOU, IBRAHIM, ME, AND LAURA

BANGKOK. FROM LEFT: LAURA, ABDOUL, AMADOU, IBRAHIM, AND ME

THREE BROTHERS

FROM LEFT: NÉNÉ, ME, AND BABA

ALL NINE SIBLINGS. SITTING: ME, DIADIA, FIFI (WHO DIED OCTOBER 2002), HASSA, AND HADI. STANDING: BOBO, OURY, KOTO, AND PATHÉ

AMADOU IN HIGH SCHOOL

NEW YORK. ABDOUL, LAURA, AND IBRAHIM

NEW YORK. AMADOU

myself wishing that my theory about air filling up the baby were true. That would be a lot easier.

Then, one day, Diadia showed up in Greenville.

"Diadia, Diadia, you're here," I cried. I had not seen anyone in my family for a long time.

"When I heard you had this baby, I began making my plans to see you," she said. She had left her baby with Néné and carried with her a single bag. She strode into the house, sure and hard, spine straight as a post, the old Diadia now, the one who always had a calling.

"Oh my God!" she said. "Look at you. What has happened? Why are you so thin?" Me? I was thin?

"You look like you could sleep for a month. Aren't you sleeping? Aren't you eating? Do this right now. For me. Lie down and I will hold the baby. You must close your eyes, Mama. You must rest. Oh my God, you are a girl and you look like an old lady. What has happened here?"

I was thin? I was tired? I had not noticed. No one had told me. Diadia was here, of all of us, the one who was sure about everything. I lay down and watched Diadia parading back and forth, Amadou cradled in one arm, Diadia, a mother now. I wanted to leap on her and kiss her face and her arms. Diadia was here! But my legs refused. Somebody has come for me, I thought. She came all this way. I loved the way she walked into the house, like she's been here before, like it's her house. I am with my family again. *Thunder cannot hurt you.* I fell off with a deep sigh, happy to rest, happy to feel Diadia around me, as though I, too, were tucked in her arms, side by side with Amadou.

"What do you feed the baby?" Diadia asked.

"He takes goat's milk and cow's milk and a little formula, but he mostly wants my milk," I said.

"Are you sure he is getting it?"

"Of course, he can stay there for hours, and he falls right to sleep there."

Diadia asked me to show her. She watched Amadou intently, saw how he grabbed on, closed his mouth, opened his mouth, closed it again, how he even smiled up at me while he was there. She watched him fall asleep.

"Mama, I don't think he's taking very much," she said. "Do your breasts ever feel hard, very hard?" I didn't know what to say.

"Let me show you."

She shifted Amadou to his side, his body facing me, no longer on his back, as I had held him. "You see, this gives him the signal that he's here to do some work, not to sleep." Diadia showed me a new way to guide myself into his mouth, to tickle the roof of his mouth. She had me sit straighter, to set myself more fully on the baby. "There is a place between you and the baby, where he knows that it is time to suck. You will see." Then I felt the powerful pull of Amadou, not the first time this had happened, but now he didn't stop. His jaws worked with newfound muscle. He made swallowing noises accompanied by a deep hum. His whole body hummed with satisfaction, even as he worked feverishly to get every last bit, and when he was finished, he licked the corners of his mouth. I was sore in a way I had never experienced, but Amadou and I slept all the way through that night.

The next day, Diadia was wild.

"How can he keep you here, no one to take care of you, he's away half the time, and no one to tell you how to do things. He can't expect you to know. He knows he married a young girl. He gives you a baby, forget school, no school. He promised Baba to give you the education you're supposed to have. But nothing. Nobody in this whole house has been to school. Traders, that's all they know how to do. Trade, make money, do more trading. That's not the Fulah life we know."

"But Saikou likes to feed the baby. He mixes up the food for him. You should see," I said.

Diadia waved her arms. She pointed to a chair as if Saikou were sitting there. I was reminded that it had been a while since I last raged at Saikou.

"He knows. He promised me, no baby until you are a woman, until you have your chance at school. And this is what he does. You are not a village girl. He gives you a baby and leaves you here in this house."

Diadia stopped abruptly. I turned to see if someone had just walked into the room. She sat and began to cry.

"What is it, Diadia?" I asked.

"I am so sorry. You are so far from the family." I hugged her tight, Amadou between us. "No one helped you," she said.

At the end of two weeks, Diadia left for Labé, but not before she got another promise from Saikou. She told him, "Get my sister out of the bush."

Amadou kept on eating. By eight months he had puffed cheeks, and his thighs were just how I wanted them, nice and fatty. A new energy came to him, and while he still watched me closely, and we went to sleep looking at each other, he soon became an explorer, crawling, hardly using his hands. People told me it was unusual for an eight-month-old to walk, but one afternoon I left him alone for a few moments. When I returned, he was up and coming toward me. I screamed, and Amadou froze on the spot. He flopped to the floor wailing, showing me that even the good parts of being a mother are hard.

When he was about eighteen months, it occurred to me that Amadou was developing, like a photograph. His eyes were evolving into soft crescents, set comfortably between a strong, wide forehead—and interesting cheekbones, sharp, but not threatening. He had a wide mouth, but overall, his mouth and chin were less distinct, and I thought this lent him a modest quality. His smile always seemed to be coming from a place far off. His mouth seemed content to allow the strength and attention to go to the upper parts of his face, his eyes, his brow, his ears, too.

It was plain to see now that his ears stuck out. Madinatou thought they were funny, but these ears made him alert and signaled to the world that he could be approached, a listener, a receiver of what came his way.

It was long past time to bring him to his grandparents, to let him receive their goodness.

This was in May 1977, when the crossing of borders involved calculated risk. Saikou had warned me that the Guinea government was distrustful of anyone coming into the country. Many people were being arrested as spies, and it was especially dangerous to take a baby, he said, and I would expose the baby to more disease in Guinea.

I left with Amadou in the back of a truck, confined over three days with many others. At the Guinea border, a guard pursed his lips at Amadou, who was dressed in a white shirt and blue pants and new shoes I had bought for his first meeting with Néné and Baba.

"You don't look like someone who has to travel on a truck," the guard said. He picked up Amadou. "His skin is too healthy and his clothes are too nice. And you, your skin is so shiny." He reasoned I must be a foreigner, and interrogated me on my plans.

"Only to see my family in Labé," I said, holding out identification papers. He shook his head, and I thought we would be brought to a police station or perhaps turned back, but Amadou chose the right time to give the guard a small smile. "Go straight to Labé and do not make any detours," the guard said with a fast folding-up of my papers.

Checkpoints at each village and town slowed the trip. The officers there held machine guns and rifled through passports and other documents, usually just to induce bribes in exchange for a swift passage. Still, the driver of the truck thought it was dangerous to travel in the daytime. In the mornings he pulled off the road, and we spent the day hiding in the bushes. After sunset, we piled back onto the truck.

We arrived at Baba and Néné late in the evening, and were engulfed by my younger brothers and sisters, Bobo, Pathè, Fifi, Oury, and the newest one, Hassah, who was nearly five. I was grateful my mother and father did not look much different. Néné hugged me, as did Baba, who usually preferred to shake hands. To Amadou, he said, "You are the first child of the first granddaughter of Karamoko Alfa to be married."

It was a calm homecoming until Koto came from college in Kankan, far in the east of Guinea. We embraced, and I clung to him, weeping into his neck, unable to stop. Finally I caught my breath, and I could sense Néné and Baba circling us with puzzled looks. Néné asked why I cried when I saw Koto but not when I saw her and Baba.

"My brother." These were the only words I managed. Nothing more would come out.

Amadou, of course, received special attention from Néné, who immediately made special dishes from fonio and maize, the best foods for a small child, she said. She also prepared large bowls of yogurt for him, and at every opportunity, she put a piece of banana in his mouth. Baba touched Amadou lightly under his chin and around his neck in soft tickles. Everyone was eager to see if Amadou had Mama's personality, and when Amadou refused to let anyone feed him and insisted always on holding his own spoon, they said, "He's got a mind of his own, just like Mama."

Néné was filled with news, much of it more than a year old. First she told me that Hadiatou's labor had been difficult. The boy, named Mauri, was very big and after he came out, Hadiatou's legs were paralyzed for months.

"And your sister cried to me in her bed, 'I am lucky you are here with me, but what of Mama?' I said, 'Don't tell me that. You want to tell me that Mama is having a baby, too?' And Hadiatou said she was just imagining, but she said, 'Suppose she has a baby just like me and you're not around.' This made me very worried, and then we heard, yes, at the same time, you were having your baby."

I learned from Néné that my friend Fatatoure, who also was one of the first to be married, lived in Conakry and had two children. Yaye Kesso was in Conakry with a husband and a baby. Many girls I knew, and boys, too, had left for Conakry. Going to the city had become almost a rite of passage for them, no matter that a place to live was ten times the cost of the same space in Labé, or that nearly everyone in Conakry lived crowded on top of one another, or that the air was filled with a muggy stench, or that thieves were known to climb over yard walls in the middle of the night. I understood why my friends had gone to Conakry. The ministries and banks were in Conakry. You could ride down the main street and see flags flying from the foreign embassies. I certainly would have preferred the clamor of Conakry to the stupor of Greenville. Conakry was where the ships came in, and where they launched. Whatever Conakry wasn't, it *was* the capital. There, often in the midst of chaos, there were possibilities.

Néné also sat me down to tell me that my friend LaFiesta, who spun with me at the Palais de Kolima and sang with me in the school play, had become sick with appendicitis and died in the health center in Labé.

Some girls did not get married. A girl I knew, with the same name as Néné's best friend, Maimouna, was in school to become a head nurse. Students at that level were referred to as "faculty." We met, and Maimouna wanted to know if I was happy. I said that it is difficult sometimes but I love Amadou. She did not understand why my father had given away a daughter who relished school. "You and I will go dancing tonight, and you can be yourself again," she said. The idea thrilled me instantly, but I told Maimouna I needed to conceal my identity.

"Don't tell anyone I have a baby at home. I don't want them asking questions."

Quickly, I changed into pants and a sleeveless blouse. I was so excited, as I ran out of the house I tripped on gravel, cutting my knee. Amadou came flying from the house, tears streaming. He squeezed his arms around my head, and he scanned my face with serious eyes, and it startled me to see an adult's worried expression on him.

"I am okay. Don't frown about me," I said.

While in Labé, I took walks with Koto. He told me that conditions at his school were far from ideal. Classes were crowded, and most people had to give bribes to avoid their expulsion. Koto would have preferred to go abroad for school, but Sékou Touré had placed a ban on students traveling overseas.

Baba, Koto knew, still cried about what he had done to "his

Mama." But Baba was not beyond his sudden outbursts and rants. Koto said that once, while he was studying for his final exams, Baba and Diadia had a terrible argument. Baba lost complete control, Koto said. He tried to hit Diadia, but Koto grabbed him, and Baba turned and struck Koto, opening a big cut on Koto's lip. Baba never apologized, but days later Néné passed a message to Koto.

"Your father wants to thank you for what you did between him and your sister. If you had not been there, he is afraid he would have done something very regrettable."

Babies have no more power to separate people from the parts of themselves that make them crazy than anyone else. You might think it would be different. The baby comes and everyone weeps and hollers with relief, and you think it might tug everyone over the threshold, away from their conceits and confusion, to their easier selves. Then you find that people cling fast to the ways they know because what else could they do?

The baby comes and everyone teaches the baby, to walk, speak, eat, love, yearn, grieve. In time, they teach the baby his past and to stand for what is right. But maybe we have it turned around. Maybe the ones already here should be the pupils and the baby the teacher. And the baby might say, "You know, where I come from, we're not so interested in what people have to say. We don't believe in a lot of talking. We consider what our eyes show us, we let it be, and then we look at something else."

I left Amadou with Néné to visit Hadiatou, now in Conakry. I had last seen her defeated, seized as a hostage. The Hadiatou I found in the city was happy, not nearly the fretful girl I knew. Her son had a big, happy face. He constantly leaped into her arms, each time a boisterous reunion. Hadiatou was now divorced from her husband and was soon to remarry. "I love him," she told me. I left Conakry after a month, relieved to know that Hadiatou had survived, and Diadia, too, and maybe even laid claim to their lives. But what about me?

Returning to the house in Labé, I found Amadou asleep, burning with fever. Red scabs covered his face, and his teeth were blackened. Néné said he was vomiting all the time. It's the chicken pox, said Néné.

"He's going to die. Néné, is he going to die?" I said, remembering Saikou's warning not to bring Amadou to Guinea.

"He will be all right. All the children have that once in their lifetime."

I put my lips on Amadou's forehead and felt a fire in him. Sweat coated him. Néné had him only in a diaper. He held a piece of clothing that was mine to his face, a green, cotton wrap, highlighted by drawings of tiny leaves. The whole time I was away, Néné told me, he never let go of it. For three days, I patted his body with cold, wet cloths. Néné managed to get chicken soup in him, but otherwise Amadou turned his head from any spoon that came near him. I slept by him, measuring his temperature with my lips to his head every half hour. When the temperature lifted, Amadou ate and ate, everything that Néné put before him, mounds of rice, bananas by the bunches, and yogurt right from the mixing drum. Pleased with his big, round stomach, he carried on tradition and jumped fully into the drum. "Look. Look," Néné shouted. "Just like Mama in Tinkin." His recovery should have cleared my mind, but unease lingered. Sick once, he could get sick again.

Back in Labé, I lived a double life. By day, I was the mother. At night, I slipped into my disguise, a regular eighteen-year-old girl, a student studying to be a doctor, or if that didn't work out, a teacher. Like Maimouna, I said, "I am with the faculty."

I spun on the dance floor under flashing lights with my friend, freed of the prospect of a dismayed Saikou awaiting my return, but not free from surveillance. Everywhere I went, Bobo followed. He was in high school, and had been designated a spy by Baba, assigned to supply reports on where I went, whom I talked to, and especially whom I danced with. "If you don't leave me alone, I will fight you," I told Bobo, but he remained my shadow, loyal to Baba.

After dancing, I sometimes found Néné sitting in the big room with Amadou asleep in her arms. I would come beside her, and cheek to cheek, we hovered over Amadou's face.

"There is something about him," Néné said one night. She shook her head. "I never knew a child like this, maybe Koto, but I don't know, a child with such wisdom about him."

"I think I see it, too, but what do you mean?" I said.

"Amadou is two now. Most children are still growing into themselves, but Amadou has, I'm not sure what to call it, perhaps it is the *mirin*, his dura. He is unusual. You see children running here and there, they haven't figured out their place yet. But Amadou, when you were in Conakry, every night he sits, he sits right here and watches Baba and me. He makes me think there is another adult in the room. I don't hear a peep from him, so maybe I go to look at him, and I see he's already looking at me.

"One afternoon, an old man, who spent his life studying the stars, happened to see Amadou and said, 'This is not a regular child. We should not call him a child. He is from the highest star.' He was very sure. He said, 'This baby should wear only white.'"

"But Néné." I wasn't sure I liked hearing this. "Is this good for a child? He is just a child. Isn't it better if he is running and playing? Sometimes I look at him, and I love him, and I see him and I wonder what he is thinking, and I'm scared for him."

Néné laughed. "Don't worry. You should have seen him with Oury and Hassah, running, kicking the ball all around, and with the other children on the street." I guessed that was right. Amadou loved to race and jump. He liked popping into laundry baskets and hiding under blankets. Baba gave him a set of play cars, and he and Oury spent hours zooming them around the house.

"A child like this is a blessing," Néné said, "because one day he can take care of you."

While I was dancing, the women of Guinea, the ones selling yogurt and rice, lettuce and fruit, rose up. They had been forced out of the markets and into a kind of hiding by Sékou Touré. Two years before he had dictated that all produce in Guinea would be sold by state-run co-operatives. And he assigned special guards to all the marketplaces to keep them clear of anyone who might try to sell outside of the system. Many women still went to the market, carrying the food beneath oversized shawls, or going door to door. Until a day in August of 1977.

A woman carrying a large container of rice went to the Madina market, the biggest one in Conakry, and sat down right in view of one of the president's special guards.

"You must leave at once," the guard said.

"The only way you can make me leave is to kill me," she said.

He tried to pull the container from her, but the woman resisted. The other women, the ones selling in secret, leaped to her defense and began beating and kicking the guard. Hearing what had happened, many other women raced to the market, and soon they were marching straight to the president's palace.

They forced their way through the gates and demanded to meet with Sékou Touré. In time, he emerged, chanting *"Pour la Révolution,"* the women's cue to chant in return. But they said nothing.

"Victoire," he roared. And the women would not say it in kind.

"You deceived us," they said. "We are hungry and tired, and all we want is the freedom to sell our food like free people."

Two things were amazing about this story.

The first was that Sékou Touré gave them exactly what they wanted. They could sell again, beginning that day. That very day!

The second amazing thing was that it was not a fable. It was a true story. It really happened.

Amadou turned two in Labé. I had made no schedule for returning to Liberia, in part because tensions on West African borders had only increased. There was news of people being shot as they tried to cross from one country to another. I did not mind waiting. I had Amadou, and I had dancing. Until Baba announced he was unhappy.

"All the nights you do this and you forget who you are. You are married. You have a son. You are not doing right by your husband." Baba demanded I return to Saikou immediately, knowing I dare not bring Amadou on the trip.

"This is all right," Baba said. "I see now you are too young. I will help you. Go back to your husband and Amadou will stay here, until he is four and he reaches the age of going to school."

"I will not do such a thing. I want to keep my child," I screamed, imagining black teeth and fevered skin. "If you force me to go back to my husband without my child, if my child gets sick again and he dies, I will never speak to you for the rest of my life."

My father's head snapped back, and he held his chin high. I wasn't sure if I had angered him or astounded him into concession. It was neither.

"You are not Allah," he said evenly. "This child will not die. He will be just fine. Just go."

CHAPTER TEN

CATCHING SIGHT OF FATE

*S*aikou kept one promise to Diadia. He lifted me out of the bushes and brought me north to Monrovia. I had never seen a place like this. Most of the streets were paved, and most homes had electricity and televisions. It wasn't hard to get from one place to the next, and once you arrived, you could see where you were. The markets were big and overflowing with boxes of Cornflakes, Wheaties, Ring Dings, Oreos, Ritz Crackers, Kleenex in a blue box, a red box, a flowered box, lots of spray cans, Lemon Pledge, air fresheners, and a dozen scented deodorants to choose from. You could walk the length of one corridor and discover a hundred products dedicated to cleaning your clothes or your dishes or your wood floor, tiled floor, linoleum floor, carpeted floor, or your car. Icy bins displayed rows of shiny plastic-wrapped containers, and only when I looked closely did I realize what all that plastic held—meat! Chicken, pork, and beef! The stores were so big and offered so many choices, you needed a rolling cart to get around, and they used brilliant white lighting, more lighting power than in nearly all of Labé. Just going shopping was an event.

More interesting were the shops on Broad Street that sold dresses from New York and California. The price tags bore fancy names in swirling letters, and just the tags impressed me. In Labé and in Seino County, price tags were a rarity. There, I would pick up a blouse, and that would set the negotiations in motion. The seller would try to size me up before mentioning a figure, gauging the customer's means before gouging her purse. I often dressed in my oldest clothes to go shopping with one thought in mind, to throw the seller off. But in Monrovia, the women dressed up to buy dresses. They dispensed their American dollars on the makeup counters with practiced nonchalance.

America was everywhere, from the currency to the racks of *Newsweek* and *Cosmopolitan* sold at the cafes to the street names, and the people indulged without self-reproach, at least while I was there. It was even part of their birthright, a few explained to me, because Liberia was created by freed slaves who came from America eager to exercise their independence. That is how the country acquired its name, "land of liberty." In Monrovia, there were also thousands of Americo-Liberians, people who had left the United States to reclaim their African roots. They brought their English with them and they brought something else—books, ideas, and an energy they could only have attained by realizing their hearts' desire. Wealthy traders from Lebanon and India lived in some of the fanciest apartments in the city, and they, too, spent their dollars freely.

Needless to say, I was a spectator to all their filled-up lives, though I did cheer myself in buying several pairs of boots and several hats. For the first time in my life I lived in an apartment, on the second floor of a building on Benson Street. It had a balcony. From there I watched the traffic of people and cars, buses and taxis. As always, Saikou did not want me out by myself. No restaurants or movie theaters for me. Even stopping for fruit carried anxiety. There I would be, squeezing a mango, delicately assessing its ripeness, telling myself "Make this snappy. Saikou will be mad." School, the thing I wanted most of all, was off-limits. He said the other students and teachers will see a girl of eighteen and not think she was married. They would have the wrong idea.

"I must go to school," I said. "It is important. It is the promise you made to Baba."

We compromised. Saikou paid someone to tutor me, in the house. This was my first English-speaking teacher, a man who looked something like the doctor in Seino County who told me I was pregnant with Amadou. Strange, just like then, I was feeling pangs in my belly.

I read a storybook in English, about a mountain climber sitting on the highest peak, recalling the fight he waged against wind and frostbite to reach the top. "What are your thoughts about this story?" the teacher asked.

"I think the story is about the struggle he went through, but I am glad it begins with him already at his destination. I liked beginning at the moment when his dream came true. Then, when I read about the hardships he suffered, I already knew everything would work out for him."

"And what did you think of the very end of the book?" he asked.

"I was surprised that after all he went through, when all was said and done, he wished only to climb another mountain, an even bigger one. It made me want to read on."

The teacher's face nearly burst with excitement. "You are smart. You understand that the writer begins with the end of the story instead of the beginning. And the best endings are not endings at all. They push the reader forward. Your husband must send you to school. You have a bright future."

The teacher didn't say as a beauty queen. But just about then, I was asked to represent Guinea in the Miss West Africa pageant. The Guinea ambassador to Liberia knew Saikou and told him that I had been pointed out to him as the wife of the big businessman from Seino County. The ambassador said I would be an ideal Miss Guinea.

Saikou came home with the news, and all I could do was laugh. "Me? In a beauty contest?"

"What is so funny?" said Saikou. "You see what is happening. You went out and the people see you. And they look at you this way."

My laughing stopped short. I could see he was serious.

"How come they choose you? How come they know you? You go out. They see you in your hats and your boots. Now they choose you, but it is simple. I will not allow it."

My head felt suddenly dizzy and heavy. A slice of a second passed when I thought my knees were buckling and I was falling. The sensation came and went, and judging by the sting in Saikou's eyes, I didn't think he had even noticed. I came right up to him.

"Hey, wait a minute. I am a human being and I can decide my life. I'm not interested in this. I want one thing. I am ready to go back to school."

"You cannot go to school."

"If you don't send me to school, I must have a divorce. I will not live this way anymore. Either you send me back to school or you send me back to Guinea." Saikou thought for a moment, a finger to his chin.

"If you want a divorce because of this condition, then I will agree, but before you do that, let's go to the doctor. I have to know you are not pregnant before you leave the marriage." Saikou was too smart to take any chances. We went to the doctor the next day, but Saikou already knew what the doctor would say.

"How could you tell?" I asked him.

"Because the same way I am seeing you now is the way you were with Amadou. Because you are rebellious when I come near you. You don't want me, you push me away, you are aggressive. This is why I think you are pregnant."

"Now what?" I said.

"Now you will have this baby."

"What about school?"

"Nothing has changed. And now you are pregnant. So stop thinking about school."

I pointed a finger at Saikou.

"Listen to me. I am ready to take this pregnancy and leave if you don't do what you promised." These words were my best attempt to scare him.

"If you do that," he said, "I will pray that you should die with the pregnancy."

And it was decided.

"I cannot let you do that, and I cannot send you to school. There will be no divorce. You are going back to Guinea. You will leave Monrovia at this time."

It was January 1978. I was in my fourth month with my second child and back on the truck. I kept going away from Saikou, but I had not left him. What I was doing now, chugging through Africa in the dark, wasn't a leaving. This was the reprimand he handed down.

Driving through the night, that was one thought. Another made me smile. I would soon be kissing my Amadou, the only male in my life who never made demands.

For bedtime, I told Amadou about the monkeys who lived in the plum trees. One day they were summoned to a meeting by the chief monkey who said it was time to harvest the plums. But the night before the harvest, while the other monkeys slept, the chief monkey, who was also the biggest monkey, ate all the fruit. When the rest of the monkeys woke early the next morning and saw that all the fruit was gone, they began to point fingers. "Who did it? Who betrayed us?" they cried, and the monkeys each said, "Not me. Not me. Not me."

"Let's go to the river," they shouted. "We will go to the river and the river will tell us."

One by one, the monkeys jumped in the river. The ones who stayed afloat would be judged innocent. The monkey who sank, stuffed and weighted down by the plums, would be exposed as the guilty one.

The chief monkey took his turn last. He jumped and immediately sank. The other monkeys pulled him out, and the big monkey said, "No, it's my robe. I have to take my robe off." He removed the robe, jumped back in, and sank again.

"It is true, you are the one," they shouted at him.

"It's my pants," he said. He took off his pants. The other monkeys laughed. When that didn't work, he removed his necklace. He sank once more. He took off his hat, his shirt, his shoes. Finally he jumped in completely naked, and sank again.

"Look at the bad monkey," the others said, pointing. And the chief monkey, who had not used his power wisely, shuffled away, his tail between his legs.

Amadou would not close his eyes until I had told him the story again and again, and each time he laughed. "Amadou, it is time for sleep," I would say. At two and a half, he would pull the covers slightly, barely disturbing them as he slipped inside. There was simplicity to his movements. I saw that he had grown in the four months we were separated. He was wider. His chest was more pronounced, and the baby fat had mostly disappeared. Néné told me that he made some mischief with her, finding places to hide behind the house, sending her out looking for him. He would pop out and say, "Néné Labé, here I am."

Up to then, he had not said many words, mainly because he could communicate without using any, Néné said. But his talking skills had developed. Néné said that he had said whole sentences. "Néné, I want my rice now." "Néné, it is time to cook the food and put it on the table." And I had been surprised by something else, that Amadou was now using his left hand to eat. He was becoming the only lefty in the family.

After my return, he fell in the yard one day and needed stitches for a cut on his forehead. Before the stitches could be removed, he fell again. The cut became worse and left behind a tiny scar. Lying beside him at night, as he slept, I promised not to leave him again. "If I ever do, just come and get me," I told him.

I drew close to him, his body warm and healthy. Néné had taken good care of him. I felt Amadou against my belly where the other baby, in the fifth month, had begun to stir. Between us, with elbows and feet, this baby made the announcement, "I am here, too."

Where Amadou had hardly moved in my belly, this baby slid, shifted, and bounced. The queasiness and joint pains I had dodged with Amadou came upon me. And my moods shifted between exhilaration and gloom nearly by the hour. Fortunately I had Néné this time. She cooked up soups and stews, mixed with boiled taro leaves, steeped in juices from a concoction of everything she could pull from her garden. At this stage, she said, my body required help to nourish both the baby and me. The baths she gave me helped settle my moods.

I was bigger, too, with this baby, but that did not stem my desire to return to the dance floor. It was the only way to be with my friend Maimouna and people my age.

"No. You cannot dance with your pregnant belly, your big belly," Baba said.

"Okay. If you say no, this gives me no harm. You gave me to this man, and I have accepted. I have respected your decision and I fulfill my role as a wife. I have my son and I am having my second child and I want to go dancing. You refuse. So instead, I will stay here all the time so you can see me."

The next morning I woke early. I wrapped myself in one long cloth, put my hair up like a crazy person, and went to sit under the mango tree. I folded my arms, and when Baba came out for the morning prayer, I was waiting, staring out, a petrified rebel determined to torment him.

Look at me, Baba. You have made the mute statue that appears before you. You cry over what you have done. Well, now you can look at me all the time, and if your deed shall ever leave your mind, I will be here, under this tree, and I will make sure you never forget.

"What is going on?" he said.

I did not look at him. I said nothing. When he returned from his office in the afternoon, he saw me in the same spot. Day after day this happened. He left with me under the tree. I ran in to get something to eat, played with Amadou, listened to music, ate some more, and ran back to the tree in time for his return.

"I cannot believe this, you are here all day," he said. "You think this will change your father's mind. I can understand why your husband sent you away." I still sat, determined to carry out his punishment. Finally, it was too much for him. He came to me, his eyes red with tears.

"Please don't do this to me. Okay, go out, if this is what you want."

"No! No way! I am not going out because you want me to be here.

You will see." He left me there, and soon I heard the sound of the radio coming from his room.

That evening, I dressed for dancing. I put on a jeans dress and boots from Monrovia. These had long, thin iron spikes for heels. Néné took one look and slapped her head. "You can't. There's no way you can walk with these."

I started walking. One. Two. Three. And I screamed.

"Néné, help me." The spikes stabbed me through my legs, into my stomach. "Please help me."

"No, I'm not going to help you. I'm going to teach you a lesson."

"I swear, Néné, I can't move. I am going to die."

"No, you are not going to die, but today you must understand that you are pregnant."

"Please, please," I screamed. I held on to the wall, crying.

Néné helped me to a chair and somehow wrenched the boots from my feet. I panted. "No more. I will stop."

One pain replaced the other. The next day, a tooth on the left side began throbbing. Hot soup made me wince. Cold soda sent the pain ringing in my cheeks and to my toes. By the following day the agony was worse, until I curled up on the floor, moaning. Amadou cried and said, "What's the matter, Mama?" I could barely lift my head to him.

Néné and Baba took me to the dentist. He said I had two choices. Either he could remove the tooth or he could fix it. He said he would put medicine in my mouth and pray for it to be better.

"Get it out!" I cried.

He took out a shiny pair of pliers and wedged it around the tooth. Not so bad, just metal scraping. Quickly came the yanking and tearing, and even the baby joined the act with swift kicks to my ribs. I was being battered from inside and out. Néné and Baba came to the door to ask what they could do.

"Go away!" I screeched. Oh God, look what was happening with me, blood and drool running down my chin, the baby choosing this time for karate practice, and this stranger's tools and fingers jammed inside my mouth. Even the dentist was sweating. "Now just another

154

second," he said. He tried with his fingers only. More ripping. More baby jabs. "Stop," I said. "I can't take any more." I went home, the tooth half in and half out, and it would stay that way until the baby came out.

My pain made me think that Baba was right in believing fate played a role in our affairs. It is the Muslim belief that we are all walking on precharted paths. Only some being or some thing with a larger purpose could have orchestrated pain streaming from all parts of me. What purpose? To teach a lesson on suffering so I would cherish my blessings? That sounded right. Or perhaps the soul can only really speak through nerve endings. My pain was deeply sown, beyond extraction. At best, it could be pulled only partway, left half entrenched, half hanging on.

Or was it simpler? Maybe I was like the big monkey in Amadou's story, found out for every wrong thought or misdeed I had ever committed, sinking inevitably to the bottom of the river.

What a beautiful thing if there were a book of fate sitting in the lap of God. And God allowed just a peek. And maybe, even, we could scan it like a menu. "That look's good. That? I'll pass on that one." What if we could pick and choose the pieces of fate we liked and purge the others? That would be the best.

The last part of the pregnancy went better, even with the obstinate tooth. Néné lavished helpings of her special tonic on me. It was reserved for the eighth and ninth months because it promised to relax the birthing muscles. Taken any earlier, it might cause a miscarriage. She mixed small fonio grains with sira ngongo leaves, which grow like grass right out of the ground, creating a smooth porridge. I ate two bowls a day for two months until late in June 1978, when, lying in Néné's bed, sweet Néné beside me, Baba praying in the yard, I gave birth to my daughter Laouratou. We called her Laoura.

CHAPTER ELEVEN

THE OTHER KADIATOU

*N*ow came the good life.

At the end of the year I returned to the apartment on Benson Street in Monrovia. Not long after, Saikou went to do business in Lomé, the capital of Togo, to the east, and in Brussels, too, leaving me alone with a small boy and an infant, but also with a maid, a new sky blue Peugeot 504, and total access to his bank account.

My reaction was swift. I raided the stores on Broad Street, and the ones on Randall Street and Benson Street. I bought the best in everything, dresses and pants suits, shoes, pocketbooks, and sunglasses. I was a regular at the hair salon. I had manicures and pedicures, and men gave me oohs and aahs as I went from shop to shop.

I met a woman from Dalaba in Guinea, also named Kadiatou Diallo, who pulled me to the cafes and the movie theaters: She even brought me to Sassa Disco, a dance club at the Organization of African Unity Village, where waiters served us sparkling water. This Kadiatou was married and had a daughter, coming on four years, like Amadou, and I marveled over the freedom she had to roam the city with me. I had a new girlfriend, and though I missed the times with my Labé friends and the shared knowingness we took for granted, this relationship with the new Kadiatou gave me something else—the chance to create a history that was mine.

She didn't know Baba or Néné. She wasn't a first or second cousin who could recite the family history. The tale of Diadia and what had happened to her, and how Baba sent away his next two daughters, one a thirteen-year-old, did not color her impression of me. When I told her, the details instantly lost their weightiness. The story parted from me easily, as if knowing the new Kadiatou had broken my allegiance to the sorrow that went with it.

When I was at school, or at the dance club, I left the children with Esther, who was officially a maid, but she was also a baby-sitter, a cook, and a seamstress. She was a seventeen-year-old Liberian.

I would say to my friend, the other Kadiatou, "I am spending more of Mr. Diallo's money."

Amadou and Kadiatou's daughter, Benette, became close companions, too. Benette was shy and had short hair, like a boy. We all had lunches and dinners together and sat around watching *Sesame Street*, the American version; an African cartoon called *Alp*, about a man with the head of a zebra. We watched *Kojak* and *Columbo*, too. We went to the Rivoli movie house, all of us, including Esther and Laoura, to watch films from India and the United States. We saw Bruce Lee carving up people and furniture with his bare hands, but just once. When we got home from that one, Amadou converted one of my hair ties to a belt around his waist and began practicing Bruce Lee chops on Laoura. "No more karate movies for you," I said.

Sundays meant ice cream at Prince's Way. We ate our treats in the car, Esther and I in the front, Amadou and Laoura in the backseat. Amadou would race through the vanilla and chocolate swirl, his favorite, and when he asked for another, I always said yes. From there we went to Sugar Beach and parked alongside the Fords and Chevrolets that most people preferred. Esther was a good swimmer, but I could not swim at all. Northern Guinea provided few settings to learn. Amadou did not take to swimming either. He had already developed a fear of water. Esther dived headlong into the ocean, while I held Laoura, and kept company with Amadou in shallow waters on the other side of the dunes. One part of me wanted him out with Esther, barreling fearlessly into the waves, but I was content to stand with him, surveying the sea and the sky and the line where they met.

At those moments, I saw Amadou growing in front of my eyes. With the expanse of the sea before us, I sensed his strength building and his vision magnifying. There was a point way out on the horizon that held him. The sound of other children's laughing did not disrupt him. His eyes remained steady. My Big Man watching over his mother and sister.

Just twenty years old, I had already learned that a mother owns instant foresight into what will remain permanent in her memory. I knew, as we stood there, no words passing, Amadou and I, and little Laoura, that I would always be able to see us together at Sugar Beach. That was my consolation for also grasping the unshakable truth that these days would never come again.

For his first day of kindergarten, September 1980, Amadou wore short pants with a shiny belt, a white shirt, and a red bow tie. He carried a red lunch box and walked into the school on Broad Street holding hands with Benette, his best friend and now his classmate. This school was not like the ones I knew from Guinea. It cost a lot, seven hundred dollars a semester. The building was a clean brown brick, and every morning someone was either washing the windows or polishing the stair railings. The hallways were filled with sunlight and trophy cases, and each morning the teachers came out to the front steps and said, "Come in, children. Come in."

The kindergarten was in the center of the city, at the bottom of a steep part of Broad Street. At the top of the road, Cadillacs and even Mercedes flowed in and out of the driveway to the Ducor, the most fashionable hotel in the city. The hotel had a swimming pool, a restaurant, and a big garden. Just bringing Amadou to school felt glamorous.

The children were Liberians, a few Europeans and Americans, and everyone spoke English. During his first week at school, Amadou's class celebrated his fifth birthday with him. He wore a cotton crown the teacher had made, and he led the other children in a parade around the room, singing a song about birds, the entire flock of kindergartners leaving a trailing of cupcake crumbs.

Amadou had a featured role, singing the main song in the class presentation of "Dressing Up."

> *I clean my shoes*
> *I fold my shirt*
> *I wash my face*
> *I wash my back*
> *I dress myself*

With Saikou's permission, even I went to school, though not a school where I could work toward a high school degree. It was a place to learn typing and basic accounting skills. But it was a start, the first time I had been a student in a classroom in more than seven years, and for Saikou a leap in trust to risk "people seeing me." I had developed a pretty girl's flair for attracting attention, and the stares and turned heads were enough for me. I moved around the city, tasting its pleasures, with the other Kadiatou. Saikou sent in his profits from abroad and I continued to spend, on silk scarves, earrings, jeweled watches, perfumes, the best skin creams and bath oils. I spared none of Saikou's money on my coming out. The Peugeot's license plate read "A41," and as I became a familiar face, people shouted "Ooh, there goes A41" when I zipped by. I bought more clothes, danced more, and Esther and I used the pool at the Ducor Hotel. I even learned to swim a little.

Everything was beautiful, except for one gnawing thought. What would Saikou say when he discovered I had swum through nearly all his Monrovia bank account? He had been away nine months, and that's a lot of time for spending money. Also, the unrest of West Africa had come to Liberia. Rice farmers, merchants, and others unhappy with the government's treatment had spilled into Monrovia in protest. They wanted their fair share. While I was enjoying a taste of freedom and easy living, thousands of Liberians were struggling for theirs.

Saikou called from Togo to say he missed me. He wanted me to come see him and look for a place for the entire family to live, if conditions in Liberia turned worse and in case a new regime made it hard on businessmen. I left the children with Esther and with Koto, who had been visiting me, and I flew to Lomé. It didn't occur to me to leave my best new clothes at home. I appeared at Saikou's hotel looking expensive from top to toe, my smooth dress, my long, braided hair, and my polished nails. Saikou could not take his eyes from me.

"I hope you didn't spend all my money," he said, not angrily. His eyes were wide, and he seemed to like looking at the woman his wife had become.

"Why?" I asked.

"Because your hair looks good and you look good."

"No. I spend some of it, but not all."

"That's all right," he said.

Adoration from Saikou was an event. He took me to lavish dinners. We sat at cafes sipping espresso. He took me to one of the finest dress shops in Lomé. He picked out a two-piece Moroccan-style dress, blue, embroidered on the sides with gold threads, and said, "Try it on." Upon seeing me in the store mirror, he lifted me in the air and right there, in public, he kissed me. Romance had come to Saikou and Kadi. He was excited to be with me, and eager to know how much money was amassed in the Monrovia account. I kept telling him there was time to talk about things like that, until time ran out.

"Now tell me," he said. "How much money is in the bank?"

I looked at my feet. "Nothing," I said.

"What was that?"

"Nothing?"

He began shaking, then screaming. Sweat instantly poured down his cheeks, or was it tears?

"Oh my God! You want to tell me that you spent over thirty thousand dollars? You spent the money? You spent the money?"

161

Saikou's panic lurched me into reality. I had done an awful thing, frittering away the savings. Perhaps I could plead guilty on account of having too much freedom. I would tell the judge that I simply didn't know what I was doing. Now I started shaking.

"I am sorry," I murmured. "I buy everything I like. I was feeling lonely and I wanted to enjoy myself."

The romance was over. He didn't talk to me for two days. I ate by myself and even talked to myself. "This time," I told me, "you deserve the punishment." On the third day, he talked.

"Anyway, you had your chance, because this money was for you. I wanted to prepare you for how to use money and to do your own business. I wanted to give you a chance. This was to initiate you into business. I wanted for you to travel from Africa to Europe, buy things, and come back and sell it. Perfumes, jewelry, anything you like, but you blew your chance."

He sent me back to Guinea, this time to a big house he had built in Labé, while he figured out the next move. This is the Guinea way, always circling back home. By that point, Saikou owned at least five houses in three countries. In Monrovia, protesters had begun to march in the streets. Some of the rallies turned violent. Stores were looted and buildings set on fire. So Saikou sent all our belongings with me, including all the furniture, the Peugeot he had bought for me, and a Mercedes he had bought for himself.

We stayed in Guinea for nearly a year while Saikou began his conquering of the globe. He fetched Aissata, his first wife, from Greenville. Enticed by a rising market for gold, he went to Geneva, Brussels, and Amsterdam to buy and sell. He opened a Swiss bank account. Amadou and Laoura asked for their father, and I told them he is a dad who travels. Then Amadou told other children "My father is a traveler," as if never being home was an occupation unto itself.

When Saikou finally came to Labé, in the spring of 1981, he had an announcement for me. He wanted a third wife. I told him, "If you want this, you will have to speak to my father, the one who gave me to you in the first place."

They met in the big room. Baba and Saikou sat in the two big chairs. Néné and I were across from them on the couch.

"I feel that I need another wife," Saikou said. "I am in many places, and I need someone to help take care of things. Nothing will change for Kadiatou. I will care for her the same as always."

Néné fidgeted. She rose slightly, sat down, bent her fingers back and ran her fingernails noisily on the couch. Saikou was her cousin and son-in-law. "I have found a girl in Conakry," he said. Néné had heard too much.

"Look. Now you look. You took our daughter fresh from school, thirteen years of age, and you said you needed a second wife because your first wife was not educated. Now you want to dump her here with two children and to choose another wife. Tell me why do you want to leave my daughter?"

"No, I'm going to take care of her like before, whatever money . . ."

"Hey! About the money? I heard the story of the money. She spent your money and that's what you deserve. If you want to get back your money, we will sell one of our houses and give the money to you."

"No, no. That is not the case," said Saikou. "I just want her to know discipline. It's not about the money."

Baba said nothing, but he glowered. His eyes inspected Saikou in a half-lidded way, and that made him all the more menacing. Either he was going to fall asleep or he was going to pounce at Saikou's throat. He held his palms out to Néné, her invitation to say what she pleased.

"It is not enough to take our daughter because of your needs," she said. "She was a girl when you married her. She is still a girl, and you leave her, all for money. You are searching for money. So it is good she spends your money. Maybe you are the one who needs teaching to. So what happened to your money is good."

Saikou turned to my father, who remained rigid in his silence. Baba nodded with the look of a man who had finally heard something that made sense. Not that he needed it, but Saikou left Néné and Baba without their further blessing.

Soon, gossip in the villages about the bad wife who had lost all of Saikou's money found its way to Labé. No, no, I thought. That's not exactly the way it was. I was left alone for nine months with two children in a strange place, after being stranded in another strange place. I would have traded in the hats and boots for anything like a normal life.

"Listen to me," I said to Saikou. "That money became like a poison in my blood. If I had a way to pay you back, I'd pay you. I hurt you, but nothing worse than what you have done, spoiling my name." It was morning. I was wearing a floor-length satin nightdress, straight from a Broad Street shop, which probably did not help my argument.

"It is deserved," he said. "You have spoiled my reputation, to have a wife who disrespects her husband this way."

"It is always about your reputation. So long as you are the big businessman, no matter what else is happening, you are happy. You leave me behind with the children like a bird in a cage and you expect everything to be kept neat and tidy. I want to get out of your marriage."

I gave a great speech. Saikou took me by both shoulders and threw me to the floor. My satin nightdress had risen nearly to my hips. Saikou loomed over me, and I thought he was about to deliver a wallop. Our maid happened to come by the door at that moment.

"Look at me lying here with my legs showing like this for people to see."

Saikou dropped to his knees and with both hands teased the nightdress back over my legs. He stayed on the floor for a while. He was a thirty-eight-year-old man. I was almost twenty-two. But a fight like this first thing in the morning, leaving you defeated on the floor, can make you feel much older. One more door had closed on me, I thought.

"No, no, no. I love you. I want to be with you. I change my mind," he said.

My debating skills had saved yet another day. Saikou decided not to take a third wife, and I got to pack everyone up again. Next stop: Togo.

The rarest of sights was Amadou and Saikou together. Since our time in the bushlands of Liberia, when Amadou was a baby, Saikou had seen his son only for interludes of a few weeks or two months at the most, sandwiched between much longer stretches away. It was hard to recall when Saikou had last held Amadou, and Laoura knew her father even less. For a while, in Togo, Saikou stayed in place. Laoura had the chance to sit on his lap, which she liked to do during dinner, and to ride high on his shoulders. He called her his little girl. For six-year-old Amadou, those kinds of opportunities with his father had passed him by. He had crossed into the age of more important considerations, and his father spoke to him about the value of Koranic studies and doing his homework with precision.

When Amadou was younger, I thought I saw traces of Saikou in his face and mannerisms, but now that they were together, their differences appeared sharper. Saikou's body had a hulking quality that I could not imagine on Amadou, even as he grew. Saikou, in silence, bore an air of entitlement, while Amadou was unassuming, trusting that things would come his way, content if they did not.

The similarities they might have shared had dissipated during Saikou's furloughs. Their conversations usually possessed the hit-and-miss rhythm of chatter between distant relatives.

"Are you enjoying school?"

"Where do you stay when you travel?"

"Do you take care of your mother?"

"What is Europe like?"

"Most important, study the Koran, be a good Muslim and take care of your family."

When we first arrived there in the summer of 1981, Togo gave us the routine of family life. Saikou went to his office in the morning, returning well in time for evening prayer and dinner. My brother Bobo, studying marketing at the University of Togo in Lomé, had come to live with us. We also had Saikou's two other children, Alfa, who was now thirteen, and Diaraye, who was nine. We lived in a big two-story brown brick house encircled by a concrete wall and an iron gate. Where the coast of Liberia was lush green, here we had as much sand around the house as grass. We always had at least three cars in the driveway, and we often ate breakfast on a bricked terrace. We had a staff, including a cook, a housekeeper, someone to help with the babies, and a gardener. We paid the normal rate to each, thirty dollars a month, and could have afforded many more helpers. Amadou went to first grade at École des Soeurs, the single French school and again the most expensive school around. On the map, Togo is a sliver, tucked between Ghana and Benin, as though cushioned from the rest of the Africa. Maybe that was just my impression, protected in the big house. But here, too, trouble simmered, and Saikou, worried about people who might envy his riches, also employed a security man full-time at the gate.

Amadou was a child of privilege, but his behavior suggested otherwise. The other children asked for new toys and bicycles, but not Amadou. When it was pointed out to him that his school uniform had torn at the back pocket, he said he had no use for a new uniform. Any license he had as the son of a rich man, he happily relinquished. When he returned in the afternoon from school, his first stop was the kitchen to talk to the cook, and he liked following the housekeeper around on her chores. He asked them about their families or he just watched them at work. He was small and fast in the soccer games, which we called football, and easily whisked by defenders. He was skilled enough to join up with the older children in the neighborhood, but he preferred to play with the smaller children. Their games had a more leisurely, free-form pace. They played, they sat, they played, they talked. This brand of football was suited not to Amadou's skills but to his nature. He liked to be coach to the smaller children.

"Something's not right," Saikou said to me. "He is playing with babies when he is getting to be a big boy. He doesn't think of himself that way."

"I don't think that's it," I said. "Amadou. He has an unusual quality that makes him special, a certain look." This was the conversation I had had with Néné when Amadou was only two, and I was finally having it with Saikou. But where Néné detected wisdom in Amadou, Saikou saw a misfit. It also bothered Saikou that Amadou spent time with the workers.

"Why does a boy want to stand in a hot kitchen, talking to the servants, when the others are running around? This is not natural."

Saikou was alarmed to see Amadou using his left hand at the dinner table and tried to convert him. "If you use your right hand, it will be easier. Just try it." Over a week of meals, Amadou valiantly ate with the right hand, spilling rice and soup on his clothes and the floor until Saikou threw up his hands. "There's nothing I can do about it at this point. I've done the best I could," he said.

Amadou did not show it the same way, but Saikou puzzled him, too. What Saikou did not notice was Amadou's stare following him after he had made one of his proclamations about the way things should be. Nor did Saikou realize that Amadou took the full measure of his father through me.

Amadou was seven when he slipped behind us, unnoticed, right in the middle of a morning argument. When Amadou returned from school in the afternoon, he waited until Saikou had gone upstairs.

"Mama, I want to ask you what happened this morning," he said. He talked slowly. "Why was my father angry?"

"Amadou, don't worry. It was just a small argument." I looked at him and thought he might break.

"I was so sad at school today. Do you think my father is still angry with you?"

"No. Please, it is nothing," I said.

He was at once nowhere and everywhere. Amadou could fall in line behind Bobo or his half brother, Alfa, or me, and we would not hear his footsteps. One night, we were watching a movie on television when a violent scene suddenly flashed on the screen. I was thankful that Amadou was not in the room. The next day he said to me, "The movie last night was not good. All those people hurting and killing each other." I would turn from a conversation, perhaps during a telephone call, and there would be Amadou, perched on a windowsill, just watching, a perfect still life.

In Togo, I supervised the staff, kept the children safe, and entertained surprise dinner guests that Saikou brought home. There were benefits for me. I had my space. I was not confronted daily with a surly, hex-fearing brother-in-law or the reflection of myself in a disconsolate first wife. My sister Fifi came to stay with me, Diadia visited, and with Bobo there, I felt close to home. And for once, there was not the constant talk of where we would shove off to next.

The life I led in Monrovia with the other Kadiatou seemed long ago. I didn't wear the boots from Togo anymore, and I gave the hats away. I stopped wearing pants. My haze had been replaced by full alertness. I was smarter, having experienced about six near divorces, the specter of a wife number three, more than a few banishments, who knows how many truck rides across the perilous West African borders, and not to discount it, the thrill of scooting down the main boulevard in my Peugeot 504 with the A41 plates. The new stability probably didn't alter anything that was about to happen, but fair to say, I was more awake when it happened.

I had another baby, Ibrahim, named for Saikou's father, born in June 1982.

The fourth one, Abdoul, named for Saikou's uncle, arrived in November 1983.

They were beautiful, different from Amadou, bigger, boisterous, right from the start noisy and fearless, sensing the freedom that Amadou, as the oldest, did not enjoy. The house clamored with children.

Saikou, though, was always one step ahead of us. This time, his search for more treasures lured him to Singapore.

At this point, still in the throes of consciousness, I might have stopped Saikou in his tracks. *You're not going anywhere this time.* I had thoughts. His own security guard could block him at the gate with a rifle. I would notify the embassy that the big businessman with all the cars was escaping from the country. I could board his flight before take-off and explain the whole story to the pilot. *You see, he left me in Seino County, Monrovia, and Labé many times over.* The pilot would surely announce, "Mr. Saikou Diallo, seat 5C, please report to the pilot's cabin to be escorted from the plane." Or I could wave to him as he left and show up in Singapore with Amadou, Laoura, Ibrahim, Abdoul, and his other children, Alfa and Diaraye. Somehow, at twenty-four, I had become the mother of six, or, more precisely, the *single* mother of six. That at least demanded another scene, another uproar.

Protest was not in me this time. I organized his clothes neatly in his bags. I packed four boubous, two business suits, and at least six safari ensembles. Amadou and I waited with him at the airport. We drank sodas, made small conversation, and soon Saikou was gone. Amadou and I drove back to the house. Amadou was now eight. "I think my father will be away a long time," he said.

"Mama! I can't see anything. It's dark! Mama! I don't like the dark!"

A nightmare came to Amadou. He yelled for me to come fast. I found him sitting up, crying as I had never seen before. Tremors ran through his neck and into his mouth. "Mama, mom, mom."

"I'm here, Amadou."

"Mama, don't leave. Stay here."

"It's all right. Lie down. You just had a bad dream. I will stay here and you will be fine." I massaged the space between his eyes until the furrows were gone and his breathing calmed. "Now, now. You have nothing to be afraid of."

He called out the next night, not as loud. I hurried to his bed and found him asleep, garbled sounds and long sighs coming from him. "Amadou, your mom is here. It's okay." His eyes popped opened and he looked at me without blinking, taking me wholly into his dream and then finally turning and finding his peaceful sleep.

The dreams kept coming. He asked me to leave a light on for him during the night. Sometimes he remembered the dreams. He dreamt about water climbing up his body, reaching all the way to his chest. I spent my nights dashing between his room and mine, and in the day, I stayed alert for clues to what had punctured his tranquillity. He was in third grade and enthusiastic about the books he brought home. Some told stories of heroic deeds by African explorers. Others detailed the growing-up years of Thomas Edison and the Wright brothers. Amadou liked history and struggled with math. His teacher said that students were required to take home one book a week, but Amadou usually brought home five or six.

In the evening Amadou liked entertaining the family with impressions of Michael Jackson. We all clapped and laughed as he squeezed himself into a ball and spun on his back. Then he would go off to bed, and before long, the nightmares came again.

Sometimes Laoura found ways to tease him. "You don't care about toys, you never want anything," she said. He called his sister Latou.

"Latou, you are too young to understand."

Amadou had developed a fascination with his half brother, Alfa, who was six years older. Alfa was uninterested in the usual talk among children, and yet he had many friends and held a leader's status. The boys his age followed him on their bicycles and allowed him to set the tone. If he wanted to stretch out on the sand, they did. If he felt like playing ball, they played ball. He might ignore them, but they still followed his cue. Amadou became one of his followers.

I saw Alfa and Amadou returning to the house one afternoon, Amadou sheltered in Alfa's arms. Alfa held a cloth to Amadou's mouth, and Amadou was coughing. I saw blood on the cloth and blood coming from inside Amadou's mouth. Amadou held a hand under his chin to catch the runoff of droplets. "Don't cry, please don't cry," Alfa said. I ran to Amadou.

"What happened?"

He pointed to Alfa. "It's my brother that punched me."

"Why would you do such a thing?" I said to Alfa.

"I don't like to play with him, but he likes to follow me. He's a child. I tell him to go away, but he doesn't. I have my friends here, and over here I have my idiot brother. I told him again and again to go away, and he looked at me. There was nothing I could do. He wanted to stay even if I hit him."

That night, Amadou suffered no nightmares, but I couldn't sleep at all. I had devised strategies for living with my isolation. If nothing else I could stand up and scream before I burst, but aloneness was something else for a soul like Amadou's, misunderstood and defenseless.

I had now been married ten years. I had wept in pain, anger, confusion, loathing, and self-pity. I cried when Amadou ran fever with the chicken pox, fearful I was not up to caring for him. Until now, though, I had never wept in fear *for* my child. "Idiot brother." "Something's not right," Saikou had said. If only Saikou knew. His son had the unusual ability to make himself as small as the space he occupied. But this did not make Amadou weak. It was your folly if you read him by how little he spoke. The key to understanding Amadou was secreted not in what he said but in what he saw.

He began to stutter then. His mouth opened but the words waited in limbo, sometimes for many seconds before they came out. He stuttered at school and at home. There were bad weeks when the stuttering afflicted his every remark and other periods when the hesitations dropped off, only to return. I tried to reason that the stuttering was simply another sign of a deliberate nature, but I did not convince myself.

The "something not right" wasn't inside of Amadou but all around him. And it wasn't just other children, who could be forgiven, or Saikou, who didn't know better. It was me. I should protect him better, explain to others his shy manner, his prescient mind, the slowness of his responses from where he gained his power. I should never have permitted him to take care of me.

The first time he was hours old. We lay on our sides facing each other. He told me not to worry about Néné and to rest up after a hard day. When I failed to give him the milk he needed, rather than protest he went to sleep, choosing not to upset me. He watched over me at Sugar Beach. He slipped like a phantom in and out of rooms, undetected, at his post. I was convinced he could turn himself into a chair or a flowerpot if that's what was necessary to shield me from harm.

From the very beginning, he knew I was a child. Did he know this about himself?

In March 1984, Sékou Touré died. Baba grieved. He said that Sékou Touré was a great man who did wrong things. "But we should not overlook his greatness."

The news report we heard in Togo said that the president had fallen ill during a trip to Saudi Arabia. He was transported hurriedly to a hospital in Cleveland, a city in Ohio, in the United States. Emergency surgery was performed, but he died from a heart attack while still recovering. He was sixty-two. The report also said that Sékou Touré left behind fifty sons and daughters.

So that's what the speeches, parades, hangings, torturing, and declarations of pride had come to. *"We have a first and indispensable need of our dignity."*

Independent from the East. Independent from the West. His dying impulse was not for an operation right there, where he was. He didn't ask to come home to Guinea for treatment or to die proudly in his homeland. I pictured him in his hospital bed in Saudi Arabia, not one of his children at his side, saying, "Get me to America as fast as you can."

After four months Saikou returned, having called home not a single time while he was away. Amadou was nearly nine, Laoura was six, and Ibrahim almost two. Abdoul was six months.

Saikou's riches had grown many times over in just the last five years, mainly because of his success in the gold market. He brought the gold from Ghana and Mali. He sold it in Brussels and Antwerp in Belgium. And he sold the gold on the Geneva stock exchange when the market was high. He was conquering the world one continent at a time. The new apple of his eye was East Asia, where he said people were mad for gemstones. A business partner had told him that the Guéckédou region on Guinea's border with Liberia held rich deposits of rubies. With Sékou Touré gone and the new president, Lansana Conté, an army colonel promising to embrace a free-market system, Saikou believed untold wealth lay in waiting back in Guinea's lush terrain.

Presto! Saikou opened a mine there. He bought bulldozers, excavators, jackhammers, and shovels by the score. He hired dozens of workers from the town of Guéckédou, paid for their food, and bought them motorbikes so they could travel to the site, thirty kilometers away. Saikou would leave again, a week or two at a time, and come back with sacks of rubies and other stones and minerals that turned up in the soil and rock. He would spill them out to show me what his industry had yielded.

Here then was the sparkling result of Saikou's life pursuit—precious minerals. I rolled them over in my palm and let them slip between my fingers. I closed my hand tight over a cool, gold nugget, and I sensed the deep earth it had come from. Saikou said that the color and texture of the stones varied, depending on how far into the ground they were uncovered. I wondered if the people who would wear these gems on their fingers and around their necks would recognize, beyond their shimmer, the stories they told.

Just holding the stones produced in me an unusual lightness. I allowed myself a smile at Saikou. I felt the vanquisher and the thief in me. Let the dictators and warlords beat their chests. We could have the last laugh, one stone at a time.

"Look at these," Saikou said.

Laid out were a dozen of the most beautiful stones I had ever seen. They were green or blue depending on how the light touched them. I saw dashes of yellow and silver in them. That was the first time I had the thought, *How much are they worth?*

I looked more closely at jewels pictured in magazine advertisements. If I was struck in some way, if I said to myself "Wow, this is beautiful," I gave them high scores. When Saikou brought home another batch of rubies, I held them up to the light and didn't like what I saw. They were dull and opaque, not shiny like the rubies I had seen in the magazines.

"Be careful, this is not good quality," I said.

Saikou was in the middle of putting them in bags that he planned to sell to wholesalers and stonecutters in Asia.

"If you look closely, they don't have the shine that rubies ought to have. Are you sure these have value?" Saikou reacted as if a fly had landed on his neck.

"Please."

"I just want you to be sure that you won't have a problem when you go to sell it."

"Kadi, please don't think about such things."

"I know a little bit and I'm just not sure of this ruby business."

Now came time to swat the fly.

"If you know a little bit, go away and use your own head! I use my head!"

"Saikou, I think these rubies are junk."

"That's enough!" he shouted. "I don't want a woman telling me what to do. You take care of the house. Take care of the children. I'll take care of the business."

The rubies were shipped to Thailand and immersed in dark soil from Chanthaburi, said to give luster and brilliance to the mildest gemstone, and cooked in ultraheated ovens to six hundred degrees, a step that was guaranteed to distill away impurities. Out from the ovens they came, and they weren't rubies anymore. They were white and small, more peanut than gem. They were worthless. Saikou had two obvious reactions, the first for his miners.

"Dig deeper," he told them.

The second was for me. "I must go and stay in Thailand," he said.

Like everything else, my Koranic studies had long ago been interrupted. Still, my father would be pleased to know that I was faithful to the daily regimen. I prayed upon waking, then at noon, midday, late afternoon, and in the evening. My old teacher, Karamoko, would be proud, too, to see how well I recited the words. But I knew little of what the words meant, beyond what I had gleaned from Baba and Saikou, and now from Amadou, who at ten liked the stories of angels flying around and the prophets who taught kindness and generosity.

I had learned one part of the Koran the hard way. Men were to be the protectors and maintainers of women, and the women were to guard in their husband's absence his children and all that needed protection. Disobedience or disloyalty by the woman gave the man the right to punish her. Didn't men appreciate the women's dilemma?

Guarding the man's children means keeping them safe and providing them with a strong home, which requires stability, a unified marriage, and assuring them of a bond with both their mother and father. How then could I remain loyal to Saikou and accept the conditions he imposed on our lives? How could I guarantee my children a relationship with their father when their father was not there?

Protecting my children for Saikou meant protecting them *from* Saikou. That meant fighting Saikou, but fighting never got me anywhere.

That's how Amadou, Laoura, Ibrahim, Abdoul, and I wound up back in Guinea in 1985 and Saikou in Bangkok. *Labé-Greenville-Labé-Monrovia-Labé-Monrovia-Togo-Labé-Togo-Labé.* As far as I knew, the Koran offered no advice on how to keep the heads of my children from spinning like tops.

Amadou's stutter worsened. He turned ten in September, a fifth grader. He still preferred to play with younger children and talk with the cook, and he discovered the old Marvin Gaye and James Brown records, in deep storage at Néné's and Baba's. His best friend was a boy named Bangali. They played football together, and when they finished playing, they talked about it. Bangali stammered, too.

At school, Amadou met up with his own version of my old nemesis, Pumpatonn. A classmate, who saw weakness in the new boy in town, chided Amadou into carrying his books. Others joined in, and day by day the load of books became heavier until Amadou could no longer carry his school bag. He could only drag it.

"What is this?" I said.

"They need my help. They don't have their own bags."

Néné and I marched to the school and told the teacher what was happening and to make it stop. Amadou was not happy I intervened. "It wasn't a problem," he said. But his bag was lighter.

On this stay, Baba seemed older. He was mostly beyond his ranting days, and he had long accepted Diadia back into his graces. Like old times, I heard him call her his New Year's Day Miracle. He said he was proud of her because she had found a good husband and was studying to be a nurse. Hadiatou did well in school and had recently married, and he held a new special place for Fifi. She was eighteen and had grown into a tall, long-legged beauty. She did not have my big laugh or Hadiatou's strong opinions or Diadia's overt charisma. She had a shy smile and carried the quiet mystery I detected in long-ago photographs of Néné.

Baba didn't cry anymore about having given me away for marriage, but he wore his regret in other ways. He recalled my report cards. He said it was a shame my first-grade teacher did not reward me with the grades I deserved. "You were the smartest one in the whole class," he said. He had relished watching me sell my candy door to door. "All our friends said how special you were."

He questioned why Saikou needed to make money all the time and said he worried about me.

"You are a good mother," he said. "You are smart. I have always known this. These are different times. What was all right for your mother is not all right for you. Look at you, dressed like an old lady. You have to live up to date, wear skirts and pants, go out and do something with your life. You cannot stay in the house."

I was twenty-six, married half my life, and had spent nearly all my life figuring out where the men had drawn the line. Once I had been allowed nowhere near it. I had trespassed occasionally and often lived on the line like a tightrope walker. Baba was now granting me permission to come clear past into unseen territory, an invitation, coming thirteen years late, that might have enraged another woman.

"Thank you, Baba. I have been thinking of this," I replied.

That's how I, without my children, wound up in Bangkok in January 1986. One thing was for sure, following Saikou this way, I was always winding up someplace.

CHAPTER TWELVE

THE WOMAN NEVER RUNS

*T*he dazzling stone you hold in your hand may, under a microscope, show marks and odd abrasions, the cut of the stone not nearly as clean as you first thought. The brilliance of the stone matters, but be wary. The amateur's eye will be won over by the glitter of fakes and imitations. The true gem has more subtle qualities. In its clarity it finds a place, the teacher said, above the pretenders.

Saikou's ruby enterprise had failed. His miners tunneled deeper. The furnace workers turned up the temperature, but nothing resuscitated the stones. He called for me, just after the new year. "Come to Bangkok. You can help me with the business, and we can go to gem school together."

"You see? I was right about the rubies."

"Just come. I am giving you this chance."

Saikou and I, at our desks, side by side, comparing notes, having a common goal. It did not seem possible, but there we were, in our flowing boubous. The school was Asian Gemological Sciences, a modern building standing among a row of shopping centers on Silom Road. The school had a library dedicated to the analysis of stones, and a dozen classrooms, each with room for about twenty-five students. In the class were Asians, Brits, maybe two other Africans, and many Americans, most of them women.

The school's short history was posted on bulletin boards throughout the building. It had been opened a few years before by a man named Rama, who on his first attempt had failed in the gemstone trade only to become wildly prosperous later. He appeared at the first class, a pleasant white-haired Thai gentleman, and said, "The key to succeeding in the business is knowledge."

"Yes, this is right," Saikou said, finding fast kinship with Rama.

After four weeks, Saikou lost his inspiration. "I have a business to run," he said to me. "You will learn the lessons here, and then you can tell me."

The teacher was French and married to a member of the Thai royal family. She wore a different ring for each meeting and I imagined her a princess with an unusual awareness of beauty.

Her lessons were not easy. Color, it turns out, is not the thing. The value of a stone is enhanced by its lack of color. A rating chart ranked the finest stones as D, E, F, G for colorless to H, I, J, K for near-colorless, down to L, M, N, O, P, and all the way to Z. I searched for the most translucent stone, but my eyes always played tricks. One was clear through and through, but not really, not when compared to the pale oval cut next to it or the lightly twinkling one, called a princess cut. Holding stones to the light, I tried to observe perfect clarity, or the thing I could not see.

I learned that while superior stones, such as diamonds, are valued for their hardness, lesser stones have their place. Topaz is white and round with the appearance of a diamond though not nearly as strong. When cut and polished and treated with a white heat, topaz reveals an inner self, a strange midnight blue. Understanding stones was like making a great discovery or learning a new language. In each stone was an idea.

After six months, I received a certificate, declaring me an official gemologist. I had the knowledge that Rama said was needed for success. For once, Saikou needed my help. I could go home to Guinea with my husband, create with him a business as true partners, and bring the family together. It was an ingenious scheme, a way to honor my husband, my children, and Islam all at once.

"I think it is time to go home for good," I said. We stood in the living room of the apartment Saikou had rented.

"Then you should go home," he said.

"I miss the children."

"I do not want you to cry about this. Go home."

"And you?"

"I have a business here. I will stay here. I will give you money for the house."

"This is not right," I said. "You are ruining the family. Our children are not here. I don't feel we should stay in Bangkok."

A week later, in July 1986, I flew off, feeling bad for me and my children, and for Saikou.

Saikou gave me money, but not enough to run the house. He said the business had drained his money, and that I should sell the furniture in the house in Labé if I needed more. I had plans, and I chose to unveil them first to Néné.

"I intend to start my own business," I said.

Néné, who had never worked outside the home, who could not read, cried at my announcement. "Good," she said. "Then you can get back the opportunity he took away."

I knew that people in Guinea did not have money for gems, so I decided it would be safer to trade in staples, like rice and sugar. Even if the venture were not a big success, it was one way to provide rice and sugar cheaply for my family. I went to Conakry and was introduced to a man named Amadou Asouma, a wholesale distributor. He agreed to sell me rice and sugar without requiring even a token down payment. Then I could resell the goods at the big market in the center of the city and pay him back when I had the money.

Amadou Asouma was a man about Baba's age. He walked and talked slowly, each word a measured thought, and he seemed out of step amid the frenzy of the marketplace. Soon after our first meeting, he thanked me for doing him a favor. He said his arrangement with me helped him meet his import quotas. I grinned.

"All right, then, I will tell you the real reason I am doing this for you," he said. He raised a wise finger and spoke so softly, I found it necessary to bend in close to his mouth.

"You are a woman," he said. His voice was a drawn-out whisper. I waited for more. "In business dealings, I trust a woman far more than a man. A man, and I learned this myself many years ago, will make the same deal you have, make his money and run away without paying. But a woman will never do that. She has other thoughts. She knows she must stay."

He paused and swallowed deeply, as though to digest his own words and prepare his conclusion.

"A woman doesn't run because she is the centerpiece of the family."

By the end of the year, I was buying by the ton and reselling in bags of fifty kilos. I opened an account in the BICI-GUI bank in Conakry. The first deposit was for 250,000 Guinean francs, and the deposits grew to millions of Guinean francs. Baba said he was happy for me. He mentioned nothing about any obligation I had to rejoin my husband.

With bags of sugar and rice, I finally had attained control in my life.

Then, in May 1987, we heard that the government, for the good of the people, had condemned forty former officials from Sékou Touré's regime to death. Talk began of strikes by students, teachers, businessmen, and workers demanding a better standard of living in everything from schools to hospitals. There were rumblings, too, that the soldiers, whom Conté had led to take control of the country, were angry about low wages. In Labé, the schools were using old books and old desks. The roads were worse than ever, and the hospitals were short on medicines.

At the same time, Sierra Leone was in turmoil. The government had been overthrown and the capital, Freetown, had fallen under a bloody siege. Refugees poured across the border into Guinea. Hundreds of men, maybe thousands, maimed, missing eyes and tongues and parts of arms, legs, and fingers that had been severed by machetes, showed up begging in Conakry.

I became nervous for my children's safety. And I started feeling sharp pains deep in my belly. I had days when the pain kept me curled up in bed. Néné forced me to sip the warmed juices of roots and cloves, easing the suffering only slightly before I was waylaid again. I knew something was wrong.

With the beginning of 1988, I sent my children back to the big house on the sand in Togo, in the care of Bobo and Fifi, and I returned to Bangkok to have a tumor removed from my uterus.

I arrived at the apartment in Bangkok, worn and sick, just a day ahead of my surgery. I felt a fever rising. I fell on the bed, craving sleep but unable to close my eyes. I saw a pair of shoes sitting neatly in a corner of the bedroom. Women's shoes. I pushed myself off the bed for a closer look. They weren't my shoes.

I opened a drawer and the picture of a smiling Thai woman stared up at me. She looked very happy. She was standing next to Saikou.

"What is this?" I demanded, flying out of the bedroom.

"This is a woman I know," he said.

"Come on, man, who is she?"

"She is a friend of mine. Her name is Siriwan."

"Are those her shoes in there?"

"Yes. She has visited here."

The fever vanished like magic, the belly pain was gone, too, replaced by an urge to break every dish and every glass in the apartment, flip over the furniture and cut the stuffings out of the mattress and all the pillows.

"She has visited here?"

Saikou breathed heavily. I noticed he had gained weight. He no longer seemed tall.

"I wanted to tell you, but I knew the right way was in person, not on the phone. I didn't know how to tell you. The woman you have seen, Siriwan, I have married her.

"It would be better if you could meet her," he said.

Meet her! I was not Baba. I was not the one to grant a blessing.

"If this is your choice, you have made it," I said. "I am not going to accept you with another wife. And I never, ever want to meet her."

The next morning they removed the tumor. The operation took five hours. I woke in a dreary fog, cataloging my misery: I am twenty-eight. I can't have any more children. I am married for fifteen years. My husband has betrayed me. I am alone.

Saikou wasn't there. I called Bobo to tell him what had happened, leaving him with a request.

"Please be sure to convey the situation to Baba and Néné."

Four days later, I phoned Saikou from the hospital. The new wife answered.

I got up, put a dress over my hospital gown, limped past the nurses, down the steps, outside, and took a taxi to the apartment.

"No, no, no," I bellowed. "You cannot do this to me. I am sick, and you go and get another girl. Why don't you take care of me? Why don't you do what you promised my mother and father? They know now. They know about you and money. If you want to destroy your family, this is what you have done. I am sick and I miss my children, and they're waiting for me, and they're waiting for you. . . ."

My voice was dying out, shrinking to almost nothing. I heard a girl's voice, Mama at five, the voice too small to reach across the yard.

Be kind, Baba. Don't be angry. Let me lie here with you. I want to listen to the radio, too, Baba.

The Thai wife stayed hidden in the bathroom, and Saikou drove me back to the hospital.

I didn't leave him.

Diadia, Koto, Hadiatou, and Bobo told me I should. They said that Néné and Baba were angry. I told Amadou his father had a new wife. He was twelve years old. He said he was helping Bobo and Fifi keep an eye on the younger children. Then he said, "Does this mean my father will be mad at you for a long time?"

"I hope not," I said.

Like it or not, hinging ourselves to Saikou's next move had become a family habit. He was the director of the show and we were offstage, waiting for him to tell us our roles and where to stand. Adding all the visits, business trips, and sudden moves, Saikou had lived in the same house as Amadou for perhaps three years in all, and less with the other children.

Ibrahim told friends that his father was one of the most important men in the world, that he knew the leaders of foreign countries and flew on their private jets, that secret missions kept him from home, but once he completed them, he would return. Ibrahim told this to his friends because it is what he told himself. He said that his father worked in a skyscraper, in a vast office encompassed only by glass. From there, Ibrahim said, his father could see for miles.

Absent, Saikou controlled the children's dreams, and their dreams controlled me. If there were a way, heroic acts I had left undone, maybe in the end I could bring my family together.

I promised to help Saikou revive his business, to move it from rubies to a larger selection of gemstones, and when this job was done, I would make my own business. He got another apartment, and I stayed in the old one. I lived on the eighth floor of the Warner Building, a high-rise at the junction of Silom and Mahesak Streets. Every day I rode the elevator down to the sixth floor where Saikou had his office. We were in the center of Bangkok and the business attracted sellers and buyers who were flying in or flying out, as well as the local traders. My routine was simple. Take the elevator down in the morning, come upstairs for meals and the five prayers, go back down.

One day I opened the door to find Siriwan in the apartment.

"What are you doing here?" I screamed.

"Oh my God. I am just getting some of my things." She had a high voice. She was younger than I had thought, twenty-two perhaps. I scanned her quickly and knew she had no chance.

A large carving knife on the kitchen counter caught my eye. I grabbed the knife with one hand, and I pulled Siriwan to me with the other. "You better not move," I said. I pushed the blade of the knife against her throat. She was thin. I could have broken her in two. She was too thin for Saikou.

"Don't ever come here again or I will kill you."

I pulled her by the arm out the door and threw after her the shoes and scarves and other trinkets she had come for. I had already gathered them in a pile. She ran down the hall crying. I knew instantly she wouldn't leave him either.

My job was to appraise the gemstones that came into Saikou's office. I told him to stay away from the African rubies and sapphires, too, and deal more in topaz and garnets. When Saikou made one of his trips to Singapore, I met with clients. Many told me that I had an unusual gift for identifying the most valuable stones.

By midyear Saikou's business was thriving. He told me I was his good-luck charm. He moved back into the apartment with me. At the end of the year, he told me to go back to Africa. He was closing the business in Bangkok and moving to Singapore to pursue his deals.

"This is what you want. You can be with the children," he said. "I will do the right thing. I will send money with you." I had seen this before, the way of the African man. Wander the bushes and leave the woman in the hut with the children. Maintain her. This was written in the holy book.

"Saikou, I still have business to do here," I said.

"It is time for you to go back to Guinea," he said.

"No. I have ideas and I want to see if they can work."

"This is the choice you make, Kadiatou, but I must tell you. Now I think you have gone too far."

Soon Baba called to say a letter had arrived for him from Saikou. Baba called it a strange letter.

"He says he has tried to keep the marriage working, but you have not followed his wishes," Baba said. "He wants to send you back to Guinea and you are not listening. He says he can no longer be married to you because of this."

"Baba, you know what has happened," I said.

"He has betrayed me," said Baba. "He promised to give you an education and to care for you properly. To think, he is a cousin of the family, and he does this to my daughter who I blessed him with. Mama, you do not have to explain. It is Saikou who must explain. He says that if we, the entire family, and the relatives we share, come to him, he will reconsider. The question is, will I reconsider?"

A week later, Baba sent a return letter.

"Sixteen years ago, I gave you my daughter when she was a child. Now you have decided you don't need her. Even her mother, after forty years of marriage, she cannot be without me, and I have never left her alone like you have left my daughter. You want to send her away to be with another wife. This is unacceptable. After speaking to my daughter, I have made my judgment, and I am on her side for the first time. You have not met your responsibility, but now I expect you to meet your responsibility. If you divorce her, you must take care of her because she is the mother of your children."

We were married in the light air of the Fouta Djallon. The women ran in the fields, the white cloth of virginity a ghost in the twilight. The young women danced and the young men beat the tribal drums to wake the chiefs and village kings, long dead. The older men murmured their satisfaction and left for their beds long before their sons, who reveled until dawn.

The divorce was simpler.

Saikou said "I divorce you" three times, and it was done.

I, the wife, said nothing.

Nothing else was required.

Every other day in Bangkok seemed to bring a celebration, honoring long-ago rulers and ancient temples. Loy Krathong honors the water spirit and is the day to wash away sins. During the Songkran Festivals, which last for ten days, people place flowers and tiny sparklers in miniature boats and watch them sizzle across a pond. At night, people dance on the beaches without their shirts. Several times a month, a party sweeps over Bangkok.

Many nights I watched fireworks light up the city from the apartment terrace. I heard their thunder, and the showers of white, yellow, and red embers, like falling stars, threw out a pale, dying light on me. Half day, half night, half real, half lost, I could not be sure if I were vanishing or reappearing. I longed for my moon to come whistling to me as it did a long time ago.

I used to watch the moon with Néné Tinkin. Then in the mornings we bathed in the natural spring. I put my hands flat and open on the rocks and watched the water break over each finger into a row of tiny streams. My grandmother's bare, wet feet slapped noisily on the path back to the hut. Néné Tinkin milked the cow while I caressed it with a branch full of soft leaves. She walked us into the field to say good-bye. I watched her become smaller as we drove off. She waved her right arm and put her left arm on her head. She always did this, and told me once it was a signal to God, to please make sure we would all see each other again.

My greatest wish had always been my simplest: to stay with the people I loved. And everything I had ever done to fulfill that had brought me here, to a balcony in a city far away with a bird's-eye view of all these people who were happier than me. In the end, I did not stay with Saikou, and yet I was not the one to leave.

January 1, 1990, I walked down Silom Road, and was blessed maybe fifty times by women who sprinkled water at me, calling Sawadee Peemai, Happy New Year. Some blessed me with love, some with health and long life. I wasn't in the mood. I liked the one who told me there was money in my future.

Before January was over, I rented an office, this one on the fourth floor of my building, and the phone rang with customers happy to hear I had reemerged. I became a broker through the contacts I had made over the last year and with the help of Bobo in Africa. We connected a mining company from Nigeria with a buyer in Bangkok, and on my first transaction, I arranged the sale of twenty-seven thousand dollars in topaz. I received five percent from the seller, five percent from the buyer. The next exchange was for fifteen thousand, then twenty-four, then thirty-two. I had capital now. I hired an assistant, a Thai woman, and decided to buy my own goods and market them. I called the new company Exotic Gem. Once a week we went to the main airport to pick up cargo loads of stones. Shipments came from the Ivory Coast and the Congo. The payments often landed on my lap in cash. One man walked in with a paper bag and pulled from it a cheese sandwich and twenty thousand American dollars.

Many days, I celebrated the deals with hugs and smiles with my customers. I rode the elevator up four floors, counted the money at the kitchen table, and wept. Who would know if bandits barged in and overpowered me at that moment? Would anyone know what had happened to Mama?

I called Bobo and said, "Please bring me my children."

CHAPTER THIRTEEN

I Love You, Unsaid

Laoura liked the mirror. She dressed up, braided her hair, and turned to see herself at twenty different angles. Her brothers were always telling her to get out of the bathroom, that she was pretty enough, and if she wasn't, looking at herself wasn't going to help. Laoura could be difficult. If everyone wanted to eat in, she wanted to eat out. If Abdoul played MC Hammer, she wanted the Beatles. Amadou wanted the channel on football. She wanted to watch "Santa Barbara." She kept her room messy. I yelled at her and she yelled back. Later we would hug and she would tell me that she loved me and that she wished her father and I had a regular marriage. She had a friend, Hinatea, whose father traveled often, too, and never failed to bring her a box of chocolates when he returned. "I'd like it to be like that," Laoura said.

I was with my children again, and finding they had changed. The boys were filled with shenanigans. Ibrahim and Abdoul discovered a crawl space above the apartment reachable with a leap onto an arm of the couch and the opening of an air vent. It was a secret channel that meandered the width of the entire building and brought them over all the apartments below. They listened in on Mr. Santora shaving, Mr. Graham singing along with Louis Armstrong, and otherwise tried to stay clear of the giant reef of electric and telephone wires that stretched the whole way. No harm was done until Ibrahim crashed through the ceiling just over the dining table of Mr. and Mrs. Robertson and their three children, who at that very moment were enjoying a big lunch. If it wasn't for Abdoul reaching out and catching him by the leg, Ibrahim would have made a terrific splash. Ibrahim liked to hang off the back of the air conditioner on the terrace, which inspired Abdoul to do it also, only he ended up pulling the whole thing out. They were clever. Before they told me what had happened, they surprised me with a home-cooked dinner.

Amadou at fifteen wasn't beyond tricks. He joined his brothers when they removed all the number stickers from the elevator buttons and then rode up and down to witness the confused reactions of people trying to find the right button. Amadou got caught swiping a newspaper from a neighbor's door and he sometimes bounced a basketball enough times to anger yet another neighbor or he blasted his MC Hammer CDs until the walls shook. And we laughed to see him dance, taking off his shirt and twirling it over his head.

Some children are born an old soul, and that part of Amadou was never far away. He lectured Laoura for giving me a hard time. "This is your mother, you must always give her respect." One time I slapped Laoura across the face, and Amadou said, "You cannot do that to my sister." For his sixteenth birthday in September 1991, he asked me not to give him any presents. His brothers liked to go to Lumpini Park, where they played roller hockey, using bottle caps as pucks, and Takro, which was something like badminton. Sometimes Amadou went with them. Other times he stayed at home and read his books. I would tell him to go out and play, and he would say, "Why? I am happy here." And then, just like that, he could surprise me.

We went to the beach at Hua Hin, about three hours south of Bangkok, on the South China Sea. Laoura, Ibrahim, and Abdoul played in clear green waters, leaving Amadou and me on the sand. I must have fallen asleep, because suddenly I looked up and there was Amadou high atop a magnificent, bronze-colored horse, sauntering along the shore.

"Amadou," I said. And he threw back his head with the best laugh I had ever heard from him.

This was not a dream. He had rented the horse. He rode past, teasing the horse into the shallow waters that he always avoided, and then went farther, breaking the horse into a gallop, leaving behind a spray of water and sand until I could barely make him out. He rode back and said to me, "I have always wanted to do that."

He had grown into a young man without losing the wisdom and humility I had seen in him in the first hours of his life. In him, I saw the composure and kindness I could never fully claim for myself, and something new, an ambition I had not seen or had not yet evolved when I left him as a boy to come to Thailand. It was not an ambition to win races or invent cures, but more a small shifting, a coming to terms with the idea that a place had been held for him in the universe. He no longer seemed as separate from his environment, and for this I was glad.

Amadou liked all things American. He began wearing Tommy Hilfiger shirts and Nike sneakers, and rooting for the Chicago Bulls. He said that Bruce Springsteen represented the dreams of ordinary people. Amadou would play "Born in the U.S.A." over and over.

I sent them all to École Française de Bangkok, a French school attended by students of foreign diplomats from Europe, Africa, and the United States. Tuition was eight thousand dollars a year, but because I had four children enrolled, the school granted me a discount by half. Amadou liked history, American history. The post–World War I period led to the Depression, he told us. People lost their savings overnight, but thank goodness for President Roosevelt. He put people to work. The attack on Pearl Harbor fascinated Amadou. "How could the United States be taken by surprise?" he said. He knew about D day and all the major events of World War II and the names of all the presidents, from Washington to Bush.

I became friends with a Guinean woman, Fatoumata Sow. She owned an African restaurant in Bangkok. She had a son, Abdoulaye, two years younger than Amadou. They both liked basketball and football, and like other friends Amadou had made over the years, Abdoulaye stuttered, too. I heard them in Amadou's room one day with Ibrahim and Abdoul discussing the American civil rights movement, and I was surprised to hear a fever in Amadou's voice.

"The changes happened only because of the action of black people," he said. "They marched and protested even while risking their lives. But they had to protest the right way or else they would defeat their purpose." He paused.

"Just think what happens to people who protest in Africa," he said.

Laoura sometimes had trouble understanding Amadou. She would overhear discussions like these and throw up her arms. One time she told Amadou that an animal in the bushes has more intelligence than he.

"How can that be?" replied Amadou with a slight smile. "Have you ever seen a mutton or a lamb sitting in a chair reading a book?"

Other times, beyond his hearing, Laoura told me there was something unusually beautiful about Amadou. "He has such a soft face, like a baby's," she said. "I would do anything to have long eyelashes like him."

Saikou still did not understand Amadou. Many times I took the children to visit their father in Singapore. Saikou said it still bothered him that Amadou was left-handed. He thought that might be responsible for his stutter. And he was at a loss to interpret Amadou's long silences. He made me angry when he said, "I think Laoura is smarter than Amadou."

My business kept growing, though after the Gulf War my customers became more cautious about spending big money and the gem trade weakened. I became partners with a Thai couple, and we began exporting cotton clothes, mostly men's shirts to the Congo and the Ivory Coast. I rented a small building in the middle of the main garment center in Bangkok and sold to retail shops. I made just ten cents on each shirt, but I sold tens of thousands. Bobo became my agent in Africa and my courier, flying back and forth. He would leave Bangkok with as much as thirty thousand dollars in bills stuffed in his pockets.

I could pay for flights for all of us to visit Néné and Baba. In the summers, I brought the children to Singapore to see their father. But we saw him there only once. He brought the children to his office. He had three secretaries, a bathroom and a shower, and his office looked down on the whole city. It was all glass, as Ibrahim had imagined.

On the other visits, we came to his apartment to find he had hired a maid to help during our stay and left an envelope with cash for the children. But there was no Saikou. He had gone on a business trip, which he always explained neatly in a note left with the money.

The monsoon season in Bangkok always felt like a surprise, probably because it stayed hot before and during the rain, and afterward, too. And unlike Guinea, where it sometimes rained without breaking for many days on end, the rainfall in Bangkok was delivered in short torrents. It would rain for maybe an hour, stop for a few hours, rain for maybe twenty minutes, stop again, and start, each time coming with a fury that put the city into a state of constant flood alert.

The storms in September of 1992 kept us inside for three days. Amadou had just passed his seventeenth birthday, Laoura was fourteen, and they volunteered to go out to the market for milk, eggs, bread, juice, and anything else we might need while we were confined. They were returning in a *tuk-tuk*, one of the three-wheel taxis that scoot around the city and are considered monsoon-proof. They were several blocks from the apartment when another shower burst and the driver said it was no use. The motor was flooded. Amadou and Laoura stepped out into the rain, in hooded coats, each cradling two bags of groceries, Amadou leading his sister home with large sloshy steps.

Through the rain, Amadou saw a man bent over his motorcycle, working frantically to repair it in water up to his ankles. Amadou set the bags of food in the water and studied the situation until he and the man found the right wire or plugged the right hole. Laoura stood in the sweeping rain, waiting.

When finally they returned home, Laoura glared at Amadou.

"What were you thinking?" she said. "We were the ones who were stranded in the rain. You put our food in the water. And did you see what the man did, the man you helped? He drove off, passed us right by, and splashed us with mud and water."

Amadou's voice was mild but certain.

"You don't understand," he said.

"Aaaaah!" she shrieked. "What am I going to do with this brother of mine?"

Amadou finished at the French school and decided to go to Singapore for a yearlong program in computer science. The program offered the opportunity to transfer the credits to an American college. Being in Singapore also gave him a chance to spend time with his father. Before Amadou was finished, Saikou left for Angola. Amadou called to say that he didn't mind. He had gone to the mosque and become friends with a group of young Asian men. He said that they shared dinners and conversation about politics, basketball, and the Koran. They celebrated Ramadan together. "They are like a family for me," he said.

I felt relief to know that Amadou was not alone, and a renewed anger at Saikou for deserting his son. My mind pictured Amadou, fatherless, adrift in a strange city, and finding a harbor with these people I didn't know, who might overpower him with their ideas. Bobo told me I was being silly. "You are afraid he will forget where his true family is, like his father."

"You are right," I said. "I am silly. This can never happen because Amadou is not his father."

In February 1993, business took me on my first trip to the United States, for just a week. I went to the Tucson Gem Trade Exhibition and then flew over brown and whitecapped mountain ridges and giant green squares to New York City. The flight came in at night, and I was struck by the clear sky. The lights of the city gave definition to the buildings and a shape to the city that made it feel welcoming and knowable.

If only my children could be with me right now, I thought, and I felt a sad pang that of all the experiences we had shared, we were not to-

gether now. The plane turned on an angle, sweeping over Manhattan, descending, and I laughed to myself to know that this was happening to me. I was in my own skin, landing in America at night with lights all around me. Amadou will be fine, I thought. Knowing him, he will be here soon and he will be telling me what it was like down there, in the middle of all that light.

I spent one day in Manhattan and one day in Atlantic City with friends who had moved from Guinea to New York. Late in the afternoon, we drifted on the boardwalk. It was slightly windy and I wrapped a kerchief on my head and leaned on a railing to watch the waves. The surf was rougher than Liberia or Togo, more like Conakry's churning waters, and much darker than the clear South China Sea near Bangkok. These waves were larger and louder than anything I had seen.

If someone had come up to me and asked how I had arrived here, I could not have said for sure.

"It's a long story." I might have tried that.

"My mother told me not to sit on my shoes in the yard, or I would face a life of travel. And I didn't listen to her." That's the best I could have done.

Facts were facts, and I was on the other side of the Atlantic, maybe right at the spot where Mrs. Aicha had aimed her steel pointer. Maybe it was a divining wand and had cast a spell right then, as I sat between Yaye Kesso and Buntu Touré. But Yaye Kesso and Buntu Touré were still in Guinea. They stayed on the road between Labé and Conakry, between Labé and the villages. The wand conveyed me, not them, leaving us all to wonder, I supposed, how the road beyond turned.

Women search back in a way men don't to see what omens they missed in their own footprints. "Just look at your own shoes," Mrs. Aicha had said, the best and worst counsel I have ever received. Nothing is more reassuring than recognizing the feet you are standing on as your own, knowing that this is my place, and I am well, and all the people I love are well. But when you look up, you may find that the world has moved along and you don't recognize where you are. Looking at the Atlantic, I sensed myself somewhere in between, walking on a bridge, halfway home, halfway to the bend in the road that hides your destination.

I turned around and there it was, gold and glistening before me, the Taj Mahal.

Goodness gracious! This is a crazy, amazing, upside-down world. I laughed almost as loud as the ocean. Then I headed for the doors, and for the first time in my life, I plopped some coins in the one-armed bandits. And I laughed some more.

Amadou came back from Singapore, a lecturer. Watching his siblings sitting around the television focused on *Melrose Place*, he asked them how they could be so engrossed.

"Don't you know these are just actors? They are people and when they go back to their houses, they cry." Amadou had returned home wearing a full beard. "Who do you think you are?" Laoura said. "Lincoln?"

Amadou preferred the news broadcasts on CNN. He woke me from a sound sleep one night in November 1995. "Did you hear?" he said.

"What, Amadou? What is it?"

"They killed him."

"Who did they kill?"

"They killed Rabin. They shot him at a rally in Israel."

"Please, Amadou, go to sleep," I said.

"What is happening to this world?" said Amadou. "He was a man of peace."

Everything worried him. Laoura came home at four in the morning from a dance to find Amadou waiting up for her. "This is not acceptable behavior," he said. "You must be thinking about your future." Later, a neighbor knocked on my door to report she had seen my daughter coming in at all hours. Amadou marched down the hall and knocked on the woman's door with a stern rebuke.

"What you have told my mother is not your concern. It is not your place to intervene."

Each morning, he prayed before showering. When the other children came out of their rooms, Amadou was already at the table, sipping tea and reading the newspaper. He would ask to know their plans, and tell them what chores he expected them to perform around the apartment. Abdoul, the youngest, did not yet have the rebel in him and was happy to please his biggest brother. Laoura would tell Amadou he was not her father. Ibrahim accepted Amadou's authority for a while, until the time Amadou made a special show of it, calling Ibrahim and me into the living room after Ibrahim had arrived home late for dinner.

"I want Mama to be here for this," he said to his brother. "Where have you been? You cannot just stay out like this."

"I don't have to answer to you. It is time you stop acting like you're the boss," Ibrahim said.

Sliding his belt from his pants, Amadou said that if Ibrahim did not change his ways, he would have to take matters into his own hands. I started to move from my seat but stopped myself. Something was happening here that needed to happen, each son expressing in his own way a desire to have a father in the house. And after years of knowing silent Amadou, a part of me was glad to see an Amadou who was so demonstrative. Still, I did not like to see my sons so angry. They jumped on each other and wrestled to the floor, rolling into furniture. A lamp came crashing down. They kept going, punching and slapping. They barreled into the intercom, smashing it to pieces. When the fight was over they sat across from each other on the floor, panting, soaked in sweat, and Amadou said, "I only want to tell you I care about you." Ibrahim, not lifting his head, said, "I know."

Amadou wanted to take care of me, too. A man I had met through business wanted to take me on a date, but I was not interested. He called a number of times. Finally, after midnight, Amadou took the phone and said, "You cannot bother my mother anymore." That was the last time he called.

Amadou wanted his brothers and his sister to pray more. He told them that it would bring peace to their lives. He told them about the prophet Joseph, whose brothers were jealous of his handsome looks and wealth. The brothers swept him away and put him into a well and declared him dead. The Egyptians found him and took him out. There was a time when women in Saudi Arabia, who saw him passing, could not resist him. He felt he needed to be away from women, and he put himself in prison voluntarily to counsel people. The lesson of Joseph was in the humility he showed, Amadou said.

My wise son, there was time to take on the weight of the world, time to consider matters of life and death and sacrifice. Please don't rush your life so much, I told him. This time belongs to you.

There was a girl, Sushi, part Thai and part German. She lived with her grandmother in the suburbs. She had met Amadou and Laoura on a Saturday afternoon at the movie theater at the Marble Crown Shopping Center nearby. The three became friends, and in time Sushi was a regular visitor to the apartment. It was clear to everyone except Amadou that he was the attraction. She would sit as close as she could to him and touch him on the shoulder or the knee when she gestured in conversation, but Amadou offered no reaction.

One night she told Amadou it was too late to travel back to her grandmother's house and asked if she could stay the night. "Yes, of course," he said. She told him that she would like to sleep beside him. "No, this is something I cannot do," he said. In the morning I found Amadou asleep on his prayer mat outside his bedroom door.

"Where is Sushi?" I said.

"Shhh," whispered Amadou, pointing to his room. "She is still sleeping."

With any other child, I would have felt only pride, but seeing him sleeping outside his door like a faithful puppy also saddened me. I wanted for him nothing more than to know the feeling of holding a girl in his arms.

My business turned the other way in the early weeks of 1996. I sent a large shipment of clothes to Tanzania, but the buyer never paid and I lost nearly a hundred thousand dollars. Somehow, the deals that had fallen into place were harder to come by, or maybe it was competition from other companies, or maybe I was just tired. The children were older, more demanding in many ways, and the apartment felt more crowded. It was not easy to be the only parent. I began thinking it might be time to return home to Guinea.

In the spring of 1996, Amadou, twenty years old, said it was time for him to go to America. He would send for Laoura, and later Ibrahim and Abdoul, after he had completed college and saved up. He had a plan that had been in the works since his return from Singapore. Saikou had relatives, mostly third and fourth cousins, who lived in New York. Amadou said they could help him find a place to live. He said he would like to go before the end of the year.

I said this was all right, and then everything speeded up. In April, I went to the American embassy in Bangkok. I paid twenty dollars and submitted the papers for Amadou's visa. We made reservations for all of us to go to Guinea. Amadou wanted to say good-bye to Néné and Baba before leaving for New York.

The family's life was changing again. I scrambled to keep business ties alive so I could remain independent once I was back in Africa. Before leaving Bangkok, I found myself almost as tired as the day I had arrived to discover another woman's shoes in my bedroom.

We found a Guinea more troubled than the one we had left. Conakry overflowed with beggars and peddlers. Girls, some no older than six or seven, offered nuts, oranges, juice, or candy. The older girls tried to sell the indigo blouses they had made, or old toys, or mattresses, anything it seemed that was expendable. Local roads overflowed with sellers and not nearly enough buyers. Men and boys banged on car windows, hoping for a hand to reach out with a few coins. The drivers slowed as they passed, more often to avoid hitting one of the children than to stop for a piece of merchandise.

The street quieted only twice a week, on Friday afternoons, when people filled the Faisal Mosque, the biggest mosque in Conakry, for the

Jumah prayer, and when the sirens blared to announce the president's motorcade passing through. The road was filled with potholes. It was hot. Garbage burned in small gullies just off the road. At night the people receded into their cramped cement houses, some no bigger than one or two rooms. The houses could not hold all of them, and so many of the men lay down where they had stood all day at the side of the road, and went to sleep.

Amadou looked at this and knew for sure there was no place for him here. This disappointed me, because a selfish part of me had nursed the hope that he would come back to Guinea and find the pull of his homeland too strong to resist.

"Here it is simple," I told him. "You can succeed here. Our money can go far."

"No," he said. "You cannot compare Guinea to what we are used to in Thailand."

Amadou belonged to many places, and he knew about the places he had not yet seen. That had been my goal in sending him to the best school in Bangkok I could afford, but I was not entirely prepared for the outcome, that he would want to venture out and embrace new experiences. I was brave, but not that brave. As it was so with my parents and my grandparents, I was torn between the pull of tradition and the temptations of my dreams.

The children of the villages came to the towns. The town's children moved to the city. And then they looked for ways off the continent. Amadou was not alone. Hundreds of young men in the early part of the 1990s had left for America. They were the modern settlers. Their families waited for them to return with stories and riches, and some did. Others came back defeated, or they didn't come back at all.

The ones who stayed, like Amadou's friend Bangali, were jealous. He was not from a wealthy family, while Amadou had studied in Bangkok and Singapore and was headed for New York City. In Bangali's eyes, there was no bigger star than Amadou.

Oury also talked to Amadou about possibilities in Conakry, that it was not all bleak. Oury had become a contractor and was busy erecting houses and buildings all around the city. He had even drawn up the first map in the history of the city, and helped give names to collapsed streets and dirt roads no one paid any mind to.

Amadou turned to his uncle, who was just five years older. "I think I can do more good for the family in America than I can here," he said.

The time to say good-bye rushed upon us.

I had planned a trip to Nigeria in August to buy gems and would still be away a month later, after Amadou's departure from Guinea.

The night before I left, I called him into Néné's room. I locked the door.

He was wearing a light blue denim shirt, button-down, two pockets on the chest. His sleeves were rolled up high on his arms.

We sat on the edge of the bed.

"We have to say good-bye," I said.

He smiled.

"I just need blessings."

"You are sure?"

"I am ready. I have the tickets, the passport, the visa. I am going to America. I want to go to America. But there will be a day when I come back and I am able to take care of everyone."

There were many people in the house, my children and Diadia, Hadiatou and Fifi with their children. We stopped and listened to the loud talking of the family.

It's not necessary for you to take care of everybody. I have learned that this is a painful pursuit. I wish for you only a mother's wish, for your happiness, the happiness of my child. You helped me grow up, Amadou, but live, please, for yourself.

I did not say any of that. I did not say I love you. Nor did he.

We did not hug. It was not our way.

I reminded him to take extra socks. I said it is colder in New York than he was used to. He smiled at me again and nodded.

"I will call you," I said.

"I will call, too," he said.

"Yes," I said. "The phone is a good thing."

On his twenty-first birthday his aunt Fifi gave Amadou the first surprise party of his life. They told me that he danced and ate all night and could not believe someone had done such a thing for him. He told Fifi he would never forget this and he pulled her and spun her to the center of the yard. His cousins and his friend Bangali, his aunts and uncles, and many children from the neighborhood surrounded them.

Someone took a picture of Amadou sitting with Néné, arm in arm. Amadou was wearing a white cap. He had a great, wide smile, and Néné beamed as if she were sitting with a king.

Three weeks later, a Thursday night, September 26, Oury drove Amadou to the airport. Amadou wore black jeans, a dark pullover shirt, and a light brown jacket. He carried a Le Sait Koran, brown-covered with raised gold floral trimming, a biography of Martin Luther King, and a navy blue suit in his suitcase.

Oury watched him walk onto the airfield to a waiting transport bus. It was a typical muggy, hazy night in Conakry. Oury could see the plane sitting out on the runway, its red lights flashing. This was an Air Afrique plane, Flight 772 from Conakry to Dakar, connecting with Flight 560 to New York. Amadou stopped as he boarded the bus and turned to catch Oury's attention. He motioned with his hands, one to his ear, one to his mouth, "I'm going to call you."

At home Néné held a note that Amadou had written for me. It was only two lines.

The solution is U.S.A.
Don't leave my brothers and sisters here.

Part
Four

≈

Where He
Belongs

CHAPTER FOURTEEN

THE CITY COMES TO HIM

*T*he taxi pulled away from John F. Kennedy Airport just before eight-thirty in the evening. It traveled on a highway and then a bridge. It was a clear night, and from there, Amadou saw the night colors of Manhattan to his left. The top of the Empire State Building was lit blue and white. Amadou noticed another building with a distinct slanted top that gave out a bright white on the skyline. The taxi turned onto a sunken highway, which became a raised highway, and the view changed. He could see the upper floors of much smaller buildings. Some he could tell were apartment houses. Others looked like factories he had seen outside of Conakry, with rows of half-open green windows.

The door to the apartment was open when he arrived. Four men were busy over plates of rice and chicken. The smell was familiar to Amadou. He stepped inside, and no one noticed him for a few minutes until one of the men looked up, a chicken bone in his hand, his mouth half-full, and said, "He's here."

They all greeted him with handshakes, saying *"Onjaramaa. Onjaramaa."* And they introduced themselves.

Mamadou Kujabi was the biggest of the four, wide at the stomach and the chest. The others called him Kujabi.

Abdou Rahmane Diallo was a distant relative of Amadou's. Salou Diallo introduced himself as a first cousin, the son of one of Saikou's brothers.

The fourth man, the one who first saw him, was Mamadou Alfa Diallo, not a relation. He wore glasses and was not too shy to embrace Amadou. "You must be tired," Mamadou Alfa said. "We have plenty of food."

Amadou said that he might eat, but first he wanted just to sit. "This is fine, but we tell you right from the start that we share everything here. If there is a pot of rice on the stove, you can feel that it is yours to take. This is the way it is for us."

Amadou nodded in gratitude, and they let him be, understanding he was disoriented and needed time to settle into his surroundings. It was a simple apartment, the door opening onto a small entranceway and the area where they ate, just next to a small kitchen. This gave way to a living room that was not wide, but it was long. It was carpeted a deep maroon, and on the walls were pictures of people in their African robes, the mothers and fathers and other loved ones the men had left behind. At either end of the living room were two doors, each leading to a bedroom.

"You're going to be in this room with me," Salou said. "Kujabi has the other room. I think you will be comfortable."

In less than half an hour, Amadou joined them at the table. They asked him how the football teams in West Africa were doing, and this woke Amadou up a bit. "I enjoy playing," he said. "Are there games here?"

"They are always playing at the park just near here," Kujabi said. "When I have time, I will bring you over there." Kujabi laughed. "Of course, I don't know I will have time. I work thirteen days, take one day off, then work the next thirteen. When I come home, as you can see, I like to eat and sleep."

"What do you do?"

"I work in a nursing home in Brewster. That's outside the city. I am there ten or twelve hours a day, and it can take me an hour each way."

Amadou ate, and the others stayed to keep him company. They spoke to him with familiarity and posed no questions.

"It is a hard life here," Mamadou Alfa said. It was his way to speak gently. He had big, popping eyes and round cheeks that gave him the look of a boy. The deep lines stretching from the corners of his eyes were a contradiction. "But right now, Amadou, you can look at each of us and you can know you are not alone. You have family here."

The phone rang, me calling from Nigeria. He told me it was cold in New York and his lips were dry. I told him to buy sweaters and socks. If he found he needed more money, I would wire it immediately. I told him to wear two pairs of socks, and he groaned a little. "I know how to handle this," he said.

"What is the Bronx like?" I asked.

"Good," he said. "But I haven't really seen it."

The line was scratchy, and I was afraid we would lose the connection. Talking on the phone created a new urgency.

"I love you, Amadou," I said.

"I love you, too, Mom," he said.

The next morning he stepped outside and could see his new home in daylight. It was simple. Two floors, redbricked, six narrow windows, a few steps to a small landing and the door. Inside, a vestibule, the size of a small elevator, enclosed by two white-painted walls and another door opposite the first in the rear of the vestibule. This door had a window square. On the left wall were four metal mailboxes, marked 1F-1R-2F-2R. Beyond the vestibule, a flight of stairs to the second floor was brightened by a skylight, but the stairway itself threw a shadow over a long corridor. The corridor led right to the door of Amadou's apartment, 1-R, for first floor, rear. His share of the rent was two hundred dollars.

This was it, 1157 Wheeler Avenue, the Bronx. "They call this the Soundview section," Mamadou Alfa told him. "Many Guineans and other West Africans live in the neighborhood."

Salou told him of a job at a company that imported computers and sold them to stores around New York. Amadou was immediately interested, and three days later, a Tuesday, Salou took him there on the number 6 train for a two o'clock appointment. This was Amadou's first subway ride, and for much of the trip, the tracks traveled above the street, providing more glimpses of the city. He passed stops named Hunts Point Avenue, Longwood Avenue, and St. Mary's Street. When the train stopped at 125th Street, Salou said they were now in East Harlem in Manhattan. Amadou started for the doors, but Salou held him back. "We've got many more stops," he said.

At the 59th Street station they switched to the N train. Amadou could feel the train turning on curved sections of the tracks, and Salou said they were moving now toward the west side of the city. They exited the train at the 34th Street/Herald Square stop, and Amadou walked out into the center of what he had imagined, New York. He noticed the buildings and the shops and the billboards, but they did not impress him. These he had seen in Bangkok and Singapore. There was, he believed, in the faces of the people and in the way they moved, a shared feeling that there was no other place they would rather be. Amadou felt his own surge of satisfaction, pleased with himself for making the decision to come here and sticking to it. He was wearing his navy blue suit.

They walked to a building on West 29th Street, between 6th and 7th Avenues, the home of Metro Group USA. And thirty minutes later, Amadou was offered a job processing orders for computers. This required a fair knowledge of computers, and it also required a strong back for carrying the units into the delivery vans. The pay was two hundred and fifty dollars a week. Amadou accepted, and before the week was over he was working.

In Manhattan! New York City!

When I called him next, I had barely said hello when he started talking. It did not sound like Amadou.

"I have a job. It's the first one I tried for," he said. He stuttered more than usual, mainly because he could not catch up with his own voice. "Everything is going just right. I feel I have started on my goal. It is not a lot of pay for here, but I feel I can save."

"I can send you money," I said. I heard serious Amadou then.

"That is not why I am here."

Saikou called him, too, and also offered to help him with money, but Amadou gave him the same response.

He settled into a sure routine. He woke at seven, prayed, showered, ate cereal or toast for breakfast, and left the apartment by eight. He walked past several houses similar to his. Some had small flower beds in front and potted plants in the windows, many had safety bars, marking homes where children lived. One building across the street at 1154 Wheeler had a simple black-lettered sign in a first-floor window: DOCTOR'S OFFICE.

At Westchester Avenue, he turned right. If he had not eaten a full breakfast, he sometimes crossed the street to get an apple or a cake at Ray Market Fruit & Vegetables and then crossed back to get to his train. Westchester was a two-way street, dominated by the steel skeleton of the elevated tracks, rusted and peeling, marred with graffiti. Amadou went up the covered steps and headed for Manhattan. He worked for nine, sometimes ten hours, and liked the job, except for the lifting of the heavy boxes, which began to hurt his back. He prayed in a storage room on a mat he kept there.

On returning home in the evening, Amadou again walked on Westchester Avenue on the way to Wheeler. His roommates had told him that this part of the Bronx suffered from crime ranging from shootings to muggings. They had also alerted him that the police sometimes singled out black men on the street whether or not they had a reason for suspicion. Amadou would see the police department's blue-and-white cars patrolling the streets and would tell his roommates that "the police were on the job."

He told Mamadou Alfa that he trusted the police, that they were not like the border guards and the police in West Africa. "In America," Amadou said, "the police know how to handle things." Many times, as soon as he returned home from work, he sat down to watch a soccer match he had taped. Everyone in the house knew not to tell him the score, or the match would be ruined for him.

On Sundays, Amadou often visited with others in the Guinea community. Some lived in the Soundview Park and Lafayette Houses, two huge apartment complexes. He had met a number of men through his roommates or through ties back home. Most of them worked long days and also shared crowded apartments. Amadou was friendly with a few Guineans who worked at the Bruckner Car Wash two blocks from the house and others who worked in the shops on Westchester Avenue. When the weather was good, he joined a group of mostly young Mexican men at Soundview Park for a regular game of soccer. He no longer called it football because he had become a fan of the New York Jets and Giants. Now he had soccer and American football, and also basketball. He had taken to the New York Knicks, too. When Kujabi had Sundays free, he gave Amadou driving lessons at a parking lot nearby. Amadou sat for a haircut every six weeks or so at Ideal Barbershop, always with Carlos Abreu. They talked about sports and Carlos saved the first chair by the window for him. Once a month, Amadou went to the Western Union office to pay the electric and other bills for everyone in the house. He was always available to fix Kujabi's computer, and he also taught himself to cook.

"I do not believe this," I told him. We spoke once a week.

"Yes, Mom. I am cooking dinner tonight for everyone. I am making rice with beef and onions. I am crushing the onions and I am also adding fresh garlic."

He and the others made for a tight band of friends. If one came home from work early, he made sure there was a warm plate waiting for the others. In the evening, they kept their doors open, always happy to receive the others. Theirs was a communion rooted in a sense of triumph for having made it to New York, constant fatigue from their long working hours, and a lingering, gray sadness for the people they had left behind.

Kujabi's father died in a car accident when Kujabi was small. Kujabi had passed the West Africa Health Examinations Board and he developed a program in Gambia to get children immunized for tuberculosis, tetanus, and polio. Now he earned eight dollars an hour as a nurse's aid.

Mamadou Alfa had escaped from Senegal after years of seeing relatives and friends wounded and killed by rebels who carried on a system

of blackmail. The rebels' policy was pay us and you will be safe. He had been forced to quit school to run a store the family owned and to care for his mother and seven brothers and sisters. The rebels targeted him, and it became too dangerous for him to stay. He imagined opportunities in New York that would allow him to send money home. First he worked at a restaurant, washing dishes and making deliveries. By the time Amadou arrived, he was working twelve hours a day for a Korean man who had an odds-and-ends shop on 14th Street in Manhattan. He sold toys, socks, hats, T-shirts, and eyeglasses from a table in front of the store. On sixty dollars a day, he supported a wife, Aissatou, and paid three hundred dollars rent on an tiny basement apartment.

To the others, Amadou, schooled in Bangkok and Singapore, had led a special life, though he barely made mention of his past. While everyone in the house confided in him, he confided only in Aissatou.

She was from Guinea, too, tall and shy like Amadou. She worked as a hair braider at a beauty salon on Westchester Avenue. She was taking an English course, and Amadou helped her with her homework. Amadou told her that his back sometimes stung with pain from all the lifting he did. He thought he might need to change jobs. He told her he worried about his brothers and sisters, and that his mother might tire out.

Saikou called Amadou regularly, and often told Amadou that he was proud of his son for maintaining his prayers. Saikou now lived in Vietnam, where he had expanded his business. Amadou told Aissatou that he wished his father had stayed home more, and that it hurt him to know his family would never be truly together.

"You know what I wish," Amadou said. "I wish my mother and father could get back together."

In the fall of 1998, by the time Amadou had been in New York for two years, our phone talks were more difficult.

"How are you doing?" I would say.

"Okay."

"What have you been doing?"

"Not a lot."

"Is work going all right?" By this point, I had stopped offering to send money.

"It is not the time to talk about it."

"Will you at least send me pictures?"

"When I am more settled."

Amadou called Ouri much more than he called me. He told Ouri that life in the United States was hard. He said that he had explored going to college to study computer science, but needed to earn more to afford school. He called the long hours, low pay, and his sore back "particulars" on his way to achieving success.

"They are just the sacrifice," he said.

In one conversation, Ouri told Amadou that he heard about many killings in New York. He said that he knew of families in Guinea who had lost their sons to shootings on the streets.

"No, Uncle," Amadou said. "This country is very organized when dealing with crime, very tough."

"Please be careful."

"It is safe here," said Amadou. "I am not worried."

It is a mother's noble conceit to believe she has the power to take her child's suffering and do it for him. It is not much more than a superstition that allows her to get through those nights when she stares out in the dark and wonders how it will work out. That part of the night belongs to the mother, listening to the sounds of the house, in quiet reverence for things she cannot see, and for nightmares that are not hers. She may want to, but she cannot step into them. The blinking lights of her child's bad dreams expose dangers that only he can confront, paths toward survival that he must choose.

At the U.S. embassy in Conakry, the young men and women stand in lines for hours, sometimes days, hoping the clerk behind the window will announce their number. A game will decide if their lives turn left or right, and even if they are unsure and scared of what happens when the number is actually called, they are more frightened of what happens if it is not. They go back to their houses and sit with their mothers, who, finally, cannot help them. Their mothers cannot conquer unemployment or a lack of sewers, electricity, clean water, and paved roads. They cannot provide new textbooks, or at least ones that are not twenty years old, and they cannot supply the hospitals with medicines or surgeons. They cannot thwart disease and hunger. Their deepest wishes for their children are nothing against the heat, the lifeless air, and poison-filled mosquitoes.

In time, the mothers hope, too, that the numbers will be called, even if it will break their hearts. Even though they have heard that some children do not come back alive.

In the Fouta Djallon, when a child loses a tooth, there is no tooth fairy planting coins under her pillow. It becomes the mother's tooth. She holds it tight and throws it over the roof of the house at night, sending with it a secret wish for her child. It is a flare, which she prays God will see. That is how a mother lives her days, sending out messages and helplessly waiting for the replies.

Amadou lied. In September 1998 he hired an immigration lawyer and applied for asylum in the United States. His application said that he was a native of Mauritania who had fled the country to escape persecution and ethnic cleansing. He told an amazing story about the death of his parents at the hands of secret government agents.

"I was not there when the soldiers came to murder my parents," he said in the application, but rather on a farm with his uncle when soldiers came for them. "They beat us with wood sticks, tied us, and dragged us to their trucks and took us to the military camp. They jailed me for two weeks in a big room without light. We slept on the floor. I was with my uncle, who was tortured to death on October 9, 1989. On October 20, 1989, soldiers took me and other Mauritanians to the river and forced us to cross the river into Senegal at gunpoint by canoe."

All the details of Amadou's story were true, even if they were not his details. He did not have to dream up the plot or the ending. He only had to look at the people he had known his whole life, his friends, his schoolmates, his teachers, and the people he knew now. He had only to recall the stories of his grandparents escaping into the mountains, leaving their dinner to burn in the pot. Or his father's story about being detained in the basement of a police station, his ability to speak Senegalese the only thing standing between him and execution. Amadou had heard about his mother and her brothers and sisters hiding in the pit as his grandmother held her youngest child, his uncle Oury, to her breast.

And how many times had I told him about the time that he, Amadou, saved us when the Guinea border guard looked him up and down and decided that at twenty months he was a threat because his skin looked healthy. And as the story I told Amadou went, "And then you smiled. Just a little smile. And if it wasn't for that, who knows what would have happened to us?"

A mother cannot know her child's nightmares or the depth of his fears. Amadou, twenty-three years old, had been blessed many times over, but you can never overestimate the power of a good story, especially when it is true.

His roommate Salou decided to move to Detroit for work there, and Abdou Rahmane moved in with Amadou from his apartment upstairs. Amadou began to spend more time in his room, sitting on his bed. The walls were a muted white, and his view from the rear apartment was the back of another house on the next street. It did not offer much sunlight. He read many books about Martin Luther King and Malcolm X. He read *Guidelines for Dialogue Between Christians and Muslims*, and while praying, he listened to taped translations of the Koran, some in English, some in French. He kept his hanging clothes in an assembled plastic closet, and the rest of his clothes in his suitcase. He kept pictures of his family in a small rose-colored album, the picture of him with Néné pressed onto the first page. And he kept the money he was saving bit by bit in a brown accordion envelope.

There remained about Amadou a certain mystery. Mamadou Alfa and Aissatou were expecting a baby soon, and Amadou did not see how they could stay in their small apartment. With Abdou Rahmane having moved in with Amadou, the upstairs apartment, the one just over Amadou's, was open. "You must move there," Amadou said.

"We cannot afford it. The landlord wants a thousand dollars just to give us the key," said Mamadou Alfa.

The next day, Amadou handed his friend an envelope with a thousand dollars in ten-dollar bills.

"Are you crazy to do something like this?" Mamadou Alfa said.

"You cannot stay in that apartment, not with a baby coming." And that was that.

Amadou's back hurt him almost all the time, and finally he decided to try something else, even if it meant making less money. Mamadou Alfa knew the owner of a shop on 14th Street, a Pakistani man who would be open to an arrangement like his, having someone sell items from a table in front of the store. Amadou liked the idea of working near Mamadou Alfa's store. They could commute together, and this work would be far easier on his back.

In September, he began taking the number 6 train to Union Square. From there he walked three blocks to C&B Convenience, just off the southwest corner of Second Avenue and 14th Street, selling everything from socks and batteries to bottles of juice and soda, Life Savers, Rolaids, gum, videotapes, diapers, birthday candles, magazines and newspapers, and pencil compasses. He was partly an extension of the store, and partly in business for himself making a start as his father the trader had on the roads in southern Senegal. Some days he made a hundred dollars, some days fifty. There were rainy days, when he made ten dollars. The store's owner, Shahin Choudhury, gave him space to pray, which he did between aluminum shelves stocked with cases of Pepsi, Canada Dry, SlimFast, and Hawaiian Punch. While working, Amadou carried house and store keys on a small chain that hung from a belt loop by his right pocket. He carried a beeper, and that helped him stay in touch with Mamadou Alfa three blocks away, often to coordinate their trip back to the Bronx.

What he liked best about standing on a street and selling was the chance to do it in New York City, in Manhattan, not too far from the South Street Seaport, which he visited once, or from the United Nations, which he planned to see. He was only twenty blocks from the Empire State Building. Working outside, he did not have to travel through the city to know it. Instead, the city came to him.

Sacir Mackic came to the store each day for his morning coffee. A shepherd from Montenegro in the former Yugoslavia, he had fled when the war started there. Amadou told him that one day Milošević would be punished, and recited for him much of Yugoslavia's history, including the rise of Tito. Amadou got to know Sarah Whitley, who lived in the building just two doors down. Sometimes he played with her baby while she shopped. He loaned forty-three dollars to a student who needed the money to pay taxes. On cold days, a young woman, Reechelle, brought him a hot potato wedge for lunch. Leila Tusuf lived on East 12th Street and came every day to see if Amadou was at his table. She hoped that he would ask her to dinner or a movie, but he never did.

In early November, I phoned to tell him that a man I knew only from business had suddenly asked me to marry him. His name was Sank and he was a shy man, I told Amadou.

"What do you think?" I said. For several seconds, there was silence.

"Give me two days. I have to think it over," said Amadou. Two days later he called.

"Mom, you have been struggling," he said. "What happened with you and my father, you are not responsible. You shouldn't have to pay a price. You should be happy. You have my blessing. Be married according to Islam." I felt a chill in me to hear my child bless me. Two weeks later I married.

Amadou's friends took photos of him, including one on the Staten Island Ferry, and another just after New Year's Day, 1999, as he stood in front of his apartment house on Wheeler Avenue. He went to see Leonardo DiCaprio in *Titanic*.

He called to say that his quest for asylum had been granted, and that meant he was eligible to receive a college scholarship and that he could open a bank account. He would be sending me the pictures I had requested, and he said he had an assignment for me.

A friend of his, he said, had shown him a picture of a girl who lived in Conakry, not far from me, and he wanted this girl to be his wife. Her name was Benti. Amadou wanted me to invite Benti to the house and to arrange for her to begin a correspondence with him, but by no means should I let her know his intentions.

She came, wearing jeans and a little sleeveless top. She had tiny braids and she was small. She had full cheeks. I thought she looked like me.

Néné told me to be very careful, that it was not easy to have a son like Amadou. He lives in a modern world where he does not need your permission, my mother said, and yet he wants to give you respect.

"He wants you to help him pick his wife," she said.

I wasn't sure. "I know Amadou. He is shy," I said.

He phoned on Saturday, January 30, to tell me that he planned to become engaged to Benti. They had exchanged letters once.

We spoke again the next day. He said he wanted to send Nike sneakers for Ibrahim and Abdoul.

"Mom, it has been a hard beginning, but I am so happy now," he said. "I have saved enough money for school. I am thinking I can start next year. All I need is your blessing."

"You know you have my blessing," I said.

"Mom, I will call you in a few days. Tonight's the big football game, the Super Bowl. I am going with my friends to watch it at a restaurant in Manhattan."

"That is good," I said, and I laughed to hear Amadou carefree.

In all, we spoke for five minutes.

"Bye, Mom."

"Good-bye."

The next day he called Oury. Amadou told him all about the game, though Oury had never seen American football.

"Denver had the advantage," Amadou said. "They have one of the greatest players ever. His name is John Elway. He can throw the ball to the exact spot he wants."

"You had a good time," said Oury.

"Yes. We went to the All-Star Café and watched on a big television. It was good. Now I'm looking forward to the basketball season. The players were on strike, but I think they are coming back soon."

Amadou told Oury, too, about Benti and the plans for college.

"They are realistic now."

"Let's talk next week," Oury said.

"I will tell you everything that is happening," Amadou said.

"Good-bye, Amadou."

"Good-bye."

CHAPTER FIFTEEN

LOSING AMADOU

Amadou worked for ten hours on Monday. He did not work on Tuesday. On Wednesday he arrived at eleven in the morning. It was an unusually mild day for February, not too cold, but Amadou was prepared anyway. Under his black Tommy Hilfiger pants he wore a pair of long underwear. Over two T-shirts, one black, one blue, he wore a white winter coat with a hood, but he didn't use the hood. He wore a red New York Yankees cap.

Fourteenth Street was busy all day and into the evening. Amadou ended up with good sales, more than a hundred dollars. At eleven that night, Mamadou Alfa was on the 14th Street bus heading for the Union Square subway entrance and saw Amadou packing up his table. A few minutes later Amadou walked to Union Square. He arrived at the house at ten minutes to midnight and went upstairs to see Mamadou Alfa without stopping at his own apartment. The door was open. A television in the living room was on.

Aissatou was away, in Atlanta, visiting a sister, and it was a rare night when there was not a pot of rice and sauce waiting for them. Amadou lay down on the couch. Mamadou Alfa was already out of his clothes, with a towel around his waist, getting ready for a shower. Kujabi came by and sat with Amadou. He asked Amadou if he planned to pay the bills at the Western Union office, and Amadou said he would do it in the morning on the way to work.

An announcer on television reported that the basketball season would finally start on Friday, and Amadou told Kujabi he couldn't wait.

Amadou said he was hungry. But he was also tired, and began to fall asleep on the couch.

Everyone was tired. Kujabi went to his apartment down the hall. Abdou Rahmane was downstairs, asleep in the apartment. Mamadou Alfa stepped into the shower, quiet as he could be, not wanting to wake Amadou.

Ten minutes later, Mamadou Alfa stepped out of the shower. He did not see Amadou on the couch and thought he had gone to his apartment. Mamadou Alfa prepared for prayer in the living room. It was just after twelve-thirty, Thursday morning.

Amadou had not gone to his apartment. He went down the stairs to the first floor, walked through the vestibule, and stepped onto the landing of the small steps out front. He might have been thinking about walking over to Westchester Avenue. He knew of a Chinese restaurant that stayed open late. Or he might have been restless after a long day of work and wanted to take a breath of air. His jacket was not zipped.

The street was quiet.

Only a few windows showed lights on. A window here and there flickered with the light of a television.

A red car came up Wheeler, from Westchester Avenue. Amadou saw it to his left. The car moved slowly. Amadou followed it with his eyes. There were four people in the car, two in front, two in back. The car moved past Amadou, by about four houses, and then it stopped and began to back up. The people in the car were men, and they were all looking at Amadou.

Amadou turned to the door. It was open, and he moved into the vestibule. His keys were in his front right pocket.

Two of the men jumped out of the car. The first man wore a dark winter jacket over a gray, hooded sweatshirt, blue jeans, and black high-topped sneakers. The second man wore jeans and a dark sweatshirt. A third then got out from the rear of the car. He wore jeans, too, and a dark pullover sweater. Finally, the driver jumped from his seat.

The first two men came up the few steps of the building to the entrance of the vestibule. They were no more than six feet from Amadou. They were tall. The third man was on the sidewalk. The driver was in the street. Amadou was now at the second door.

One man, the one closest to Amadou, pulled out a gun and began to shoot. The second man pulled out a gun, and he began to shoot.

Amadou was falling.

He fell.

More bullets came, from the other men, one on the sidewalk, and the last firing from the street.

The first two men each fired sixteen bullets, emptying their weapons. The man on the sidewalk fired four times, the man on the street, five. Forty-one shots in all.

Nineteen bullets struck Amadou. Several bullets struck the stairway beyond the vestibule, including one that went through the stairs through another wall and lodged in a wall in Amadou's bedroom.

It was sixteen minutes before one in the morning, February 4, 1999.

The four police officers, members of the New York City Police Department's elite Street Crimes Unit, were taken away, complaining of ringing in their ears.

Mamadou Alfa, on his knees, was shaken from his prayer. He went into his bedroom. He heard the voice of a man screaming, *"Fuck. Fuck. Fuck. Fuck."* He turned aside the curtains and looked to the street below. He saw a red car double-parked and a man standing behind it. He saw another man, to his left and across the street, standing next to a parked car, and he seemed to be pounding the car, as if he were confused, Mamadou Alfa thought. He saw a police car farther down the street to the left. Mamadou Alfa went back to finish his prayer.

Abdou Rahmane was awakened by bamming at his door. He opened the door in his underclothes to find police officers standing there. They said they needed to talk to him.

"Put on your pants and your shoes and come out with us," one said.

He thought Amadou had come home and gone to bed. He saw a crowd in the vestibule, and he saw something that alarmed him on the floor.

He ran back to the apartment to get Kujabi, whose bedroom looked out onto Wheeler. Somehow, he had slept through the gunfire.

"What is it?" Kujabi said. He was half-dressed.

"There's a man lying in the hall. I think he was shot."

"What do you mean? I didn't hear anything."

"I don't know," Abdou Rahmane said. "He might be dead."

Kujabi quickly put on a shirt and rushed out. The hallway flashed red and white from police lights on the street. There were police officers in the hall and in the vestibule. Kujabi approached them.

"Do you know this man?" one asked.

Kujabi came closer. He saw that the man's jacket was unzipped. He saw blood on the man's chest. He turned his head to look again. He looked into the man's eyes. He could not make them out.

And then he knew. He dropped to his knees and sobbed into his own chest.

Mamadou Alfa, upstairs, heard a knock at his door. It was a police detective with questions.

"What's your name?"

"Did you hear any noise?"

"Where were you?"

"How long did it go on? How many shots?"

Mamadou Alfa said the shots rang out too fast for him to say. He was tired.

The detective left and came back in a few minutes with a New York identification card.

"Do you know this guy?" the detective asked. It was Amadou's card with his picture.

"That's my brother," Mamadou Alfa said, and he felt something grabbing in his throat. "How is he related to this? Did something happen to him?"

The detective lowered his head and went back downstairs.

Mamadou Alfa tried to steady himself. "Okay," he thought. "Whatever happened, happened already."

He went down the stairs. He could see someone lying on the floor. He saw Kujabi.

"Where's Amadou?"

Kujabi pointed.

"That is Amadou lying down there."

And Kujabi said, "Wasn't he sleeping upstairs?"

People with badges were everywhere, in the vestibule, the hallway, on the stairs, on the sidewalk, and up and down Wheeler. Their questions continued.

"Does he carry a gun?"

"Does he smoke?"

"Where does he work?"

"What are his activities?"

They went to Amadou's room. They lifted his mattress and emptied all the clothes from his bureau drawers onto the floor. They emptied his closet and opened his books, and they flicked on his computer.

When they were done, they drove Kujabi and Abdou Rahmane to the police station in the middle of the night.

"Who might have done this?" they asked.

"Did he have any enemies?"

They kept at it until the sun came up, determined to uncover the secret life of the man they had killed.

That night, unsettled dreams fell over my house and my family. Néné dreamt that the calf wanted to drink milk from the cow, but there was no milk. The mother could not feed her offspring, could not help him.

Laoura dreamt that Amadou, rowing in a canoe, said he was dead and that he offered the bread he no longer needed. She told me she had a pain in her head. I brought Tylenol and a bottle of water to her. I pulled the cover sheet up over both of us and fell asleep holding her.

Ibrahim saw a hand reaching for him. "Who was that?" he asked me in the morning. "I pulled his hand, but I couldn't save him."

Something was coming. My own sleep in these days was jangled and filled with sweat. I had caught my own eyes in the mirror, hollowed and older and pleading for a reprieve.

The phone started early, one call and another and another. The callers gently wished me off the phone. They said someone had phoned with news from the States and that they wanted to speak to the man in the house.

Where was Amadou? Shouldn't he be in bed? Why was there news from America? It was morning here and night in New York. Amadou would be sleeping. How could harm have come to him in his sleep? No. No. Yes, it could be something. Why would someone call from New York in the middle of the night? He was hurt. He was in a hospital and he needed me. He was sick and he didn't want to make a fuss. He was just sick. People get sick in America. They have good doctors there. No. No. They asked for the man in the house. That's how it is. They never give a woman the bad news. Amadou had an accident in the road. He was badly hurt. Maybe he was dying. No. Don't think that, because if you have those feelings, reality will follow. Cry, and then it will be over. The feeling will pass. No. Don't cry. Nothing is wrong. Nothing happened.

"What's wrong, Mom?" Laoura asked. Her head still pounded.

"It's Amadou."

"What?"

"Nothing. I don't know. I can't tell you."

Laoura pulled me to her. The seconds raced under my skin. The phone rang again, as we knew it would.

My child. My child. Were you hungry? Had you gone out for something to eat? Were you tired from working? Had you needed to feel the air on your face? Were you cold? February in New York must be cold. Had you wanted to talk to me? Is that why you went outside? What did they look like when you saw them? Did you talk to them? Did they understand you? Did you stutter? I imagine you might have stuttered. They didn't understand you, and you wanted them to know who you were. You wanted to say "I am Amadou." But the "A" got caught.

"This is my door, this is my doorstep," you wanted to say.

Four men approached you. They were dressed darkly. Who were they? Could you tell? Did they have faces?

One must have seen your face. How ridiculous, this one must have thought. He had wanted to tell the others that there was no danger here, only an angel. Wasn't there just one like that who could bring peace? Just one of these men could have turned to the others and told them they had gone too far. We don't need to bother this man. We are not looking for a man like him. Let us be on our way. Trouble is not here. Let's go and allow the revolutions of the earth their order.

I don't hear the voices of these men. It is I, my own voice. I will reverse the planet. Allah will allow me. He has given me my mother's strong arms. What is this business about forty-one shots? My arms are stronger than the wind or gravity or the pull of the moon.

"Mama," Laoura says. "Mama, I am here for you." She wipes my eyes. She holds me, keeps me from falling.

No, Allah. Don't do this. Please help me stand. I am the mother. Do not leave me like this. I'm fighting. I'm fighting, kicking madly. Don't you see? Do not make me a child again.

The first ambulance worker to reach Amadou, only four minutes after the shooting had begun and ended, did not find much blood. He knelt beside him, cut open his two T-shirts, and noticed a wound in the center of his chest at his heart, but no real bleeding, just a small stain. He noticed two holes on Amadou's left side and no blood there, but realized he had no chance to revive him.

Amadou was lying with his head and shoulders propped slightly against the left corner of the back wall, his legs stretched to the center of the vestibule, when the emergency worker came to him. The dull brown skins of used bullets surrounded Amadou's body.

The ambulance worker noticed Amadou's right hand, slightly opened, cupping a tiny pool of blood like an offering.

Amadou was kept in the vestibule for many hours. Photographs were taken and a video was made. And finally, at about seven in the morning, he was placed in a white body bag and removed from his apartment house to the Jacobi Medical Center in the Bronx. He was taken to the basement of a single-story building and slided onto a refrigerated drawer, one of fifty in columns of four and five, and pushed into the dark. He was given a case number, BX9900498, and declared a "Police shooting. Multiple."

At nine-thirty, Dr. Joseph Cohen met Amadou, who had been transported to a stainless-steel table in a small room lighted by a few round fluorescent ceiling bulbs. This room was called the Autopsy Suite. Its main feature was a single panel, containing a sink, suction hoses, and a cutting station. This was called the Autopsy Wall Unit. Photos were taken of Amadou first clothed and then unclothed. To undress him, a technician delicately removed the body bag and each item. Fragments of bullets fell clattering from the clothing and the body bag onto the table.

A case like this, Dr. Cohen knew, would take deliberateness. He noticed holes scattered on Amadou, some with the appearance of dimples, others ringed by small circles of blood. There was a little more blood on the left side, but no massive openings and no wounds to the face or head, even though Dr. Cohen had found two holes in Amadou's Yankees hat, one likely from the bullet going in and one going out of the hat.

He told himself to "circle the table," as he usually did before beginning an examination. "Get to know him." He noticed that Amadou was not big, or especially stocky or especially thin, and was in good athletic

shape. He dwelled on Amadou's face and found it pleasant, and with a wise aspect, even in death.

He spoke to Amadou, something he had done with other people, but only rarely. "This won't be so bad," he said. "You are a fine-looking young man."

They stayed together for several hours into the evening, Amadou and this gentle man.

Dr. Cohen found nineteen gunshot wounds. Three of them he labeled "penetrating," meaning they remained in Amadou's body. He identified sixteen as "perforating," meaning they had cut a trail through Amadou and come out someplace else. Altogether, then, this meant that the police officers had put thirty-five holes in Amadou.

Dr. Cohen then had the difficult job of tracing the paths of the bullets even as they crisscrossed throughout Amadou's body. Some came in low to one side of Amadou and exited high. Others charted a more even course. Of the nineteen bullets, fifteen struck Amadou in the back or his sides. Just four entered him in the front, three striking his legs and one piercing his chest, missing the heart itself but making a one-and-a-half-inch gash in the aorta, basically tearing it apart. Dr. Cohen found blood spilled into Amadou's chest cavity, roughly two and a half quarts, nearly half of all the blood in his whole body.

That's why so little blood seeped from the other wounds, Dr. Cohen reasoned. There wasn't enough blood left, also causing Dr. Cohen to think that the bullet to the chest was the first to strike Amadou. If not, then at least one or more of the wounds would have produced greater bleeding.

This bullet also passed through Amadou's left lung before crashing into Amadou's spine, paralyzing him on the spot.

Dr. Cohen's job was to break down just a few seconds of chaos into a reasoned, imaginable sequence. If this bullet had been the first to hit Amadou, as Dr. Cohen believed, and had paralyzed him, it meant that Amadou fell instantly, his body now at the mercy of gravity.

And that would explain at least in part why so many other bullets entered his body haphazardly and to his back and sides. The shots kept coming while Amadou was falling and even after he was down. Dr. Cohen found that four bullets had struck Amadou in the feet, including one that entered through the *bottom* of his right foot.

One bullet also traveled through Amadou's diaphragm and spleen, grazed his left kidney, and cut through several loops of the small intestine. Several bones were broken, including the right elbow, the right leg, the right arm, the pelvis, and one rib.

Dr. Cohen needed a second day to complete the exam, when he moved deeper inside of Amadou. "We are finished now," Dr. Cohen said to Amadou. "I am sorry for this tragedy."

In all, it took Dr. Cohen seventeen hours in the Autopsy Suite and several weeks more to determine scientifically what Amadou's broken-hearted mother and stricken loved ones already knew. He never had a chance.

CHAPTER SIXTEEN

SEEING HIS LIFE

ive days later, I was in New York.

The plane set down at about one-thirty on a Tuesday afternoon. Sleet rapped against the plane windows, and I saw blinking lights from a line of police cars sitting on the airfield. This must be for an important person, I thought. We had been told that someone from the Guinea embassy would meet us, but a police officer came aboard to ask for Mrs. Diallo and said he had been assigned to escort me from the plane. I came down the steps and was swallowed by people with titles, an ambassador, a woman from the mayor's office, an executive somebody, a lawyer. Their faces were lost on me. A large woman hugged me. I knew her face from Conakry. Her name was Mahawa Bangoura of the Guinea embassy.

"We can't let her go with them." I heard that from the mayor's person. I felt myself being pulled into the mob.

I grabbed hold of Mrs. Bangoura's arms.

"Don't worry, I'll be following right behind," she said in my ear. "Be careful. Don't speak to them."

They put me in a van. My husband, Sank, was with me, and my uncle Korka, a brother of Baba's. The mayor's person sat in front. She talked on a cell phone. She told someone I had landed and was with her. The lawyer was there. He had short hair, maybe freshly cut. He spoke on a cell phone, too. He said he was *my* lawyer. I looked at him. He said my husband had called from Vietnam and signed off on hiring him.

"He did what?" I said.

"I'm your lawyer."

"Oh."

We entered a highway. Then we were on small streets, and someone said we were getting close. The van windows were darkly tinted, but I could see walls stained with grafitti, gated storefronts, and buildings with windows boarded up. I felt the rumble of a train over my head, and we passed between the grim girders that held up the tracks, bolted like a giant's feet into the pavement. It was like looking into a dark dream. Amadou never told me it was like this.

The door of the van opened and I was stepping out, and now there was a crowd, heads everywhere, hands, too, reaching for me, everyone dressed thickly in winter clothes, no place to move, cold air and hot breath, cameras raised over the heads, flashing at me, gray television cameras and silvery microphones. I didn't see Mrs. Bangoura. I didn't see anyone, anything particularly. Nothing was distinct, vague shapes, vague faces, and then one stood out, a young man, his voice traveling through the crowd.

"Look at me. Look at my face. I am your friend. I am your son. My name is Frankie," he said. For a second I saw a clean face that bore no urgency, and I saw Amadou.

The tide pushed me up steps. I heard myself calling, *"Amadou. Amadou. It's your mom. Your mom is here."* Then someone said to me, "Mrs. Diallo, this is the corner where he was lying." I was in the vestibule of 1157 Wheeler. I dropped into a crouch.

"Leave me here," I whimpered. But they didn't. I was pressed forward, through a dark hallway and into my son's apartment.

They showed me to his bedroom. Amadou never told me how small a room he lived in. A small space separated two narrow beds. Someone had folded a few of his items into small piles on his bed. I recognized an olive green T-shirt he had worn in Thailand. I brought it to my face and

I smelled Amadou sitting beside me. I smelled a pair of jeans, a few shirts. I held a sweater close.

Many people came in and out of the bedroom. I met Mamadou Alfa and Abdoul Rahmane. Their eyes were red and tired. Faces watched from the doorway. I reached into Amadou's suitcase, which was sitting on the floor, and pulled out several books and a prayer rug. A black leather jacket hung in his closet beside a blue windbreaker. A pair of brown suede shoes and worn sneakers sat in a corner. I found pictures of him, some taken in just the last week, that he had not had a chance to bring to the photo shop. It had fallen to Mamadou Alfa to do it for him. In one picture Amadou wore a necktie. In another, taken the day of the Super Bowl, he was smiling broadly. In his room, there was an envelope where Amadou saved his money. In all, there was three thousand dollars.

Other young men appeared. "Did you know Amadou?" I asked.

"Yes, I knew Amadou," they said. I cried at the simplicity of the words. *I knew Amadou.* My life lived in those words.

The people with cell phones took me back in the van, and two men in suits, wearing earpieces, joined us. They were from the police department. They took me to a hotel, brought me past more cameras stationed on the sidewalk, to the tenth floor. They told me the city was paying for my stay. The earpiece men told me to wait in the hall because they needed to check the room. Numb, I stood there. Not until I was inside the room, in a chair, my feet throbbing, my body broken, did I think, maybe the men put something in my room.

Visitors began arriving. Many had settled in New York from Guinea, and though I did not know them, they talked in familiar ways about Conakry, Labé, the villages and the roads in between. Mohammed Diallo, the president of the Guinean Association in New York, told me that the community planned to stand behind me. I told him that I wanted to be with the community, and he smiled and said that was good.

I was introduced to the Reverend Al Sharpton and told he was one of the most influential leaders in the African American community. I had never heard his name, but I was impressed that such an esteemed person had come to see me. He said that he would provide me with whatever I needed. "I will give you my full support," he said. To me, this meant he understood the wrongness of what had happened and would help me, a stranger in need. He said that he had just come from a rally in support of Amadou. I had been to something like a rally only once, long ago, when I chased Sékou Touré's car at the stadium. Reverend Sharpton placed a call to Chicago and handed me the phone, saying Jesse Jackson wanted to offer his condolences. He, too, said he supported me.

I was exhausted, still raw from the rain, jittery from all the hands grabbing at me at the airport. I closed my eyes and I saw cameras flashing, cell phones and earpieces, heads at Amadou's door, long black microphones staring at me as if they had eyes, men spying under my bed.

Everyone wanted to give me support, or did they just want me? I asked myself the question, not knowing what it meant. "I'm not comfortable," I told Sank. "I feel like a hostage here."

"Whatever you want," he said.

Reverend Sharpton was still there when the man from the van with the short hair and the cell phone came to see me.

"You're my lawyer?" I asked, only half-remembering what he had said.

"Your husband called from Vietnam and he approved," he said.

I had not slept in days. The trip, through Mali and Brussels, had taken fifteen hours. I thought my ankles might crack and fold up beneath me if I stood. Going to sleep would give me nightmares. Staying awake gave me nightmares.

I lifted myself from the chair, creaking and bent like an old woman. I summoned the might to straighten, and I pointed a finger, and the voice that came from me startled even me, for in all the screaming, fighting times of my life, I had never known my voice to be touched by the devil's madness.

"You are not my lawyer!

"I will hire my own lawyer.

"Nobody tells me what to do.

"My husband? My husband? My husband is here with me.

"I may be just the mother, but I make my own decisions.

"Go away!"

I could feel my muscles snapping and curling like they were dying. Everyone, go away now. Please. Don't you see what has become of me? Don't you see that I am turning into a rag doll, or are you blind?

People, well-meaning, kept coming and going until around midnight and one person was left—not Mrs. Bangoura, but a comforting figure like her. Her name was Delores Blakely, and she said she had spent her life fighting for people like Amadou. She said that the community was coming together behind me. She had seen images of me crying on the television news.

"That's a disgrace they put that on," she said. I sat with her on the couch, clutching the photographs of Amadou.

"I don't want you to be alone," Miss Blakely said. "If these people harm you, everyone will think it was because you didn't come out of shock. No one would ever know what happened to you." She screened all the phone calls. She ordered a plate of rice and chicken and insisted I eat.

I told Sank that Miss Blakely suspected something would be done to us, and I let her spend the night. I stayed on the couch with her. I wept into her chest. I wanted Néné to walk into the hotel room, side by side with Baba.

Miss Blakely stroked my hair and my back. "Thank you so much," I said. She said that everyone in the community called her Queen Mother. That made me smile. She called me Mama.

"No one can hurt you while I'm here," she said.

I told her about the two men from the police department who checked the room. I told her I was scared to stay in this hotel. It was about two in the morning. She got on the phone with Reverend Sharpton. "Mama wants to go," she said.

"Who will pay for this?" I asked.

"The community," she said.

I was scared and I was tired. I did not like this place. I said yes, take me to another hotel.

≫≪

Noise be gone.

It is time now for me to be with my son.

He lay on a silver table set on crisscrossing metal legs. He was covered in a white robe. An incense candle burned. His lips were sealed. They were beautiful lips. I touched them, and my fingers cried. The long eyelashes that his sister envied were asleep. His head was back. I saw little hairs around his mouth and on his chin. This silent body has gone through a lot, I thought. I wished he could tell me what happened, but he could not, and maybe that was better. I did not want him to remember it or see it still. None of that, my silent boy.

Tears fell, but the sound was snuffed out, like crying into a pillow.

Others from the family filled the space around me at the funeral home. It was Thursday, February 11, a week after the shooting. Saikou and Amadou's half brother, Alfa, had arrived. I wished I could have been alone, but I was thankful for the privilege to see Amadou once more. Alfa, twenty-nine, offered me his shoulder to lean against.

"I saw my brother," he said, in awe of the truth of it. "He's here."

I placed my palm on each part of Amadou's face, as though comforting him with a moist compress. I saw the tiny scar on his forehead, from when he had fallen and received stitches as a small boy. I placed my hand over it. He was cold, of course. I looked down on him with gentle tears. So nice to encounter you.

The robe covered him to the neck. I wanted to pull it away to see him, but with all that force going into him, I could not bear what I would see. I let him be.

The Koran says that when a good person dies, the angels come to retrieve the soul and escort it to heaven. I prayed over Amadou, wishing that the angels had come quickly that night and sped him away before he could feel a thing.

We went to the store on 14th Street. The day was covered in clouds. Mr. Choudhury, the owner, showed us in with a graceful hand. Many people who said they had become friends with Amadou stood nearby in a warm half-circle.

"These are some of the things he sold," said Mr. Choudhury, holding up a tray of videos and battery packs and other items packed in plastic. From floor to ceiling, I was surrounded by bright boxes of cereals, cartons of cigarettes, baby food, pet food, whatever it seemed could fit on the shelves—socks, hats, playing cards, cigars.

"This is his prayer rug and back there is the room where he prayed. And there, out front, is where he stood and sold."

I dropped down and grabbed onto Saikou to keep me from falling.

"This is who they are talking about," I cried. "Amadou, my baby."

I wanted to grab Saikou by the neck and say, "Why didn't you tell me? He didn't have to live in this place, the Bronx. He didn't have to work so hard."

Where my sobs were stifled at the funeral home, now they erupted. I held tight to Amadou's prayer rug.

"What was he doing here, trying so hard to make it?" I said. "This was not necessary. He didn't have to feed us."

The next afternoon we went to the Islamic Cultural Center for the Friday-afternoon prayer, the *Salat al-Jumah*. I sat in the balcony of the mosque, on the floor with dozens of women, separated as always from the men. There was hardly an unused space in the hall, and no leftover pockets of air. They carried a wooden box that held Amadou to the front of the mosque. The imam led the prayer for the dead, reaffirming our faith in God, and I was relieved to let God hold my suffering for a few moments. The women seated with me said something about the mayor and the police commissioner having come through a side door. "Who invited them?" somebody said.

Saikou stood by the podium, shaking hands with Reverend Sharpton and the imam. Saikou was never far from center stage. I liked being with the women.

Private grieving eluded me in New York. After the service, Reverend Sharpton said to me, "You have to go to a rally."

"What rally?" I said.

"At my headquarters."

"When?"

"Now."

I entered a small auditorium to the chanting of "Am-a-doo! Am-a-doo!" When the people saw me, and then Saikou, they clapped and stomped. Reverend Sharpton promised he would fight for Amadou and for all young black men targeted by the police. And he said, "We have to hear from the mother." I had not planned to speak, and as I rose, my hands and my knees shook.

"I am standing before you," I began. I saw mostly black people, but many white people, too. I saw children, many young men about Amadou's age, and, mostly, women who I knew were mothers, too. "I am standing before you because you have given me courage. Everybody has prayed and grieved for Amadou. And I want to thank you."

I took a deep breath.

"We have to work together to save all our children," I said. I did not know where these words had come from. I turned to Miss Blakely, the Queen Mother. I had given her some of Amadou's books to keep near me.

"Here," I said. I held up his Koran and a book on computers, another on Martin Luther King, and *Guidelines for Dialogue Between Christians and Muslims*.

"These can tell you a little bit about who my son was," I said.

Dazed, I found a moment's renewal by reminding everyone that in the midst of our pursuit of justice, there was a boy who had a life worth knowing about.

Hushed conversations whirled around me. "She should talk to the press." "She should say nothing." "She must appear." "She's too tired to appear." There was always a van waiting outside the hotel to take me to an event that no one had told me about in advance. Amadou would have told me not to worry, that everyone needed me almost as much as I needed them.

My hotel room was on the thirty-second floor. Saikou was staying on the tenth floor. On the Sunday after our arrival, we held a meeting in his room with Reverend Sharpton and perhaps a dozen other advisers and lawyers who all seemed to have been called by someone, but not me. I was comforted to see that Johnnie Cochran was one of them. I knew about him from having watched occasional news about the O. J. Simpson trial while I was in Bangkok. I thought of him as a celebrity, a big lawyer in the United States. He was dressed in a dark suit. He handed me a signed copy of a book he had authored, and he said, "I will fight for you."

The room simmered with arguments. The first lawyer Saikou had contacted said he had the right to be the lead counsel. Cochran said that was not acceptable for him. Other lawyers chimed in, everyone trying to carve out a section of the case. An administrator of Amadou's estate had to be chosen in case we decided to file a lawsuit. Saikou put papers in front of me and told me to sign.

"What is this?" I said.

"I've chosen someone to administer the estate."

"How can you do this so fast, and without consulting me?"

"We will have to settle on our lawyer, but I will name the administrator."

"You cannot give me orders," I said. "I have my own ideas." I rose to leave and felt Saikou's hand heavy on my arm. He pulled me back.

"Now you want to be the big man and make decisions," I said to Saikou. Cochran and the other lawyers were involved in their own discussion. I did not think they heard me. "But you haven't even seen Amadou. You don't care about anything, and now you fly in and think you will take control."

Saikou said he wanted to appoint a cousin of his as administrator.

"I want Bobo," I said.

"No, Bobo is your brother. He cannot defend my interests."

239

"He can't defend your interests?" I said. "Bobo has been defending your interests all along. He took care of your children when you were not around and acted as their father." In the end, we compromised on a third choice, the Reverend Wyatt Tee Walker, a civil rights pioneer who had worked closely with Martin Luther King. And we officially hired Johnnie Cochran to be our chief lawyer.

That night, I left for Guinea with my husband, Sank; my former husband, Saikou; Reverend Sharpton; and Miss Blakely. I was thankful for a first-class seat that separated me from more than fifty journalists and many Guinea officials who were also making the journey. I found a small retreat in the strong sound of the plane engine. I fixed on it and, pushing back, I thought only of Amadou, resting below me in another part of the plane. I closed my eyes and sailed all the way home with him.

CHAPTER SEVENTEEN

"I Am the Mother"

All of Conakry was there to hail the return of the *setté*, filling the tarmac at the airport, calling his name, desperate to embrace his mother. Modest Amadou had returned a hero. I descended from the plane into the crush of all the people who wanted to fall on me to express their sorrow. It was my new fate to be taken into large crowds, to be grabbed at, and smothered. Conakry was hot as usual, and I felt myself tipping. I heard, somehow through the thick air, the voices of the women who knew me. I heard Néné saying, "My child is tired. Help her. Help her." And Hadiatou saying, "I just want to touch her." I could not see them.

Nothing came into focus until I heard Laoura. "Mom, don't leave me. Don't leave me." She was locked arm in arm with Ibrahim and Abdoul at either side.

My children. My children.

God bless them and keep them as they are now, joined at the hip.

The crowd would not retreat and I thought I would be trampled. Government ministers, lined up in their best robes, shouted, "Order. Order," having come for the chance to give me their official handshakes. But they were overwhelmed. I was about to fall when I felt the arms of Ouri around me. I grabbed his neck and then I was moving backward, carried again in a way that was familiar, for my own good. I looked at my brother and I knew his thoughts.

"Yes, you sent him," I said to him. "You were the last to see him, and today he has come back."

At four in the morning we began the journey to Hollandé Bouru, where Amadou would be buried, in the village of his father. First, we stopped at the morgue. We sat in vans provided for us by the Guinea president, the whole family, and many others waiting for the men to come out carrying the coffin of Amadou into a long, gray van.

To sit in the middle of night and watch your son be carried into the funeral car that would have waited another eighty years for him: If God knows a greater sorrow than this, then bind me and take away my eyes so that I will never see it. If someone can dream up a worse torture than crawling up the Fouta Djallon in the middle of night, behind your dead son, then try it on me now and see if I flinch.

I worry if Amadou is all right, if he has been bumped or moved on the spiraling, cracked roads of the mountain we cannot see. If this is so, then have my door swing open and let me fall from the edge of the cliff.

By sunrise, we began to see people lining the road to see the caravan and to wave at Amadou. We passed a grade school in Mamou and saw the faces of children in rows at the windows, calling, *"Whoooo. Whoooo,"* the sound of the siren given in respect to the mourners' convoy.

Here, at nearly exactly this point, is where, as a girl bride, I crashed on the motorbike with my new husband and plotted my getaway. I knew finally how far-fetched an idea this was, how all my schemes to take flight were built on foolishness, an exaggerated faith in my influence over the way things happen. I had traveled often and far, and the journey had brought me back to the spot where once I had skidded to the ground.

We came for Baba. He had been waiting in Labé to join us for the trip to the village. He was wearing a long dark robe. I stepped from the van, and Néné said, "Here is your father."

I grabbed him and cried and hoped he would throw his arms around me and squeeze and kiss me all over my face, and tell me he was finally over the mood that made him shy. I saw him next to Néné. I had spent days muffled and baffled in crowds. I wanted to scream to Baba, "Please hug me!"

I didn't. I cried softly, "Baba. Baba."

"Don't cry," he said. "Just pray to Allah."

The next van pulled up behind us, and when Ouri appeared, my father took one look at him and began to weep. I watched without anger, but with curiosity. Soon I saw Koto, who learned how to be alone early. The way we held each other, the monsoons could not have knocked us over.

North to Popodara, then northeast to Saikou's village. We left the vans outside the gate to Hollandé Bouru and walked in a procession behind the casket. We were met with the unreal sight of large satellite dishes and antennas looming over the huts and the big house that Saikou had built there. There were at least a hundred journalists. All the villagers were there, the same people, I imagined, who had danced around me at my wedding. The babies were now mothers, and the women who had seen me peek from under my veil were the old people who surrounded me now to shake my hand. Here where I first learned to fly, the constancy of one generation nudging out the other, everyone staying put, seemed to live on.

I saw Ibrahim and Abdoul at a distance, and this made me want to cry, to see Amadou's brothers at his funeral, but each put a finger to his lip and shook his head to say, "No, Mom. Do not cry."

The people assembled for the funeral service, many from surrounding villages, sitting on the grass around the simple grave that was now Amadou's. It was dug from a clearing, not far from where Saikou's father was buried, and in the shade of branches filled with plums. The plum trees touched and held hands over Amadou.

"I thank everyone for coming and bringing sympathy and prayers," Baba said. "When a child is blessed, the mother and father are the source of that blessing. I want all of you to remember that. When my grandson came to see me the last time, we prayed together, and this made me proud."

Abdoul told everyone that Amadou was the kindest person he ever knew. Ibrahim said that Amadou had been his teacher.

I heard none of this. Ouri told me later what the men had said, because I was not there. I waited at Saikou's house with Néné and Laoura, prohibited by custom from attending my son's funeral. Many years before, women had been allowed at funerals, but the men often told a story about a woman so overcome with grief she threw herself into the open grave of her beloved. From then on, in the name of myth, the women were kept at a distance.

When Ouri came to me, I knew the service was over. Now, I thought, the body is gone and the soil is on top.

Later, I saw Saikou greeting a long stream of people, five hundred, perhaps more. Of them, only a handful had known Amadou, but Saikou was the grandson of the man who built Hollandé Bouru and the richest man they knew. In a flowing robe, he smiled and shook the hands of the people. When he was finished, Saikou said he wanted Laoura, Ibrahim, and Abdoul to stay with him in Hollandé Bouru. Laoura, desperate not to spend a night in the village, said that she had to return to Labé to take medicine. Ibrahim and Abdoul stayed behind.

Over three days, Saikou told them how his grandfather had built the village with the profits from cattle trading. Saikou walked with them over the length and width of the village, and together, the two sons helped their father measure the land.

I left in the van, imagining that, given the chance to speak at Amadou's grave, I would have talked only to him. I would have said, "Good-bye" and "I love you." I would have done this to show the people that it is good to be soft with your children, even the eldest son.

When Ouri told me about the funeral, he said there were plum trees, but he said nothing about the trees holding hands. That part, I made up for Amadou.

He became the "unarmed West African street vendor."
Amadou Diallo, the unarmed West African street vendor.

Kadiatou Diallo, the mother of the unarmed West African street vendor.

Who were these people? I did not recognize them with their new tags, which gave neatness and order to the implausible, the unexplainable.

Here was a man killed by police officers while standing in front of his own house.

To make sense of this, you would have to reinvent what it means to behave in a reasoned way. Or you could describe it in ways that make it familiar and help it to fit into a workable picture. Consign Amadou to the role of the African immigrant that you think your readers will expect and presume a level of protocol by the police, and the story does not carry the same shock.

From the beginning, it was said that Amadou had been sending money home to his family. We were described as poor and from the villages. It was said that Amadou was poorly educated and did not speak English well.

Details from nameless police officials were offered with the specter of absolute truth, unquestioned. Nearly all the stories I saw flatly said that the police had mistaken Amadou's wallet for a gun. They said that Amadou's beeper and wallet were found next to his body, but of course there was no way to know this.

The officers were depicted as having been on the prowl for a suspect in a series of rapes in the Bronx, but no one mentioned that the last of these rapes had happened nine months earlier. The police said that Amadou had been acting "suspiciously" or in an "agitated" manner, portrayals that created a lingering impression of someone who had unnerved the officers by behaving unpredictably.

Why wasn't that scenario turned around, to help people see what had happened from Amadou's perspective? He was the one standing on his doorstep, watching four men in jeans, sneakers, and hooded sweatshirts leap out of their red car, heading straight for him. *They* were the ones who acted unpredictably.

What would the newspapers have written if *Amadou* had been wearing a hooded sweatshirt bounding from a car after midnight?

Suspicious African man in hooded sweatshirt startles police by jumping out of car.

None of this hurt me as much as *unarmed West African street vendor.* This label stole his story. To call him West African revealed nothing. He had lived in three different West African countries, in five different towns or cities in Africa, with subtleties that made each one distinct. He lived in two different cities in Asia, had studied in the best schools in these places, and had been part of a neighborhood in New York for nearly two and a half years, selling, buying, eating, rooting for teams, kicking a ball in the playgrounds, going to the movies. Didn't that give him even the slightest claim to being not just a West African but a New Yorker, too?

Stories about the shooting could not accommodate the picture of someone selling goods on the street who hoped to one day do something better, or to allow for the idea that Amadou's father had begun his fortune precisely in this way. The faceless, hunched-over, soda-selling *street vendor,* rooted to the sidewalk in good weather and bad, was someone more expendable than the actual young man, college-bound, a world traveler. Someone like that you would have to stop and think about.

Most misleading of all, to call Amadou *unarmed* was to suggest the inverse, that his natural state was *armed.* The media would not refer to the pie maker who was robbed as the *unarmed baker* or the bank teller as the *unarmed bank employee.* So why Amadou? Why was he given that tag? For only one reason that I could think of: because the police said that they *thought* he was armed. In other words, the police, through their actions, *not his,* framed Amadou in a context that was wholly not of his making. By taking this fact—that he did not have a gun—and turning it into a label for him, the police were given the right to define Amadou and the light in which he would be seen.

I like to imagine how people may have perceived the situation if I had been allowed to define him with the label of my choosing. He would have been the *good-hearted, stepping-out-for-air, loved-by-his-mother young man.*

Or the *determined-to-make-it-on-his-own-no-matter-what example-setter for his sister and brothers.*

When you read that, the actions of the police officers, hurtling onto the street and up the steps of 1157 Wheeler, seem much less coherent. At the least, it makes you wonder what they were thinking *before* they noticed a man standing on the front steps of a house on Wheeler Avenue, before they turned onto the street, or whether a white man standing on the same steps could possibly have come to the same end.

Joining up with the black community in New York was not second nature for me. Delores Blakely told me that for many years she had worked with Queen Mother Moore, a legend in Harlem who had fought for reparations from the United States for slavery. Miss Moore's grandfather had been lynched, and her grandmother, a slave, had been raped by a white man. The anger expressed by people at rallies for Amadou was built on a history that I did not have and could not know, no more than they could know the specific terror of hiding in a pit, thinking that soldiers with guns and machetes were on their way. But the distinctions in our suffering were based more on fate than anything else. Their ancestors had been taken away to suffer the horror of slavery, and mine, through nothing but a slight accident of geography, stayed free, and lived to suffer the hardships of Africa.

Our pasts and our futures now intersected through Amadou. As parents, grandparents, brothers, and sisters of black men, we shared the same anger and fear. If my grief was more immediate, theirs had lasted lifetimes and become their companion, something that walked with them always. I met other mothers who had lost sons to police shootings and to drugs and other kinds of violence. I learned that it was not unusual for black men to die from shootings in New York, and I was shaken to discover that Amadou had become the *thirty-ninth* young Guinean man to be flown home from America in a coffin in the last five years.

The rallies kept on. More than a thousand people, black and white, were arrested in protest of the police, and six weeks after Amadou's funeral, the officers were indicted for murder in the second degree and reckless endangerment. Wounded and stricken, I could not always bring myself to go to the demonstrations. I stayed home to cry and pray, and I blessed everyone who marched and shouted, blessed them all for doing a mother's work.

Late in April, Cochran's office sent me a notice of claim he had already filed to let the city know he was planning a lawsuit. I called and said, "Johnnie, why did you file this without asking me?"

His voice shifted, in a way I knew well, though I had never heard this tone from an *American* man.

"Young lady!" he said. "I will not tolerate you talking to me this way."

"Whoa, Johnnie," I said. "You cannot speak to me this way. I am your client. And when this is all over, no matter what happens, I want to be able to shake hands with you."

As the months passed, I met with him only two, perhaps three times, and I received few calls to keep me abreast. Rightly or not, I felt I had been waved away, dismissed as the bush girl who should just go back to the wilds. I told Johnnie Cochran I needed to have more input in the case. I had an idea to create a foundation for Amadou, to provide scholarships for young Guineans to go to college in America, as Amadou had dreamed. Then he said it. Johnnie Cochran told me that until the trial began, it would be a good idea if I went back to Africa. In these words, I heard the commands to go back to Labé, to leave Bangkok, to abandon my schooling, to discard my ambitions. I felt silenced again by another man who would let me know later what was best for me. Johnnie Cochran had earned a deep respect in the African American community, which I understood. But I could not endure a repeat of my own history. I decided to move ahead without him.

Every part of my life had changed in a few months. My business had come to a stop. Wanting them close, I had sent for Laoura, Ibrahim, and Abdoul, but I had them stay in Maryland to avoid the commotion in New York. Every day seemed to bring a headline, debate, some rumor, speculation, and criticism. *The mother was fighting with the father. The father was fighting with the lawyers. The lawyers were fighting with each other.*

In Guinea, people learned how to hide from danger and turmoil. I had hid in the bushes and in trucks, behind houses. When it was necessary I hid from anger, sadness, and jealousy. As a girl I hid from the dark at night, and sometimes, in the day, I closed the door of my room to hide from the light. Everyone I had ever known had hidden from something, husbands from wives, wives from husbands, from bullies and mosquitoes. Hiding was nearly a part of the culture.

I wondered if there were a hiding place from my despair. Maybe I could find the other Kadiatou Diallo, the one I knew in Monrovia during rare freewheeling days, and I might try on her life the way she and I tried on dresses and scarves in the stores on Broad Street. *That* Kadiatou, the one I knew then, did not carry the freight of someone else's expectations as did *this* Kadiatou, a fact that removed the dread from her choices. Her decisions, as I remembered and imagined them, carried no cost, no thought of what might have been if she had gone a different way. She already had my name. I could slip into her skin unnoticed and return to Sugar Beach, sheltered from censure and loss. Were it only possible on the mourner's watch.

I was discovering that the mourner's wish to detach from her grief is complicated by a desperate longing to keep the pain close. For me, grief was not all bad, because Amadou lived there now, terror bound up with my sweetest thoughts. I wanted to wake up a thousand years removed from my sorrow, and yet I wanted no time to pass, fearful that every vanishing second took me further from Amadou. There were no hiding places in my grown-up life, no backyards to run to, no village flames that burned the whole night through.

The trial of the men who shot Amadou began a year after his death, in the winter, in a stone gray courthouse. I took a seat on a long pew that had the cold feel of a doctor's examination table and watched the lawyers, defendants, and witnesses discuss the hard technicalities of the case. The lighting on Wheeler Avenue, the lighting and dimensions of the vestibule, the speed of the guns the officers used, their line of vision, the role of gravity. They concentrated on the physics of how forty-one bullets could fly out of four guns faster than it takes a mother's heart to skip a beat. It focused on the blip in time when all sense was lost, when the officers somehow saw something that was not there.

If the officers made a poor judgment, if they reacted too quickly, it was only because they believed themselves to be in mortal danger. Any man in that situation would have reacted likewise, in an act of pure self-defense. That was the heart of the message that emerged from all the questions, all the back-and-forth. We were no longer in the Bronx. The courts had moved the trial upstate to Albany, where there had been less publicity, less furor, and where, I was told, the power of the police was seen not as a responsibility but as a right.

I sat between Pathè and Bobo, and I wondered how the matter of right and wrong had become so narrow and simplified, so wanting for common sense. The events that ended in the death of Amadou did not begin at the moment he and the officers met at his door.

These officers were members of the Street Crime Unit, which some called an elite branch of the police department. The officers had one job, to remove guns from New York streets, but because people with guns do not usually announce themselves, do not walk down the street with their guns in plain view, the officers' main technique was to stop people and frisk them, just like the border patrol officers in West Africa. The officers here watched for the look in somebody's eyes, the pace of his walk, the intentions he conveyed with ordinary movements. And unlike most New York City police officers, who work for years in one neighborhood and learn its tempo and patterns, these officers were strangers nearly everywhere they went. If they had just a small sense of Amadou's street, they would have known that young families lived there with small children who rode their tricycles on the sidewalk. They would have known that many African men lived there and that after working long hours the men might want to relax on their front step.

They might have realized that four *white* men roaming around in an unmarked car were more threatening in this neighborhood than a black man standing in front of his house.

At the trial, I heard that, before encountering Amadou, the officers had already had a busy night. They had raced to the aid of another group of officers, only to find they were not needed. They chased a man who had been standing in front of a building. Upon seeing them, the man ran into the lobby and got away. Then they stopped another man on the street, searched him for a weapon, which he did not have, and minutes later they came to Wheeler Avenue. The officers themselves offered this description of their night as a way to show that they had been performing their jobs routinely, and that Amadou would have avoided a confrontation if only *he* had behaved differently.

I saw their night another way. The officers had acted normally, but normal meant stopping people on a hunch, a theory, pushed along by their own racing pulses. It seemed to me that the officers moved along, mumbling that they didn't like the look of one man or another, their decisions based not on any kind of police science, but willy-nilly, on guesswork. When they finally came to Amadou's street, one of the officers turned to the others, according to this officer's testimony, and said, "I've got something on the right."

Primed as they were, to them, Amadou was *something on the right.*

Their technique, if you could call it that, invited a deadly outcome. Everything they did, the whole approach of this special unit, showed a willful disinterest in acting wisely, calmly. Hunched in their car, peering out from their hooded jackets, everyone they saw—every black man they saw—looked sinister. Those frantic, horrid moments when they say they took Amadou as a threat, were not something that *just* happened. The officers, through everything they did before even seeing Amadou, created these moments. It was a story in their heads that they brought to life.

This idea was lost at trial. Nor did the trial address why other police officers, on the night of the shooting, turned Amadou's room upside down or why they asked his roommates if he carried a gun or if he smoked. The trial avoided the question of what detectives had in mind when they asked his roommates if Amadou had any enemies, acting as if they were prepared to hunt down the suspects while knowing exactly who the killers were.

The end of the trial drew close with the heft of inevitability. The jurors were never taken to 1157 Wheeler. They never saw the vestibule, were not given the chance to picture a man standing there, trapped, no place to turn, no escape route, gray, metal mailboxes, walls pressing in, no last corner to find a breath. The trial might have held some intrigue. The murder scene held none. The officers were found not guilty.

The judge then made a proclamation. "The book is closed," he said. "It will be open to no man and no woman."

I stayed in my seat as the courtroom emptied, holding tight to my brothers. I thought of standing and saying, "Judge, you have not introduced your guests. Let me introduce myself. I am the mother."

I was afraid he would look down at me from the bench and see nothing more than a bewildered black woman. I did not budge.

CHAPTER EIGHTEEN

STILL TALKING

*Y*ou decide on the people you will love early. No storms or upheavals can change this. Once you recognize your people, you will always be able to find a place of peace. Néné Tinkin let me know this when I was small. She was also Kadiatou Diallo. She stood in the natural spring that blessed the village with the clearest water on earth, and she told me that I was a beautiful girl. She lifted her face to the sun, and I knew that the sun itself was graced. We ate bananas off the trees, and she told me that, as the grandmother, she could see into the future and knew that I would be well long after she was gone.

Once, a teacher told me that the best stories start at the end. This might be true, though I have also heard that everything that happens to us when we are babies determines who we are, or that the story laid out by our grandparents is our story. You might as well start at the beginning, because it will tell you everything you need to know. Maybe, finally, it doesn't matter where you enter the story or even the order in which you tell it, as long as you enter. My mother told me not to take my shoes off in the yard or I would be faced with constant travel. Baba looked proud when he swung the bush chickens over his shoulder. Baba sang well. Amadou loved riding on a horse. In Bangkok, Amadou had a teacher who taught him English and introduced him to books about Martin Luther King, Malcolm X, and the successes in the black man's struggle for his basic rights. Once, my license plates said "A41." I lived many years before I saw the meaning in that.

There was a day in Bangkok, just before we returned to Africa. I was tired, knowing that with Amadou's plans to discover America, my children and I would soon be separated again. I came upstairs to lie down on the sofa and fell fast asleep. I dreamed many things in fast motion. I saw Néné running across a yard filled with diamonds and topaz. I saw myself racing for a plane. I saw Amadou galloping to me. He was gallant and strong.

Suddenly, my eyes opened. Amadou was sitting at my feet. He was watching me.

"What's wrong?" I said.

"Nothing." His eyes stayed on me. He smiled and said, "Mama, go back to sleep."

We talk even now, and he comforts me still. My praying carries messages for Amadou, that Allah will have mercy on him, that he will purify Amadou of sin and bring light into his grave. I have told Amadou that Ibrahim went to the movies one night in New York, and I was afraid that something would happen to him, and that it bothered me to give fear a shelter. Ibrahim came home and told me he had enjoyed the movie, and that a small piece of fear hung on his shoulders as he walked back along Third Avenue, but that he cast the fear away. Amadou told me that this is the right way. He wanted his brother's shoulders light.

Ibrahim, Abdoul, and Laoura are all in college. Each works, and they support themselves in an apartment they share. They come and go, take phone messages and leave food on the stove for each other. Ibrahim grew out his hair for a while and talked about getting an earring. Abdoul struggled at first with his studies. He has a feel for computers, the way Amadou did. Laoura had thoughts about marrying, but decided not to. They have regular problems, time to time they aggravate me, but they're here now, I've told Amadou. They've staked out their position.

I know now the goodness Amadou saw in New York, and I am glad to live here. People stop me on the sidewalk to say a few small, kind words, and I know their faces the way we knew the faces of the people who came to see us from the villages surrounding Diontou or Tinkin, when we arrived in the middle of night. Their hands, brushing over me to tell me I was welcome and understood, were maybe the best part of growing up in Africa. There was always some place where a girl or a boy could go where someone would be waiting to touch them lightly, to hold them safely in their palms. I talk with people about Amadou. I tell them about other young men and women in lines, waiting for their numbers, for their chance to follow my son. The people tell me this is right and good.

One afternoon, when the trial was done, I found myself in a taxi. It was springtime.

"Take me to East 96th Street," I said.

"No problem," the driver said.

I detected an accent that sounded familiar. Perhaps the driver was from Africa. I looked out the window. I wished Amadou and I could have shared springtime in New York.

I put my head back and my eyes met the license posted on the back of the driver's seat. *My heart! My heart! What will become of my heart?*

The name of the driver was Amadou Diallo.

He was older than my Amadou. He was heavier. I asked him where he was from.

"Labé," he said.

I cried.

"Please forgive me," I said.

"I know who you are," he said. "You are the mother. A mother does not have to apologize."

Amadou Diallo is a common name, shared by generations of West African men. In America, I discovered, Amadou Diallo would be a John Doe, another way of saying: Everyman.

*T*he preparation of this book was an exercise in remembering, a stirring of the soul to recall whispered thoughts, conversations, and ideas long forgotten, quiet to go with noise. A family's life holds the threads of forebears, and is woven through the legacies of villages, towns, countries, entire passages of time. It fell then to the authors not merely to rely on the power of reminiscence. We found it necessary to become investigators, to position ourselves as best as possible in the footprints of grandmothers and grandfathers long gone, brothers, sisters, aunts, uncles, cousins, friends, colleagues, and mentors.

The roads and houses, dirt paths, schoolrooms, huts, woods, markets, and hospitals described in the book were traveled to and visited by the authors. Our research began and ended at 1157 Wheeler Avenue in the Bronx, and in between we moved, notebooks in hand, through Conakry and into the mountains of the Fouta Djallon, from Labé to the villages, including Diontou, Tinkin, and Hollandé Bouru. We went to Paris to meet with friends and relatives whose recollections and knowledge complemented ours. We traveled to Maryland and of course to the places Amadou had come to know in New York.

In contemplating the research of Amadou's time in New York, we had at our fingertips mountains of articles, essays, and editorials, but we resisted taking a look at them, at least at first. For one thing, these stories typically emphasized his death at the expense of a detailed portrayal of his life. They also amounted to a body of labels, received wisdom, and caricature. We wanted to do our own reporting, our own discovery or *rediscovery* of Amadou. We went to where he worked, shopped, played, where he learned to cook, where he rode the subway, where he prayed.

We conducted more than two hundred interviews, and we relied on diaries, letters, and photographs dating from the 1920s to 1999 that took us through many parts of West Africa, Asia, and the United States. We researched the interlacing histories of West African, tribal and Islamic culture.

While the book flows out of original research, we also enjoyed the benefit of many works that came before this one. They included: *A History of Islam in West Africa,* by J. Spencer Trimmingham; *Ambiguous Adventure* by Cheikh Hamidou Kane; *So Long a Letter,* by Mariama Ba; *Doctrine and Methods of the Democratic Party of Guinea,* by Sékou Touré; *Strategy and Tactics of the Revolution,* by Sékou Touré; as well as many of the writings of Martin Luther King and James Baldwin.

Throughout, the heart and mind remained the most important resources for *My Heart Will Cross This Ocean.* Everything else we did held the purpose of reminding the world that everything that unfolded in these pages happened not in the imagination but to real people and in real places you can find on a map.

ACKNOWLEDGMENTS

*O*ur greatest blessing is to be surrounded by so many bright and caring people who grasped the importance of this book and shared with us the sense of mission behind it. Their work, insights, and support slashed through the tears and doubts. Our conviction became theirs. Their confidence became ours.

Elisabeth Kallick Dyssegaard was our editor. She is a visionary, who knew that this story could be told in a new way. She was kind and patient with her writers, tender and wise with the material. Before her, Anita Diggs saw the potential, and she too has our gratitude and admiration.

Christy Fletcher is our literary agent, in the fullest sense. She is a superb agent with a true *literary* eye and ear. She and the amazing Carlisle & Company were a beacon for this project. Thank goodness for the thoughtful and tireless Liza Bolitzer.

We were reinforced by the research and journalistic instincts of Christian Red, Vivian Liao, Carla Sapsford, Matthew Strozier, Benjamin Lowe, and Miriam Tribble.

Caren Sanger stepped in to provide exquisite judgment as a reader and listener for cadence and context.

Carla Baranauckas lent us her refined editing talent and her rousing, contagious spirit.

Amy Karafin shared her keen intelligence about the land and the people of West Africa. And Julia Cheiffetz was an invaluable help in moving the manuscript through the editing and publishing pipeline.

We treasure the calming friendship and sheer expertise of two wonderful writers, George James and Lili Wright.

Our friends at the Columbia Graduate School of Journalism helped us too by providing time for the completion of this project and enthusiasm for the work.

We found support along the way too, from the reporters and editors of *La Lance*, an independent newspaper in Guinea. The Guinea Embassy in New York and the United States Embassy in Conakry provided us with safe passage. The American Cultural Center in Conakry generously pointed us to new ideas and resources.

Old friends, neighbors, schoolteachers in Labé, Tinkin, Diontou, Hollandé Bouru, Paris, and New York opened their homes, shared their food joyfully, and bestowed our endeavor with their prayers.

We also want to thank Bob Conason, Tony Gair, and Howard Hershenhorn for their advice and friendship.

This book grew and flourished only with the love of our families, who tolerated our absences and understood our single-minded focus. They nourished us with simple words: *You can do this. Just tell the story.* Martha, Jonah, and Rosa provided us with light.

Laoura, Ibrahim, and Abdoul did the same, sifting through their memories, conjuring their dreams, while missing and aching for their brother. For this, they will always be heroes.

KADIATOU DIALLO, a frequent lecturer, is the founder of the Amadou Diallo Foundation (www.amadoudiallo.org) to promote racial healing through educational programs. Born in Guinea in 1959, she now divides her time between New York City and Rockville, Maryland, where her three younger children are in school.

CRAIG WOLFF is an assistant professor at Columbia University School of Journalism and a former reporter for *The New York Times*, where he was part of the team that won a Pulitzer for coverage of the 1993 World Trade Center bombing. He has contributed to *The New York Times Magazine*, *GQ*, *Rolling Stone*, and the *Daily News* (New York).